# THE GREAT CANADIAN BUCKET LIST

## ROBIN ESROCK

### ONE -OF-A- KIND TRAVEL EXPERIENCES

To Naomi,
Enjoy!
Robin Esrock

Thomas Allen Publishers

*Books of Merit*

*For my late grandfather, Abie Esrock,*
*and my father, Joe Kalmek*

Library and Archives Canada Cataloguing in Publication
Esrock, Robin, 1974-, author

The great Canadian bucket list : one-of-a-kind travel experiences / Robin Esrock.

ISBN 978-1-77102-301-6 (pbk.)

1. Canada--Guidebooks.  2. Esrock, Robin, 1974- --Travel--Canada.
3. Canada--Description and travel.  I. Title.

FC38.E86 2013          917.104'73          C2013-902859-5

Editor: Janice Zawerbny
Cover and text design: Tania Craan
Cover images:  Robin Esrock; Nansen Weber; Chrystal Kruszelnicki/RCMP;
              T.J. Watt; Éliane Excoffier, Ed English

Published by Thomas Allen Publishers,
a division of Thomas Allen & Son Limited,
390 Steelcase Road East,
Markham, Ontario L3R 1G2 Canada

www.thomasallen.ca

ONTARIO ARTS COUNCIL
CONSEIL DES ARTS DE L'ONTARIO
50 YEARS OF ONTARIO GOVERNMENT SUPPORT OF THE ARTS
50 ANS DE SOUTIEN DU GOUVERNEMENT DE L'ONTARIO AUX ARTS

We would like to acknowledge funding support from The Ontario Arts Council, an agency of the Government of Ontario.

We acknowledge the support of the Canada Council for the Arts, which last year invested $157 million to bring the arts to Canadians throughout the country.

We acknowledge the Government of Ontario through the Ontario Media Development Corporation's Ontario Book Initiative.

We acknowledge the financial support of the Government of Canada through the Canada Book Fund for our publishing activities.

13 14 15 16 17 5 4 3

Printed and bound in Canada

# CONTENTS

# INTRODUCTION

**bucket list:** *A list of things one hopes to accomplish in one's lifetime.*

Although the idea is ancient, the expression has quickly entered popular culture thanks to the 2007 movie starring Jack Nicholson and Morgan Freeman. Two men with terminal cancer decide they're sick of dying, create a list of all the things they've ever wanted to do and promptly run off to try to do them. Two of the greatest actors of their generation also challenge the audience: why do we need death to remind us it's time to start living?

One spring day as I rode my scooter to work, a car drove through a stop sign, causing me to crash into its side, executing a poor swan dive over my handlebars. In the process, I mangled my bike and cracked my left kneecap. It was, by far, the most painful physical injury I had ever experienced and, without doubt, the luckiest break of my life. Literally using the intermediary of an unexpected vehicle, Fate had decided to shake me out of my stupor. I had been stuck in an unsatisfying desk job, my romantic life a shambles, wrestling daily with the feeling that time was running out and I would never get the chance to see the places and do the things I'd always wanted to see and do. All that changed with the accident, and the fortuitous $20,000 insurance settlement that accompanied it. It was just enough to convince me that, pinching a few pennies and selling off more belongings, I could act on my dreams and make them a reality. The scariest day of my life was walking into a travel agency and booking a solo, twelve-month, round-the-world ticket to five continents—a ticket to visit all the places at the top of my bucket list.

Bidding friends and family farewell, I went off to hike the Inca Trail and visit the Taj Mahal, drink beer in Prague and sweet tea in Istanbul and sail down the Mekong River. Determined to record every moment of this one special year, I wrote long reports, edited photo galleries, reviewed my accommodations and interviewed every person I met—uploading it all to a simple website I called Modern Gonzo, in honour of my journalism hero, Hunter S. Thompson. One thing led to another—newspaper columns, a globally syndicated TV show—and here I am, veteran of over a hundred countries on six continents, more travelled than any one person deserves to be.

Yet the more I experienced abroad, the more I was intrigued by my adopted home. Immigrating to Canada had been a bold move, but as a travel writer, I had spent the greater part of my Canadian life exploring just about everywhere else on the planet. My words and images had introduced millions of people to far-flung destinations, but rarely to the country that had welcomed me and allowed all this to happen in the first place. *The Great Canadian Bucket List* is my attempt to rectify that situation.

This is not a guidebook, although it will inspire you with ideas, furnish some tips and, through an accompanying website, help you plan and even book your own itineraries. This book is a personal journey to discover what makes Canada—so large, so underrated—the special country it is. The list that follows, spanning every province and territory, was personally selected with an eye for the extraordinary, the unique and the quintessential. My profession and experience had trained me to research each item with an educated, selective eye, always asking, Why does this activity/experience belong on the Nation's Bucket List?

With a few exceptions (I am only one man, with a very, very limited budget), I endeavoured to experience everything first-hand, so that I could bring you along on the journey and not just rattle off facts from Wikipedia. Spanning adventure, culture, nature, history, food and oddball, there is something here for everyone, of all ages and abilities, of all incomes and interests. You will undoubtedly notice horrific omissions, but I'm certain you'll also learn something new. My job, as a travel writer, has always been to inspire and inform — and, I hope, entertain in the process of doing so.

Devising a nation's bucket list is an epic responsibility, and so I'm looking forward to your thoughts about everything I missed, and also to your confirmation about when I got it right. A National Bucket List is only as strong as the people who create it, and the people who believe in it.

This book is for Canadians interested in their very, very large backyard. It's for students preparing their dreams, and for boomers and empty nesters finally living them. It's for our guests, so that they too may know where to find the good stuff, and for new generations, to help them see the blessings this country has and why it's important not to squander them. There are so many people to meet, so many kilometres to explore, so many adventures to jump into. Canada isn't going anywhere, but each passing year reminds us that we most certainly are. You don't always need a car accident to wake you up to the possibilities that surround you (although it certainly helped in my case). All you have to do is turn the page.

Robin Esrock
Vancouver, B.C.

# USING THIS BOOK

You will notice this book includes little information about prices, where to stay, where to eat, the best time to go and what you should pack. Important stuff certainly, but practicalities that shift and change with far more regularity than print editions of a book. With this in mind, I've created online and social media channels to accompany the inspirational guide you hold in your hands. Here you will find all the information noted above, along with videos, galleries, gear guides and more.

By visiting www.canadianbucketlist.com, you can also join our community of Bucket Listers, with exclusive discounts to many of the activities featured in this book, options to build them into customized Bucket List itineraries, as well as interactive forums to debate the merits of these, and new adventures on the Great Canadian Bucket List. When you register, you can unlock the entire site by entering the code BUCK3TL15T, or simply access each item individually with the START HERE link at the end of each chapter.

## DISCLAIMER

Tourism is a constantly changing business. Hotels may change names, restaurants may change owners and some activities may no longer be available at all. Records fall and facts shift. While the utmost care has been taken to ensure the information provided is accurate, the author and publisher take no responsibility for errors, or for any incidents that might occur in your pursuit of these activities.

# BRITISH COLUMBIA

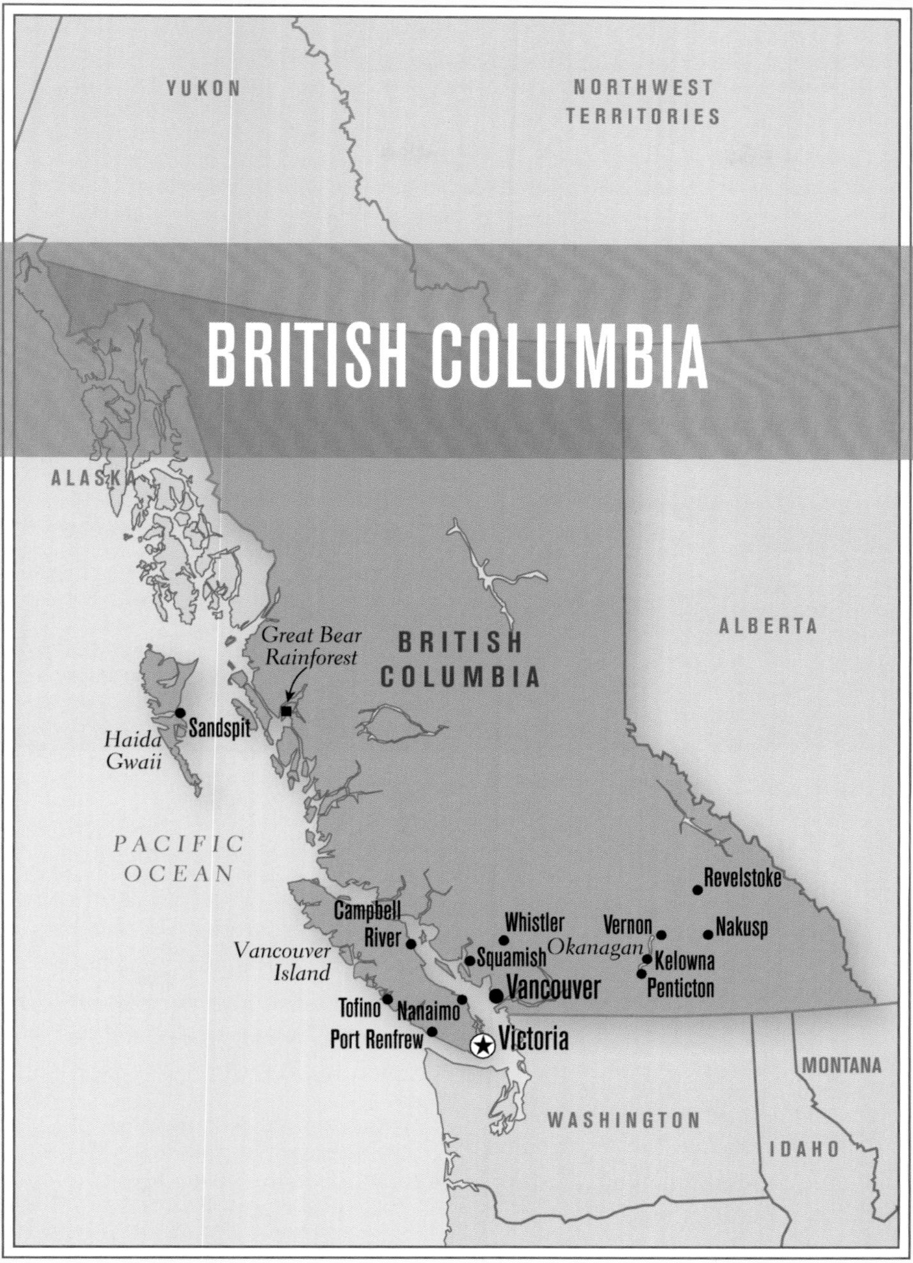

YUKON

NORTHWEST TERRITORIES

ALASKA

Great Bear
Rainforest

BRITISH
COLUMBIA

ALBERTA

Haida
Gwaii

● Sandspit

PACIFIC
OCEAN

Revelstoke

Campbell
River

Whistler

Vernon

Nakusp

Vancouver
Island

Squamish

Okanagan

Kelowna

Vancouver

Penticton

Tofino

Nanaimo

Port Renfrew

★ Victoria

MONTANA

WASHINGTON

IDAHO

# SAIL IN HAIDA GWAII

West of British Columbia's west coast, beyond the boiling water of stormy dreams and on the knife's edge of the continental shelf is a 280-kilometre-long archipelago of unsurpassed myth and beauty. A region of mountain, creeks and towering trees, these Pacific islands are inhabited by a culture whose uniqueness means its art is instantly recognized, its language found nowhere else on Earth. When I set off to discover the best of Canada, I asked fellow travel writers what tops their own National Bucket List. More often than not, the answer was Haida Gwaii.

Flying into the sleepy village of Sandspit, I catch a ferry over to the $26-million Haida Cultural Centre to place my next adventure in some context. Here, I learn about the two Haida clans—Eagles and Ravens—and how they balance each other in marriage, trade and even death. I learn about the importance of western red cedar, how imposing "totem" poles were carved to tell legends, honour men and identify homesteads. I learn how this proud warrior nation, whose seafaring and ferocity have been compared to that of the Vikings, was all but exterminated after a century of European contact, in a deadly cocktail of disease and cultural genocide. Of the Haida who thrived on these islands, 95 percent disappeared, but their descendants are staging a remarkable comeback. First they reclaimed their art, which is recognized worldwide as a pinnacle of First Nations cultural expression. Next they reclaimed ownership of their land, in an unprecedented deal with the federal government, so that the Queen Charlotte Islands became Haida Gwaii (Place of the People). Now they are relearning their language, before it too becomes a ghost echoing in the forest.

It gives me a lot to think about as Moresby Explorer's 400-horse-power Zodiac speeds down the coast into the vast protected realms of Gwaii Haanas Marine Conservation Area Reserve and Haida Heritage Site. I am late for a date with Bluewater Adventures' 21-metre-long *Island Roamer*, where I will join a dozen tourists from around the country on a week-long sailing expedition. This 1,470-square-kilometre national park reserve, unique with its steward-ship from mountaintop to ocean floor, can only be accessed via boat and float plane. Only two thousand visitors are allowed each season. Founded in 1988, the reserve was a hard-fought victory for the Haida over political roadblocks and multinational logging companies busy shearing the islands of their forests.

I hop on board to find new friends deeply fascinated with the culture, wildlife and beauty, and relishing the comfortable yacht in which to explore it. The islands of Gwaii Haanas boast forty endemic

## The Day the Springs Sprung

On October 27, 2012, the largest earthquake to hit Canada in over six decades was recorded off the coast of Haida Gwaii. The massive offshore quake, which measured 7.7 on the Richter scale, rattled the region, but fortunately there was no damage to property or people. There was, however, a natural casualty. The hot springs in Gwaii Haanas National Park, located on the aptly named Hotspring Island, mysteriously dried up. Fault lines and fractures from the earthquake were blamed for the disappearance of this popular attraction. The good news: locals and seismologists are optimistic the springs will return. ➤

species of animals and plants, a haven for twenty-three types of whale and dozens of seabirds, and dense old-growth temperate rainforest. Sailing the calm waters between the coves and bays of the park's 138 islands, we spot humpbacks, seals, sea lions and a large family of rare offshore orcas.

Bluewater's Zodiac or kayaks deposit us onshore to explore forests of giant western red cedar, hemlock and Sitka spruce, the ground carpeted with bright green moss and fern. We walk among the ruins of an old whaling station in Rose Harbour and pick up Japanese garbage on Kunghit Island, blown in with the raging storms of the Pacific. In Echo Harbour, we watch schools of salmon launch themselves from the sea into the creek, and a huge black bear (Haida Gwaii boasts the biggest black bears found anywhere) lick his lips in anticipation. We do the same on the yacht, with chef Deborah serving up fresh coconut-crusted halibut and other delights from her small but fully equipped galley.

As an eco-adventure, Gwaii Haanas deserves its reputation as a

"Canadian Galapagos." Yet it's the legacy of the Haida themselves that elevates this wild, rugged coastline, a history best illustrated by the remarkable UNESCO World Heritage Site on Anthony Island, now known as SGang Gwaay. Haida lived here for millennia, but after the plague of smallpox, European trade and residential schools, all that remains, fittingly, are eerie carved cedar mortuary poles. Facing the sea like sentinels with the thick forest at their backs, they make it an unforgettable and haunting place to visit, and all the more so for the effort it takes to do so. The five Haida village National Historic Sites in Gwaii Haannas—Skedans, Tanu, Windy Bay, Hotspring Island and SGang Gwaay—are guarded by the Watchmen, local men and women employed by the community and Parks Canada.

James Williams has been a Watchman at SGang Gwaay for almost a decade, showing visitors around and enthusiastically describing the history of the village and the legacy of the poles. He tells us how the Haida attached supernatural qualities to the animals and trees that surrounded them, hence their culture borne out of tales featuring bears, ravens, eagles, killer whales, otters and cedar. Unassuming in his baseball cap, James discusses violent battles with mainland tribes, the Haida acumen for trade, canoe building, and their interaction with European sea-otter traders, which ultimately killed off the animal and very nearly finished off the Haida themselves. Today, these weathered ash-grey mortuary poles are maintained to honour a tradition that once thrived and shows signs of thriving again. Tombstones that seem older than their 150-year-old origins, they remind me of the stone heads on Easter Island, the stone carvings of Angkor. Trees rattle in the onshore breeze as the forest slowly reclaims the remains of abandoned cedar longhouses. Isolated for months, James gifts us with some freshly caught halibut as he welcomes some arriving kayakers. With Watchmen having to live in solitude for months at a time, it is not so much a job as a calling.

Each abandoned village is different, and each Watchman reveals more about this rugged west coast wonderland and the people who call it home. By the end of the week, both the land and its stewards have woven a spell over us. Designed to last the length of a single lifetime, old Haida totem poles will not last forever. Fortunately, the protection of Gwaii Haanas, by both the Haida people and Parks Canada, along with the deep respect paid to both by operators like Randy Burke's Bluewater Adventures, ensures this magical archipelago will remain on Canada's Bucket List for generations to come.

**START HERE:** canadianbucketlist.com/haida

# HIKE THE WEST COAST TRAIL

I'm overjoyed I experienced the West Coast Trail, but happier still that one of the world's great hikes didn't kill me. Hikers come from all over the world to challenge themselves on this rugged 77-kilo-metre trail. Shortly after I left the trailhead, I was convinced every one of them must be insane. Case in point: the few wild animals you might encounter are those most likely to eat you—bears, wolves and cougars. The path is treacherous, the weather notorious, and every year about one hundred hikers are evacuated with injuries. Born out of a life-saving trail created alongside the Graveyard of the Pacific, where over one thousand ships have run aground, the West Coast Trail is nonetheless a true Canadian challenge, in all its hurt and glory.

## Tips for the Trail

Rub Vaseline on your feet every morning to avoid blisters

Pack more hot chocolate

Bring tea bags

Bring wraps to make meals go further

Plastic bowls work better than plastic plates

A walking stick and gaiters are essential

Bring fire gloves for the campfire

Instant mash and rice works great as a meal

Don't bother with towels, a sarong will do

Bring knee or ankle guards if you think you might need them

Fruit bars are worth their weight in gold

A small bottle of hot sauce goes a long way

Bring an extra battery for your digital camera

If weather permits, take a day off and relax

Do your research

Speak to other hikers as you go for more info ➤

Snaking up the Pacific Rim National Park from Bamfield to Port Renfrew, you're far removed from roads, stores or civilization. That's why park rangers patrol in helicopters and boats looking for wounded hikers suffering from sprains, slips and hypothermia. Given that 15 centimetres of rain can fall in just twelve hours, the well-marked trail can quickly become a quagmire of thick mud, sharp rocks and slippery boardwalks. So why would anyone actually add this to their bucket list? To find out, I joined a group of seven hikers, allocating our supplies according to our body weights. All our trash would have to be burned or carried out, while lunch would consist only of GORP (granola-oatmeal-raisin-peanut) and energy bars.

Within the first exhausting hour, evacuation didn't seem like

such a bad idea. The rain was holding off, but the path was streaked with roots and knee-deep mud pools. Then came the wooden ladders, some of which climb as high as twenty-five metres.

With my knees creaking under the weight of my 25-kilogram backpack, I stumble into camp seven hours later, collapsing in a heap.

"The nice thing about hurting your ankle is you forget how much your back and feet hurt," says my friend Andrew, who is dealing with a sprained ankle and receiving absolutely no sympathy. Each man's pain is his own. The key to success, according to Kyle, our veteran hiker, is preparation. We have all the essentials: walking sticks, gaiters, camel packs, dehydrated food, good tents, a water pump. "Inexperienced hikers are usually the first to go," a park ranger tells me. "This is not the trail to break in new boots."

We build our campfires beside driftwood benches and bathe in freezing streams. All food is locked in communal bear lockers overnight, and one morning we awake to find fresh wolf prints next to the tent, just in case we thought we were alone. Halfway into the

## Canada's Top 10 Trails

In a country blessed with a staggering number of hikes and trails, here are some of the best:

1. West Coast Trail, BC
2. Bruce Trail, ON
3. Skyline Trail, AB
4. Fundy Footpath, NB
5. Meewasin Valley Trail, SK
6. East Coast Trail, NL
7. Tombstone Traverse, YK
8. Les Laurentides, QC
9. Mantario Trail, MB
10. Chilcoot Trail, BC

week-long hike, my pack begins to lighten and my muscles harden. I stop kvetching long enough to admire the massive Douglas fir trees, the sea arches, limestone cliffs, waterfalls, sandy beaches, crystal tidal pools bristling with luminous purple starfish and green anemones. The camaraderie with fellow hikers from around the world, met along the way or in camp, tops up this natural inspiration. Sharing tips on what to expect up ahead, we're all pushing our mental and physical limits. Each day we hike between eleven and seventeen kilometres of challenging terrain.

At the end of the week, food consumed and camera batteries low, I trudge along the final twelve kilometres to the end, grateful for the extra-strength painkillers. Our group is haggard, dirty, sore — and utterly elated. "Few finish this adventure pain-free," reads a popular hiking website.

Why is the West Coast Trial on the bucket list? For the challenge, the beauty, the communal spirit and the opportunity to say, "Yes, I did it, and it didn't kill me!"

**START HERE:** canadianbucketlist.com/wct

# DIVE A SUNKEN BATTLESHIP

With the press of a button, I descend into the cold, dark murk of the Pacific. It's a far cry from the warm turquoise waters of Papua New Guinea, where I learned to scuba dive among hundreds of tropical fish. Yet the waters off the coast of Vancouver Island are renowned for offering some of the best diving on the planet, with no less an authority than the late Jacques Cousteau rating B.C. as the second-best temperate dive spot in the world, behind the Red Sea.

To see if he was right, if emerald oceans can compete with sapphire seas, I will have to adapt. In these cold waters, dry suits are a necessity, as they allow you to remain dry in an airtight bubble, adjusting descent and ascent through air valves. This kind of diving also requires extra training, which is why I call on Greg McCracken, one of B.C.'s top instructors, to introduce me to the submersible wonders of Canada.

What makes the diving so special in B.C. is how big everything is. Orange sunflower starfish the size of dinner tables, forests of bright white plumose anemones, giant octopus, wolf eels and big-eyed cabezons. Forget the tropics; divers in B.C. immerse themselves in the clear, clean waters of another planet—and you can keep your jeans on. Greg picked out one of the most spectacular dives on offer: the sunken destroyer HMCS *Saskatchewan*, sitting upright on the ocean floor not far from the ferry port of Vancouver Island's Departure Bay. The Artificial Reef Society of B.C. is a world leader in the art of creating environmentally protective reefs, having sunk six ships and one Boeing 737 in B.C. waters. Such reefs attract indigenous marine life, creating a sustainable and attractive destination for scuba divers.

It's a crisp early morning when Sea Dragon Charters' dive boat anchors to a buoy alongside a slither of rock and sand called Snake Island, home to 250 harbour seals. Two huge bald eagles soar above us. We suit up, bulked by our layers, resembling alien superheroes attached to all manner of pipes and tanks. Even though the water is a brisk seven degrees Celsius, I'm surprised at how insulated and comfortable dry suits can be. After descending twenty metres, we see the first anemones, rocking in the breeze of the ocean currents. A huge lingcod is perfectly camouflaged against the reef. I soon realize the reef is in fact metal, part of the 111-metre-long *Mackenzie*-class destroyer. Our flippers propel us forward, and I see the old canons, now exploding with marine life. There are huge spiky copper

## British Columbia's Top Dives

Greg and Deirdre McCracken, owners of B.C.'s Ocean Quest Diving Centre and two of the province's most respected divers, list their Top 10.

1. Browning Wall (boat dive)—Port Hardy
2. Skookumchuck Rapids (boat dive)—Egmont
3. Steep Island (boat dive)—Campbell River
4. Rentate Reef (boat dive)—Barkley Sound
5. Dodd Narrows (boat dive)—Nanaimo
6. Race Rocks (boat dive)—Victoria
7. HMCS *Saskatchewan* (boat dive)—Nanaimo
8. Wreck of the *Capilano* (boat dive)—Comox
9. Whytecliff Park (shore dive)—Vancouver
10. Ogden Point (shore dive)—Victoria

rockfish, purple California sea cucumbers, assorted sculpins and thousands of dancing brittlestars. Two hundred and thirty officers once lived aboard this ship. Since it was sunk in 1997, local marine life has gladly taken the officers' place.

We swim through the control deck, descending to twenty-nine metres, before making our way back to the midship buoy, keeping an eye on our air supply. After making the required safety stops to avoid decompression sickness, we climb on board the boat elated. "The size and abundance of marine life in B.C. really sets it apart," explains Greg over hot chocolate. "You experience things underwater here that you just can't experience anywhere else."

Just a few hundred feet away from the battleship is another artificial wreck, the world's second-largest upright reef and one of B.C.'s most popular diving locations. The HMCS *Cape Breton* is a 134-metre-long World War II Victory ship, built for action in 1944 but converted into an escort and maintenance ship soon after. After languishing for decades, she was cleaned up and sunk upright onto a flat seabed off Snake Island in 2001. Once again we suit up, check our air pressure, add weights to our belts. The *Cape Breton* is a massive wreck to explore and cannot be done in one dive. You feel like a budgie exploring a double-decker bus. Greg hand signals to a long corridor, and I follow him through it, peering with my flashlight into various rooms, noticing the fish, plants and sponges that have moved in. We hover over the engine room skylights, but as much as I'd like to explore the playground below, Greg warned me that this area is only for technical, well-trained divers. When you're thirty metres below the surface connected to life by an oxygen tank, it's best not to argue.

A half-hour later, we ascend once more to the warm tea and smiles of the *Sea Dragon* crew. They're used to huge smiles lighting up the faces of divers emerging from the depths of British Columbia.

Diving should only be attempted with the proper training, available across the country. If you have chronic ear problems, as I do, look into a product called Docs Pro-Plugs. These handy vented plugs are worth their weight in underwater treasure.

**START HERE:** canadianbucketlist.com/scuba

# SURF IN TOFINO

Canada may be a cold northern country, but Canadians can still live for the surf, philosophize about the rhythm of the ocean and call each other "dude." Tofino is not Malibu or Haleiwa, but then Vancouver Island is not California or Hawaii. This laid-back surf town demands a commitment to the waves, not sun-bleached hair and bikinis. When you surf in a full-body wetsuit, pretentiousness dissipates.

The town sits on the wild west coast of Vancouver Island, battered by volatile weather that washes up debris along its long sandy beaches, shredding trees in the surrounding Pacific Rim National Park. Storm watching is a popular pastime in the spring and fall,

# Surf's Up

Vancouver Island's west coast may be Canada's most popular surf spot, but there are alternatives around the country:

**Nova Scotia** Surf the cold, wild Atlantic off the 1.5-kilometre-long Lawrencetown Beach, located about a half-hour's drive from Halifax. Writer, poet and legendary local surfer Lesley Choyce tells me sea ice often freezes to his face, and it's definitely not a place to learn in winter. Still, it's a friendly community, dedicated to the Atlantic and the waves that "peel off in perfection on those magic, glassy-clear days." Surfers also congregate at Martinique Beach, and farther north at Ingonish Beach near Cape Breton.

**Ontario** The Great Lakes are big enough for summer storm systems to kick up a swell. Surfers gather on Lake Superior's north shore around Stoney Point, Park Point and Lester River to challenge waves up to 4.5 metres high. Similar conditions might be found at Lake Erie's Wyldewood Beach in Fort Erie.

**River Surfing** No ocean, no lake? River surfing is surging in popularity. There are river surf communities outside Calgary and Edmonton, and on the Winnipeg River in Sturgeon Falls, Manitoba; surf schools take advantage of Habitat 67, a standing wave in Montreal's Lachine Rapids that can reach as high as two metres. ➤

best enjoyed from the large picture windows of the Wickaninnish Inn, one of the finest hotels in the country. Tofino offers whale watching, hot springs, artisans and hikes in old-growth forest, and for Canadians embracing surf culture, there's no better place to be. Although the climate can be extreme, the surf community is unusually friendly. The beach break is kind to beginners, and one of the most popular local surf schools is called Surf Sisters. Visitors from southern surf towns enjoy the fact that territorial testosterone is kept to a minimum.

Insulated from head to toe, I enter the ten-degree-Celsius water. Although waves can reach up to ten metres high, today is a gentle introduction to the art of riding them. Just several metres into the waters of Cox Bay, I sit on board and admire the unkempt beach cradled by a wind-battered forest. There are no bars, clothing stores or hard bodies glistening in the sun. Instead of birds in bikinis, a bald eagle soars overhead. It's my first time on a surfboard, and while the waves may be timid, I still spend the afternoon wiping out, falling off my long board with the grace of a flying ostrich. When I do stand up, for just a moment, the heavens sing hallelujah, and an eagle swoops by to give me a congratulatory wink. Maybe I've swallowed too much of the Pacific and I'm not thinking straight. What does it matter? Without the attitude and pushiness, sans the ego and tan lines, surfing the wilderness of Vancouver Island keeps your soul warm just as surely as a wetsuit. Even if you don't manage to get up.

START HERE: canadianbucketlist.com/tofino

# TRACK THE SPIRIT BEAR

Pacific Northwest Airlines' amphibious Grumman Goose splashes down into Barnard Harbour, and clearly, the Great Bear Rainforest is in good spirits. Absent on this fine mid-September day is the notorious west coast weather, replaced by a beaming sun striking the Pacific Ocean like a spotlight on a mirror ball. What's more, the familiar face I'd seen at the Vancouver airport's south terminal is booked as a fellow guest, a man who passionately knows this area, and its conservation, better than most: David Suzuki, Canada's most respected environmentalist. And while I'd heard much about the King Pacific Lodge, reputed to be perhaps the finest fishing lodge in B.C., the sight of

Todagin Mountain, a wildlife sanctuary in the sky that anchors the nine headwater lakes of the Iskut River, main tributary of the Stikine. Todagin is home to the largest concentration of Stone sheep in the world. Because the herd is resident in all seasons, the mountain is also home to an astonishing number of predators: grizzly and wolf, black bear and wolverine. So rich are the wildlife values that hunting by rifle has been forbidden for decades. Unfortunately, open-pit copper and gold mining on the very flank of the mountain threatens to bury pristine lakes in toxic tailings. See Todagin while you still can, and if enough Canadians do, perhaps we might still stop this egregious violation of the Tahltan homeland.

Wade Davis
Author, Explorer in Residence
National Geographic Society

this spacious, floating luxury hotel buttressing the dense forest of the coastal mountains is magnificent.

Guests are arriving from around the world to explore this unspoiled temperate rainforest, stretching 70,000 square kilometres from northern B.C. to the Alaska border. Within its borders are hundreds of islands, dozens of First Nations communities, vast amounts of wildlife and a peculiar animal that has long captured the public imagination. A bear with a coat as white as snow, roaming the forest creeks like a mist in search of substance. A bear so rare that fewer than one thousand are said to exist, with a spirit so powerful it has never been hunted or trapped. This rare kermode bear, commonly known as the spirit bear, has a recessive gene that gives it a distinctive white coat. Not an albino, not a different species, just a family of black rainforest bears that pass on a trait for a distinct appearance, like a tribe of redheads living in the Amazon.

We settle into the lodge, pampered by the friendly staff, outstanding cuisine, gorgeous views and cozy wooden surroundings. Some of us have arrived with hopes of hooking giant halibut, or taking the lodge's helicopter into the mountains for an unforgettable day of

BRITISH COLUMBIA ↑

19

hiking or fly-fishing. Others are here to see the hundreds of humpback, orca and fin whales that feed in the rich sea channels. We can also visit the Git Ga'at, the closest First Nations community, to meet elders and learn about their fascinating culture in Hartley Bay. Or pop over to a unique, isolated whale research station to hear eerie hydrophonic songs of local migratory whales. Each May, King Pacific Lodge's summer season begins with a 24-hour, 130-kilometre tow to its protected location on Princess Royal Island. Each September, when millions of salmon begin their final journey up the very creeks in which they were born, the great bears that give the region its name come out to feast.

It's an hour-long boat ride along the tidal zone of Princess Royal, crossing the whitecaps on the channel that separates it from our destination, Gribbell Island. Docking against the rocks, we are greeted by a man who has lived and worked with the spirit bears his entire life. Marven Robinson is the go-to guy for the kermode, the man who introduces film crews, tourists and journalists to this magical animal. Marven personally constructed wooden platforms along Riordan Creek in places that least disturb the bears but still allow visitors to observe them in their natural habitat. "I'm here to protect the bears," he says, "not the people."

Supplied with sandwiches and hot soup, we begin the wait. Marven talks about his calling, how hunting black bears with recessive genes is a major threat to the kermode. David Suzuki tells me about the fight to save the region from becoming an oil supertanker highway; how, despite huge financial incentives, the First Nations have joined conservationists to say enough is enough: protecting Great Bear's natural resources is more important than a short-term paycheque. All this in surroundings that are jarringly beautiful, reminding me of idyllic photo-wall papers so popular in the 1970s, the kind that depicted the tranquil forest of your dreams. Below us, hundreds of pink salmon are spawning, squirming against each other, darting upstream. It's the abundance of this food source that Marven knows will draw the bears, eventually. In the meantime, we talk *sotto voce*, swatting the bugs away from our faces.

Finally, a ripple of excitement. A large black bear is making his way downstream. It stops, swipes a mouthful of salmon from a pool, tears it to pieces. Slowly, the bear ambles along the river, stopping right beneath our platform, oblivious to our quiet presence. Privileged to be a guest at a spectacle that takes place all over the coast, I hear the sound of memory cards filling up, and then an excited whisper: "There it is!"

A large kermode male, all 135 kilos of him, six years old by Marven's reckoning, is following in the footsteps of the black bear. Ethereal, pink-nosed, with cream white fur at odds with the earthy tones of its surroundings, the kermode chases salmon in the pools, spraying drops of water that reflect the early afternoon sunlight. Suddenly the black bear charges aggressively, sending the kermode into the mossy adjacent banks. Unperturbed, it re-enters a few metres downstream and continues its hunt for as many as eighty fish a day. Finally, both

## Welcome to New Caledonia

I once visited a friend on a little slice of France located 16,000 kilometres east of Europe, in the South Pacific. Governed in Paris, New Caledonia has tropical beaches, strong cheese, great wine and locals who can't quite believe their luck at having been born in such a place. It could have been ours . . . the name anyway. Simon Fraser originally wanted to call the new British crown colony on the Pacific coast "New Caledonia," since the mountains reminded him of the Scottish Highlands. Alas, Queen Victoria nipped that idea in the bud, as Captain James Cook had already claimed his New Caledonia in the South Pacific. ➤

bears wander off, leaving us spellbound by our good fortune. There's no guarantee you'll see the spirit bear on any given day, and more than once on my Canadian journey I've found myself facing the wrong end of the barrel of fortune. But not today.

The First Nations have always protected the spirit bear, believing it has a powerful effect on all who are lucky enough to see it. My encounter left me inspired by the power of true wilderness, along with all the creatures who inhabit it, protect it and nurture its future. Creatures like the Gitga'at, Marven Robinson and David Suzuki. Creatures like the folks at King Pacific, our local guide George's granny (with her "65-plus grandkids!") and the couple who live in isolation at the whale research station. Creatures like the kermode, which radiate magic, and bring it all together.

**START HERE:** canadianbucketlist.com/spiritbear

# SNORKEL WITH SALMON

Next time you order sushi, spare a thought for the miracle of Canada's Pacific salmon. Half a billion of them, returning from a 5,000-kilometre journey in the open ocean, ready to spawn in the very gravel, in the very river, where they themselves once hatched. In the process, they must survive a who's who of salmon addicts—seals, sharks, eagles, sea lions, bears—and, of course, human appetites. Leaping from pond to pond, battling predators, starvation, suffocation, overcrowding and fierce interspecies competition, their backs hump, their noses hook, and their skin turns red as finally they are ready to mate. Having accomplished this extraordinary feat of derring-do, they promptly die. Why these kamikaze pilots are drawn to the rivers of British Columbia is still something of a mystery (Atlantic salmon don't die after mating), but it certainly has something to do

with B.C.'s abundance of fresh water, filtered by its wealth of temperate rainforest. As the spent bodies of salmon wash downstream, they continue to feed up to two hundred species in the forest. Some 80 percent of the nitrogen found in forest soil can be traced to salmon, nitrogen vital for hemlock, spruce and cedar to grow. Delicious as they may be (smoked, barbecued, fried or grilled), there simply wouldn't be a B.C. without its annual salmon run. A salmon run you can witness first-hand, underwater, each year with Destiny River Adventures in Campbell River.

Suiting up in full-body wetsuits for a two-hour journey downstream, Jamie Turko and his crew transport us on whitewater rafts to the base of the river. A hydroelectric project regulates the Campbell River's water supply, making it a particularly safe river in which to do what we're about to do. Which is: hop in the water with masks and snorkels, point our arms downriver, float with the current and immerse ourselves in this little-seen world of salmon—hundreds of thousands of them.

Jamie, who has run salmon snorkelling tours for over two decades, explains the differences between the five species: the mighty chinook, the chum, the sockeye, coho and pink. We'll mostly be seeing pink salmon today, interspersed with giant chinooks, along with opportunist rainbow and steelhead trout (yet another predator for nature's ultimate survivors). This enormous bounty of fish means we won't be alone. Locals line the banks with their rods, catching their seasonal quota, or catch-and-releasing in hopes of hooking a true beast (a 32-kilogram chinook was caught in the area in 2010). Locals

## Acquiring the Taste of Salmon

Packed with protein, omega-3 fatty acids, vitamins and minerals, a diet rich in salmon is considered to be an extremely healthy one. Salmon is cited as being beneficial for everything from arthritis and dry skin to heart disease and Alzheimer's. But when it comes to cooking, the five species of Pacific salmon are not created equal. Ask any local and they'll tell you: the firm, pink and oily sockeye swims way ahead of the pack. ➤

watch us with a mix of curiosity and envy, for once we enter the brisk current of the river, we can see exactly where the fish are. And boy, they are everywhere.

Wetsuits suitably disarm the 10°C water as we enter the river. From above, I had seen streaks of grey darting in the green-brown water. Underwater, there are salmon everywhere—walls of them, floors of them, cities and towns and planets of them. Despite the obstacles that began the moment they were born, in just one corner I see enough survivors to assuage a feeling of guilt. Certain stocks are threatened, and the debate over farmed salmon versus wild rages on, but today there seems to be a fish for every Tom, Dick and hungry Harry.

We raft over some gentle rapids and enter another section of the river, where the current carries us into more schools with a feeling that is part buoyancy, part flying. For a moment I feel like a fish myself, nervously watching for rocks, large predators and deceptive bait. Most of all, though, I'm just having fun, in awe of a creature that deserves credit for its role in west coast culture. A creature that, against all the odds, finds itself on the Great Canadian Bucket List.

START HERE: canadianbucketlist.com/salmon

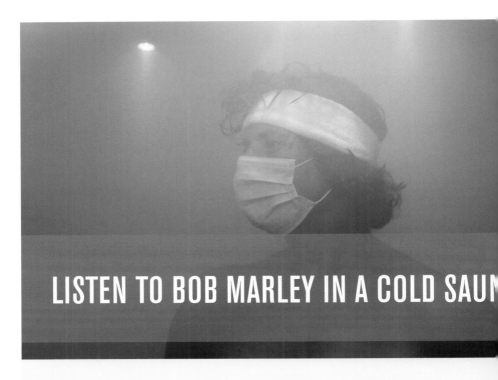

# LISTEN TO BOB MARLEY IN A COLD SAU

You too can enjoy the health benefits of freezing to death. And benefits there must be, otherwise guests wouldn't pay for what they're paying for at Sparkling Hill, a pretty, Austrian-style resort located near the interior town of Vernon. Owned by the Swarovski family and adorned with $10 million worth of their crystals, Sparkling Hill has an ambience that is distinctly Old World Luxury, even with the crystal fireplaces, stunning pools and themed steam rooms in the award-winning KurSpa. I'm wooing my wife with these facts in the four seconds it takes before her panic attack sets in. To be fair, we are half naked in a small room with the temperature a frosty -60°C. Sorry, that's the second room; her real panic attack hit in the third room, at -110°C. Hey, she's Brazilian, they freeze to death quicker than the rest of us.

A visit to North America's first cold sauna provides a treatment in something called cryotherapy, which activates biochemical, hormonal and immune processes to give your circulatory and nervous systems a healthy kick-start. Sports stars apparently swear by it, whereas I was just swearing, deeply, under my breath, while my eyelashes froze and my nasal passage turned to ice. Strictly monitored, my wife and I are told to wear bathing suits, supplemented with gloves and slippers. In order to prevent any humidity, we enter the cold sauna through three separate rooms: the first a balmy -15°C, the second -60°C and the final corker -110°C. Here we must walk in small circles for three minutes, encouraged by a bundled-up spa worker. Ever jump into a freezing

## How We Freeze to Death

As soon as your body gets cold, blood moves away from your skin and extremities to protect your core. Shivering is a mechanism to generate warmth, and it gets intense once your core temperature begins to sink. Welcome to hypothermia. The good news is that hypothermia is typically associated with moisture (our bodies lose heat about twenty-five times faster in water than in air), which is why the cold sauna is so well insulated, air current free and perfectly dry.

When the body temperature drops from its normal 37°C, horrible things start to happen. Lose five degrees and you'll lose consciousness. Once you hit 21°C, your lights might go out permanently. Inside Sparkling Hill's cold sauna, sticking around longer than the prescribed and therapist-monitored three minutes is a bad idea. Just two to three minutes in, your body surface temperature plummets to -2°C, but your core remains comfortable. Once your time is up, relief, warmth and comfort are just steps away. ➤

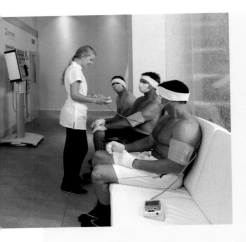

cold lake? Multiply the shock by ten, and go ahead and punch yourself in the neck for good measure. My wife freaks out, and the spa worker quickly ushers her out to safety.

Meanwhile, I continue walking with three old ladies in a tight circle, all of us trying not to touch each other in case we fuse. Bob Marley is blasting from in-sauna speakers, "stirring it up," as it were, with images of frozen corpses washing up on the beach. As I twitch with cold, nipples ready to break off, my testicles having retreated deep into my pancreas, the three minutes come to an end and we rush out of the chamber. Time may fly when you're having fun, but when you're freezing to death, a single Bob Marley song can sound like a James Joyce reading. Here's the best part: once you exit the cold sauna, you are not allowed to hop in a hot tub or steam room. I assume it's because the rush of blood would explode your head like a champagne cork. Rather, we are told to rest in our robes and drink a warm cup of tea.

While you need multiple treatments (sold in blocks of ten) for the cryotherapy to be effective—flash-freezing muscle inflammation, improving joint and muscle function, and relieving skin irritation—one visit was perfectly adequate for my purposes. My wife did (eventually) forgive me, and once again I learned that what doesn't kill you only makes you appreciate the bizarre things people pay good money for.

**START HERE:** canadianbucketlist.com/coldsauna

# EXPLORE AN OLD-GROWTH FOREST

These days, it's hard to impress kids who have grown up on PlayStation, music videos and television cocktails spiked with attention deficit disorder. Show them a great mountain, a sweeping beach, a lush forest, and chances are they'll be glued to their text messages on the cellphone you regretted the minute you bought it for them. Fortunately, Mother Nature still has some tricks up her foliage when it comes to impressing children, and it's doubtful cellphone coverage will interfere at all. Yes, they're just trees, kids. But look at the size of them!

The giant red cedars, Douglas firs, hemlocks and spruce trees that survive in the old-growth forests of British Columbia are truly

## Canada's Biggest Trees

According to the Ancient Forest Alliance, the town of Port Renfrew is the go-to place if you're looking for the biggest trees in Canada. Near this Vancouver Island town you can find the planet's biggest Douglas fir and biggest spruce tree, as well as the biggest tree in the country, the Cheewhat cedar. Located within the Pacific Rim National Park Reserve, the Cheewhat is 56 metres high, 6 metres in trunk diameter, and has enough timber volume to create 450 regular telephone poles' worth of wood. ➤

impressive. Somehow, these trees have survived the colonial building boom and the modern logging industry, and now range in age between 250 and over 1,000 years old. "This tree was here before Marco Polo explored China, before Shakespeare . . . em, before Harry Potter!" Fantasy is an apt means to capture a kid's imagination, because standing between 800-year-old Douglas fir trees—towering up to seventy-five metres high in Cathedral Grove in Vancouver Island's MacMillan Provincial Park—you can't help but feel you're on another planet. The forest moon of Endor comes to mind, although I'm dating myself with *Star Wars*. Perhaps the kids will prefer Avatar Grove, fifteen minutes away from Port Renfrew, so named for this ancient red cedar and Douglas fir forest's resemblance to the planet Pandora in the blockbuster *Avatar*. Surrounded by a drapery of ferns and moss, with a soundtrack of chattering woodpeckers or bubbling brooks, a spell of peace and space envelops adults as well. When the kids get tired of trying to hug a trunk that can accommodate the linked hands of eight people, bedazzle them with a contorted red cedar known as "Canada's Gnarliest Tree." Keeping with the theme, it looks remarkably like Jabba the Hut.

According to the Ancient Forest Alliance, a B.C. organization working to protect these natural wonders (and support sustainable forestry practices), less than 25 percent of the old-growth forest on Vancouver Island still exists, and only 10 percent of the biggest trees

that you might find on a valley bottom. Some studies have shown that conserving old-growth trees might be more economically viable than slicing them down for furniture. Meanwhile, the few remaining stands in the province are still threatened with clear-cutting, including Avatar Grove. The emotional and childlike wonder that accompanies hiking an old-growth forest certainly belongs on the National Bucket List. Unfortunately, we have to add the caveat: "while they still exist."

**START HERE:** canadianbucketlist.com/oldgrowth

# GO HELI-SKIING

Welcome to a place where a person's worth is measured in vertical feet. It is surrounded by mountains, waist-high powder and the *whomp-whomp* sound of a helicopter. Heli-skiing has been on my bucket list ever since I discovered how much fun it is to strap on a plank of polyethylene and launch oneself off a mountain. Having gone through the meat grinder of learning to snowboard, the idea of being dropped off at the top of the world to float over virgin snow seems a just reward. Thus I found myself at the Canadian Mountain Holiday's K2 Rotor Lodge in Nakusp, among a group of Americans on a Mancation, folks proudly addicted to the "other" white powder. How else to explain the guy celebrating his six-millionth vertical foot with CMH? Or the sole Canadian who has visited every one of CMH's eleven heli-skiing lodges? Using a helicopter as a makeshift ski chair doesn't come cheap, with trips costing north of six thousand

feet. This eye-popping price tag didn't dissuade dozens of well-to-do snow fiends to visit CMH each season.

## Tips for Heli-Skiing

- The more fit you are, the more fun you will have. Start training as early as possible, focusing on cardio and muscle strength.
- Make sure your boots are worn in and comfy. This is not the place to break in a new pair. And make sure you pack them in your carry-on luggage, just in case.
- CMH veterans sing the praises of yoga classes as having increased core strength and flexibility, improving their skiing.
- Drink water on every heli-run. Keep those muscles hydrated and prevent fatigue.
- The free stretch classes before breakfast are gold. Warm up and iron out the stiffness before each day begins.
- Book off enough time to get used to the powder and physical demands, so you can truly enjoy the magic heli-skiing delivers. ➤

dollars. "My wife goes on cruises, I go to the mountains," explains Mike. One guy has flown in from London, England, for four days of powder. That's if the weather plays ball.

It's late February, and the avalanche risk is high. The snow is plentiful, but conditions mean "we only have an area about eight times the size of Whistler available to us, as opposed to one hundred times," explains affable mountain guide Rob.

We watch a safety video, which pretty much explains all the ways heli-skiing can kill you: avalanches, tree wells, decapitation by skis. We practise avalanche drills and rescue, get fitted with receivers, radios and shovels, and finally head to the Bell chopper we will come to know so well. I see grown adults behave like little kids, clapping their hands with glee. Wind, visibility and terrain dictate where the helicopter can land, but it appears to be able to settle gently on pretty well anything. We exit, the chopper taking off right over our heads, and the Selkirk Mountains surround us in blue-sky mountain glory.

I strap in, barely containing my excitement, and proceed to have the worst run of my life. Powder, I discover, is not a groomed ski hill. Heli-skiing and -riding require new techniques, new muscles and instincts. My group of heli-veterans patiently pull me out of tree wells, traverses and snow burials. Every muscle is burning as I battle my physical demons, determined to master the challenge. This is why you don't go heli-skiing for one day. Besides bad weather that can ground you for days, you need several days to enjoy the diversity of runs and snow, and to progress in your ability. We ski runs called Drambuie and Cognac, In Too Deep, Lobster Claw and, my favourite, Little Leary. I had expected just a few rides in the helicopter, but we average about ten a day, the pilot somehow landing the copter just a few feet from our heads for the return flight to the top of the mountain. Like the skiing itself, it's a thrill that doesn't get tired. We whoop and bird-call through the forest, making sure nobody is lost, over fresh powder that stretches in every direction.

By day three, I've found my groove. Early morning stretching classes (and fabulous food) at the lodge help the muscle woes, and now I'm carving in deep pow, slaloming pine and hemlock trees. "That was the best run so far," says the guy from England after just about every run. I'm taken with the routine of each day: wake up, stretch, eat, ski, soak in natural hot springs, drink beer, eat dinner, retire early. No wonder these guys keep coming back, and work so hard to be able to afford to do so.

Atop a mountain on the final day, crystals glittering in the air as skis click into their bindings, I soak in a post-adrenalin, post-exhaustion, sense-of-achievement high. It's been a once-in-a-lifetime week of sport, companionship and natural beauty. A highlight on the Great Canadian Bucket List, and my first fifty thousand feet of CMH vertical. Strap in, there's still a long way to go.

START HERE: canadianbucketlist.com/heliski

# POWDER DOWN IN WHISTLER

When it comes to North America's largest and most highly rated ski resort, one word comes to mind: *epic*. Epic terrain. Epic snow. Epic dining. Between Whistler and the adjacent mountain, Blackcomb, you've got 8,100 acres of skiable terrain linked by the world's longest and highest lift system, the 4.4-kilometre-long Peak2Peak. That's over 50 percent more terrain than any other ski resort on the continent, and the reason you'll find long lineups with visitors from around the world. To ensure the first line of the day will be mine, I pick up a Fresh Tracks ticket, which offers a breakfast buffet and early loading privileges at the top of the mountain. I've still got egg in my mouth when I hear "The runs are open!" This initiates

# Canada's Top 10 Ski Resorts

*Scott Birke, editor of* Snowboard Magazine Canada, *drops in the ultimate Canadian ski and snowboard destinations.*

1. **Whistler Blackcomb, BC:** For its two massive mountains with over 200 runs, world-class terrain parks and some of the best slackcountry in the world.
2. **Red Mountain, BC:** Since you can drop in anywhere 360° from the top and as long as you don't go below the mid-mountain cat track, you're good to go.
3. **Whitewater, BC:** The trees over on Glory Ridge are so perfectly spaced and free of people that you'd think you're out of bounds.
4. **Fernie, BC:** Big bowls, tons of gullies to slash and lots of snow? No-brainer here.
5. **Lake Louise, AB:** For some of the most majestic views ever and its great expansive terrain.
6. **Le Massif, QC:** For its super snowy micro-climate, steep west coast–like terrain and killer views of the St. Lawrence near its widest point.
7. **Kicking Horse, BC:** Sixty percent of its runs are rated black and double-black. 'Nuff said.
8. **Revelstoke Mountain Resort, BC:** At 5,620 feet of vertical, it's the highest drop in Canada. Oh and it gets tons of snow.
9. **Marble Mountain, NL:** It's a gem on the east coast with enough great runs and charm to make the west of the country jealous.
10. **Tremblant, QC:** Party: Where else do people dance on tables in bars and not get thrown out by the help . . . ➤

a school bell–like atmosphere as everyone grabs their gear and races off to Emerald Express.

Having only discovered snowboarding in my late twenties, I still get a kick taking lift rides surrounded by shark-fin alpine peaks. Among the kids are adults with permission to behave like children, whooping at the top of the world and then bulleting down the mountain on planks of fibreglass. I'm not one for throwing myself into the challenging Double Diamond bowls, although there's plenty of that to go around. Rather, I choose to glide down the blues, in seventh heaven on my favourite runs, Harmony Ridge, Peak to Creek, the

Saddle and Spanky's. Riding the impressive Peak2Peak Gondola can be unnerving, especially in the glass-bottom carriage. The reward is worth it. Blackcomb offers heaps of snow, with accurately named runs like Jersey Cream and, yes, Seventh Heaven.

The entire experience has a tendency to make other resorts pale in comparison. Factor in the nightlife, festivals, world-class restaurants—Barefoot Bistro's nitro ice cream is something to experience on its own, as is their $1.4-million wine cellar—along with endless backcountry Nordic trails and thrills at the Whistler Bobsleigh Centre, and it's always a powder day for Whistler on the National Bucket List.

**START HERE:** canadianbucketlist.com/whistler

# STROLL THE SEAWALL

"Can you imagine, some people actually live here!"
I overheard that comment from one of the eight million people who visit Vancouver's Stanley Park every year, during my first stroll along its 8.8-kilometre paved seawall. When the sun is beaming, the park, and the city, has that effect on people. It's the first place I take visitors to the city, the first and most powerful impression I can give them. One second we're surrounded by apartment buildings, and the next we're in a tranquil forest, with stellar views of the North Shore mountains, or the sun reflecting off the glass of buildings downtown. If you look at the view of downtown and Stanley Park from across the Burrard Inlet on Spanish Banks, Stanley Park looks almost exactly the same size as downtown, a perfect balance of nature and city. With a half-million trees, two hundred kilometres of trails and attractions such as the world-class aquarium, some of the city's

best beaches, manicured gardens, Pitch n Putt and concerts under the stars in Malkin Bowl, there's plenty to do in Stanley Park. Some might argue—under their voices during hockey season—that this is Lord Stanley's greatest legacy.

For the Great Canadian Bucket List, simply walk or pedal around the seawall, taking in the views of mountains, city, ocean, birds, people. It's something to appreciate in all weather, but on a warm summer day it will probably make you want to live here too.

**START HERE:** canadianbucketlist.com/stanleypark

## The Wind Bomb

In December 2006, a powerful windstorm blew in from the Pacific, flattening forty-one hectares of Stanley Park forest and damaging Vancouver's beloved seawall. Aided by public donations and scores of volunteers, $10 million was invested planting fifteen thousand new trees and shrubs, rebuilding parts of the wall, upgrading the road and improving park trails. The park's famous Hollow Tree was restored with a $100,000 private donation (and concealed steel pipes). ➤

# TASTE THE OKANAGAN

I'm on an electric-assist bike scooting alongside vineyards, the wind in my hair. It's a honeymoon of sorts, but since my wife and I cannot afford jet-setting to Tuscany, we drove four hours from Vancouver into the B.C. interior for our very own Canadian wine adventure. Certainly, there is nothing in Tuscany that remotely resembles the sparkling 135-kilometre-long Lake Okanagan. Neither do Tuscan wines benefit from the "lake effect"—a cooling of the temperature caused by the lake's deepness. Wines in the Okanagan's Lake County more accurately resemble those produced along the Rhine in Germany. Yet, as in all great wine regions, the caramel-coloured countryside here has the fragrance of a farmers' market. Summers in the Okanagan routinely bake the landscape above forty degrees Celsius. And while the rest of Canada deals with harsh nine-month winters, Okanagan summers last from April to October. This might explain why the region's largest city, Kelowna, has become one of

## Wine in B.C.

British Columbia produces over sixty types of varietals, the most popular reds being Merlot, Pinot Noir and Cabernet Sauvignon, and the most popular whites Pinot Gris, Chardonnay and Gewürztraminer. The province boasts five wine regions: Okanagan Valley, Similkameen Valley, Fraser Valley, Vancouver Island and the Gulf Islands. ➤

the fastest-growing cities in North America, attracting everyone from tech start-ups to celebrity chefs.

Visiting over the years, I've always been surprised by just how beautiful this part of the world is, and how good the wine can be. A sommelier at Mission Hill, the region's biggest vineyard, tells me that the enjoyment of wine is all about context: where you are, how you feel and whom you're with. Years earlier, I romanced a girlfriend in the Okanagan by visiting wineries in the back of an immaculately restored apple green 1953 Cadillac convertible. It was one of a hundred classic cars owned by Garnet Nixdorf, who offers chauffeured tours to vineyards around Penticton. Talk about context!

There are over 120 wineries in the Okanagan, many opening their doors for summer tastings, with patio restaurants and artisan stores. Everyone has their favourites: Gray Monk, Burrowing Owl, Summerhill, Cedar Creek, Sumac Ridge, Dirty Laundry, Red Rooster, the rock 'n' rollers at Ex Nihilo. Wine is a taste to be acquired, and the Okanagan provides ample opportunity to do so.

While you're in the area, consider renting a houseboat to float on Lake Okanagan, complete with wet bar and Jacuzzi. On a sweet summer day, lounge on the thick carpet of grass below Mission Hill's watchtower with a chilled glass of white wine. It's balm for the soul. And a lot cheaper than flying to Italy.

**START HERE:** canadianbucketlist.com/okanagan

# LET IT HANG OUT ON WRECK BEACH

For all its natural wealth, Vancouver still has a reputation as a city allergic to fun. Transplants will be quick to tell you how polite yet unwelcoming the city can be, how rules and regulations suffocate events, and how the orchard of civic spirit is chopped down by City Hall in case of that one bad apple. And then you get Wreck Beach. It gravitates on the city's most westerly point like antimatter, like anti-Vancouver. To get there, you must journey to UBC (the University of British Columbia), find parking and walk down the 473 stairs of Trail Six as exhausted people pass you on the way up. At the bottom, you'll notice two things: a beautiful beach, and a motley collection of naked people.

Wreck Beach is clothing optional, but it is more than that. It's a community, dedicated to keeping the beach clean, the conduct becoming and the creeps out. While it's impossible to buy food on

# Nudity in Canada

Canadian law states it is unlawful to be nude in public, or dressed in a way that offends public decency. That includes you, Justin Bieber. Fortunately, there are places where we can run around in the buff, such as municipally approved clothing-optional beaches, and any place where nobody cares to call the authorities. Toronto's Hanlan's Point joins Wreck Beach as an official clothing-optional beach, while nudists gather unofficially at Crystal Crescent Beach (Halifax), in Oka Park (Quebec) and at naturist resorts around the country. ➤

the sand of any other beach in the city, here you can pick up a cold beer, a pizza, a bison burger, a veggie wrap and even a cocktail from enterprising and spritely vendors in the buff. Kids run amok, safely observed by their parents and friends. Groups gather around logs, playing guitar and Frisbee, reading the paper or debating politics. Smell the tang of marijuana in the air, hear the beat of a drum, and be surprised that the majority of bodies belong to the weathered and leathered, not the rebelliously young. It can get really busy on sunny weekends, and increasingly tourists are finding their way here too.

Yes, City Hall, some people cannot hold their liquor and shouldn't be allowed to toke on the beach. But the vast majority of Wreckers are quite capable of looking after themselves, and deal responsibly with someone who steps out of line. When the police raid, as they seem to do more frequently, word rolls up along the beach to help everyone avoid a violation fine. They're just doing their jobs, but I've seen officers handle a wayward beer with far too much aggression, rightly earning a "shame on you" from nearby students and grandmas. Wreck Beach may not be everyone's cup of chai, and not everyone deserves all the freedom that it offers. Yet here is proof that beautiful Vancouver can let its hair down and bask in the sun without burning down the house. Have fun responsibly, and don't forget to apply sunscreen. Yes, there too.

**START HERE:** canadianbucketlist.com/wreck

# FLOAT THE PENTICTON RIVER CHANNEL

M any years ago, I spent an afternoon floating on a rubber tube
down the Mekong River in Laos, toasting my fellow floaters
with cold Beer Lao, waving to locals on the riverbank and celebrating my good fortune at having discovered such an activity in the
first place. I thought I'd have to return to Vangvieng for that simple
pleasure, until I saw the river channel linking Lake Okanagan and
Skaha Lake in Penticton. Rubber tubes were floating down the canal
like twirling Froot Loops in a bowl of cherry cola. Every summer, the

seven-kilometre channel fills with locals and visitors. Gliding on your back in the sun, a clandestine bottle of wine chilling at your side, you can take three to four hours to float the entire length, where a handy shuttle service awaits to return you to the entrance parking. Any inner tube, air mattress, raft or floating device will suffice, available at stores around town or for rental from the shuttle service. It's shallow and safe, with a halfway point to exit in case the sun is a bit much or the weather turns.

The river channel makes it onto the bucket list for several reasons: Firstly: This is not a water park but the fortunate by-product of a dredge built to control flooding in the 1950s. Secondly: It's relaxing as hell, free as air, and can be as social or meditative as you wish. (If you're lumped with a loud group of spotty teenagers, pull to the side in the two-metre-deep water and give them some distance.) It may not be as exotic as the Mekong River, but the accommodation and dining choices in Penticton are much better, trust me.

START HERE: canadianbucketlist.com/tube

# CLIMB THE GRIND, HIKE THE CHIEF

Vancouverites have a special place in their hearts for physical pursuits. These are people obsessed with the outdoors, since it's among the best cities in the country, weather-wise, in which to enjoy it. Despite the "granola with my yoga" reputation, Vancouver also offers more demanding physical challenges. Take the Grouse Grind, "Mother Nature's Stairmaster," running 853 metres up the side of Grouse Mountain over a distance of exactly 2.9 kilometres.

At some point in your life, you've been physically exhausted—leg muscles burning, sweat stinging your eyes, mind full of blame. Well done, you've just reached the soul-crushing quarter-way sign on the Grouse Grind. The Grind is a walk in the park, and by walk I mean slog and by park I mean mountain. In front of and behind you, you'll see others stuck in the same elevator from hell, but not to worry, everyone is too polite to panic. What's more, many will be dressed in form-fitting stretchy pants, because the Grouse Grind is not only a natural workout, it's become an unlikely pick-up joint for yuppies hell-bent on maximizing the tone of their glutes.

Among the 100,000 people who undertake the Grind every year, count on seeing at least one of the following during your visit:

- A young parent seriously regretting the idea that doing the Grind with their toddler on their back would be fun.
- Asian tourists who heard about one of the city's most popular hikes and had no idea what they were getting into. Typically wearing Hello Kitty sandals.
- A hiker well into his or her seventies who seems to be having no trouble whatsoever.
- The despair when people reach the quarter-mark sign.
- Someone arriving at the sad realization that there's no view, and nowhere to go but up.

Regular Grinders time themselves, with the average being about ninety minutes, and the current record an astonishing 23 minutes 48 seconds. My personal best up the 2,830 uneven dirt stairs is fifty-five minutes, but to be fair, I was drunk and in the mood for self-loathing. The reward for your calorie-decimating workout is typically beer and nachos at the Grouse Mountain bar. Take off, put on. Fortunately, it's only ten dollars for the gondola ride down to the parking lot, where you'll find a mix of exhausted, sweaty hikers and tourists reaching for their noses. If a Vancouverite asks to take you on the Grind, be prepared for a physical gauntlet. Or lie, with the reliable excuse, "I've done it, just over an hour, isn't it a bitch of a hike, wow, once was enough!"

Alternatively, there's another climb that's just a fraction less admired by Vancouverites: the Stawamus Chief, or, simply and respectfully, the Chief. This giant granite monolith sits seven hundred metres above the Howe Sound, overlooking the town of Squamish on the Sea to Sky Highway between Vancouver and Whistler. World renowned with climbers who scale its impressive rocky face, hikers and day walkers can go around the back and climb to the Chief's three summits, where they'll find a truly staggering view of the fjords and coastal mountains. The well-maintained trails can be rugged and steep, with handy iron chains and ladders adding to the sense of adventure. Pack a picnic for the top, and marvel at the beauty that stretches out in every direction. You don't even have to rough it. Opening in 2014, the Sea-to-Sky Gondola offers a restaurant, coffee shop and an easy way down.

**START HERE:** canadianbucketlist.com/grind

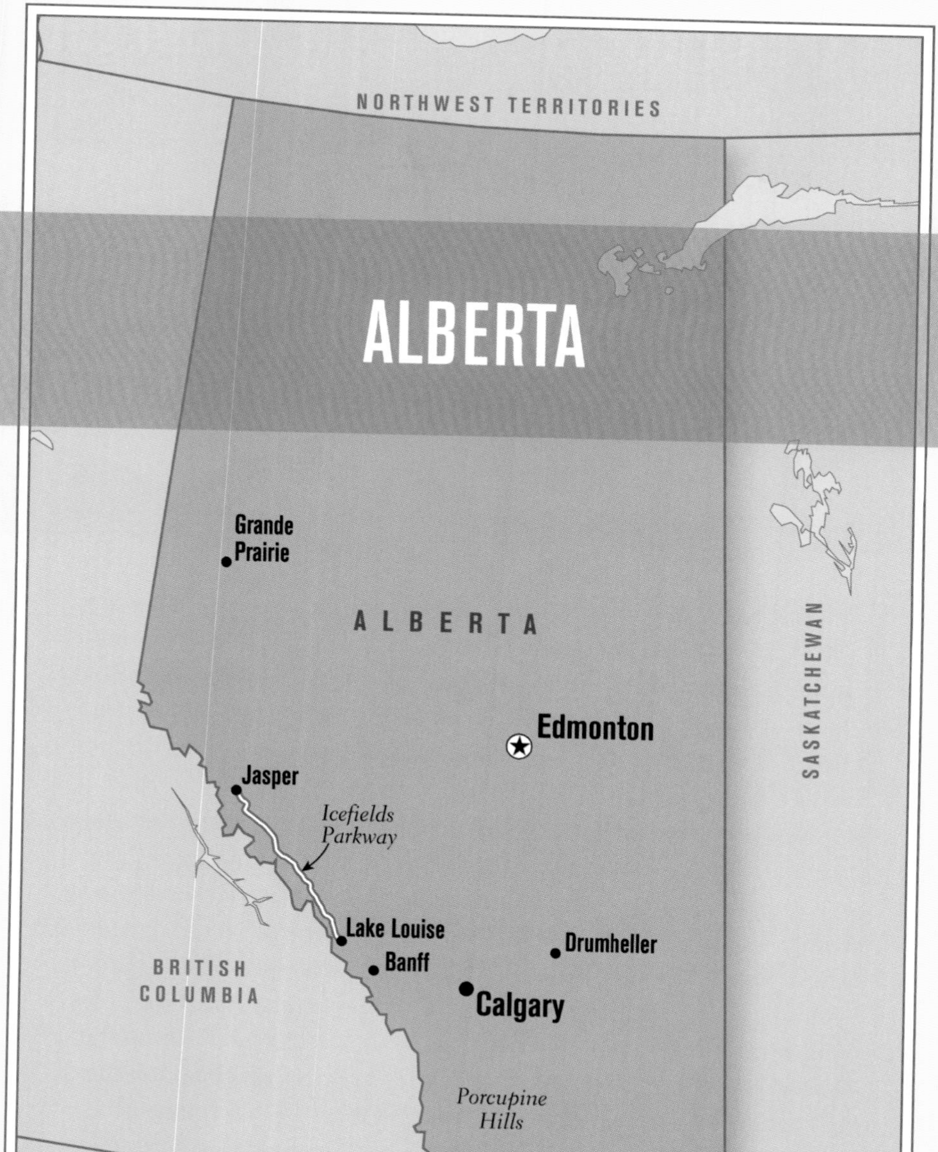

NORTHWEST TERRITORIES

# ALBERTA

Grande
Prairie

ALBERTA

SASKATCHEWAN

⭐ Edmonton

Jasper

*Icefields
Parkway*

Lake Louise

Drumheller

Banff

BRITISH
COLUMBIA

Calgary

*Porcupine
Hills*

WASHINGTON   IDAHO

MONTANA

# EXPERIENCE THE CALGARY STAMPEDE

It may be many things to many people, but there's no denying the Calgary Stampede—that ten-day Cowtown spectacle—is something to experience before you die. For those who have been, or locals who live it, I don't need to explain why. For the rest of you, take it from a city slicker who came to love his inner yahoo, and to wear his white hat, buckle and boots with pride. Here's why:

The festival attracts millions of people, from western Canada and beyond. Among them are party animals, herded through gates into wild nights at Cowboys, Nashville North and other venues around town. They see the Stampede as an excuse to drink beer, dance on sticky floors, flirt with the opposite sex (in boots), perhaps go home with them, wake up, hate themselves and repeat it all the following day. Strangely enough, older celebrants don't stray too far from the above, perhaps preferring smaller venues such as Ranchmans or bigger concerts like the Round Up. It's one of the world's biggest parties, if you're into that sort of thing, which the Stampede is more than willing to provide you an excuse to be.

# Tips for a Stampede

1. If you don't have boots, get a pair at the Alberta Boot Company, which has been furnishing cowboys and their accountants for over thirty years. That pain you feel breaking them in makes you a better person.
2. Pick up the traditional Calgary White Hat at Smithbilt, official hat maker for the event, and for the stars. Do not take it off, even when you sleep.
3. Never say *Yeehaw*. It's *Yahoo*. Remember that, or face a world of shame.
4. Line up for free bacon pancakes and festive chit-chat each morning at Flour Rope Square. Do not make fun of the clowns.
5. Win a prized item from China along the midway. Donate it to a kid, but not in a creepy sort of way.
6. Ride the abnormally fast Ferris wheel, pet an animal, visit the exhibitions, watch a miniature horse show, eat lunch in the Big 4, gear up for the rodeo.
7. Stay for the Big Show and fireworks.
8. After that, interact with local wildlife at Cowboys, Nashville North or Ranchman's. ➤

Next, the Stampede is the World's Richest Rodeo. Before I understood exactly what the rodeo is, how it works and who's behind it, I always rooted for bulls and horses. I'd yell at my TV set: *Throw that bastard off you and trample him in the mud!* I'm sure I'm not alone, but that changed when I decided to actually see what was going on for myself. Interviewing riders, judges, farmers and vets, I found myself busting one rodeo myth after the next. No, the testicles of the animals are not strung up to make them buck. No, rodeo animals seldom get hurt and receive the best possible medical attention when they do. Yes, riders have the utmost respect for the animals, and bear the brunt of the injuries. No, the animals are never overworked, but are bred for their bucking ability, and live out their days like champions in the pasture. And yes, it's dangerous, as even a mechanical bull will snap your wrist. It's always difficult to lift a veil of assumptions, but having finally learned more about the rodeo, I see a timeless confrontation between man and beast, in fierce but relatively harmless battle, catering to and supported by the very people who work with animals in their daily lives. Animal rights activists may still want to string me up by my testicles, but I'll say this: go check out the

ALBERTA ↑

rodeo, meet the people, see the animals, and form an educated opinion.

Finally, there's Cowtown itself: Calgary. Over the years I've visited the city during Stampede, I'm always impressed with the community spirit behind the event. The free pancake breakfasts. The parades. The exhibitions. The Young Canadians. The performances. The volunteers who make the event tick, taking unpaid leave from work in order to do so. "Any time you can give back to the community, and help them out a little bit, you get something out of it," TV's Mantracker Terry Grant tells me. He's been a volunteer at the Stampede for years.

During my second Stampede, I was hell bent on breaking in a pair of boots and never left the hotel without my white hat. Before that, the only time I'd ever dressed like a cowboy was at Halloween parties, but here I can slot right in. Boots make me stand taller, puffing out my chest. The cowboy myth (see Ranch Vacation, page 62) still holds power in our modern age.

Certainly there are those who avoid the Stampede like a warm pile of cow droppings, but there's no denying the sheer energy that shakes up the city. Boots and hats are everywhere, kids have cotton-candy grins, the midway is buzzing. Like many items on the Great Canadian Bucket List, the Stampede is likely a saddle that fits some better than others. But as a true Canadian celebration of Western roots and community spirit, you can't miss it.

**START HERE:** canadianbucketlist.com/stampede

# SKI IN A UNESCO WORLD HERITAGE SITE

Canada has sixteen UNESCO World Heritage Sites, and it's safe to say that visiting them all should be on the National Bucket List. After all, these are places of unique physical and cultural significance worldwide. Still, a bucket list should transcend the thoughts of a committee, even if they get it right, and especially when they get it wrong. Some World Heritage Sites I've visited around the world consist of little more than historical rubble. Some sites are miss-them-if-you-blink-really-that-was-it? And some, like Banff National Park, are just so staggeringly gorgeous they belong in another category altogether.

In any season, the Canadian Rockies is the picture postcard of Canada. Vast carpets of forest, gemstone lakes and mountains with views waiting to kick you in the plexus. It took genius, and considerable Canadian elbow grease, to set up three different ski resorts in the park: Lake Louise, Sunshine and Norquay. Come winter, you can literally slide down the wilderness that surrounds you.

Lake Louise, the third-biggest ski resort in Canada, is View Central. Enjoying the resort's runs, I often had to stop and plop my butt in the snow simply to admire the vista. I was determined to hit every lift in one day, which I did, and was not disappointed. Thanks to its location inside a national park, respect for the environment takes precedence over the ambitions of a leisure corporation. Perhaps this is why Lake Louise is owned by one family, with patriarch Charlie Locke being the first guy to scale all ten peaks in the area. Here is a mountain for people who love mountains: million-dollar views, not million-dollar condos.

Closer to Banff town centre is Sunshine, a smaller resort famed for its champagne powder. Staying at the Sunshine Mountain Lodge, Banff's only ski-in, ski-out boutique lodge, it's easy to awake each morning to catch "first chair" and reap the rewards. For skiers and snowboarders, simply catching first chair is one for the bucket list, anywhere, especially with a dozen centimetres of fresh snow on the ground. Sunshine has the kind of snow that makes your skis smile. This from a guy who grew up in Africa, who first saw snow as a six-year-old during a freak storm in Johannesburg, and was told to hide under his school desk in case it was ash from nuclear fallout. True story.

For all the snow in Canada, and the resorts that offer world-class conditions without even trying, what's the big deal about the UNESCO designation? You probably won't ski among moose and elk (although one instructor tells me his girlfriend once saw a wolverine). Sunshine, Norquay and Lake Louise—the Big Three, as they

## Canada's UNESCO World Heritage Sites

1. Head-Smashed-In Buffalo Jump, AB
2. Historic District of Old Quebec, QC
3. Landscape of Grand Pré, NS
4. L'Anse aux Meadows National Historic Site, NL
5. Old Town Lunenburg, NS
6. Rideau Canal, ON
7. SGang Gwaay, BC
8. Canadian Rocky Mountain Parks, AB
9. Dinosaur Provincial Park, AB
10. Gros Morne National Park, NL
11. Joggins Fossil Cliffs, NS
12. Kluane / Wrangell–St. Elias / Glacier Bay / Tatshenshini, NT
13. Miguasha National Park, QC
14. Nahanni National Park, NT
15. Waterton Glacier International Peace Park, AB
16. Wood Buffalo National Park, NT/AB

co-market themselves—look like typical resorts, with lifts and quads and young Australians sweeping chairs in exchange for a season pass. There are après-ski bars serving craft beer and knee-high plates of nachos. So how is this different, you may ask? It could be the views from the chairs at Lake Louise. It could be the snow at Sunshine. It could be the homeyness of Norquay. It could even be the proximity of iconic and grand Canadian hotels: Fairmont's Banff Springs and Château Lake Louise. On investigation, I can confirm it's all of the above, wrapped in a shell of deep respect for its surroundings—safe, protected, but available to be enjoyed.

**START HERE:** canadianbucketlist.com/skibig3

ALBERTA ↑

# HUNT FOR DINOSAURS

O h, what irony that the fiercest creatures ever to roam the planet have been unearthed, literally, in Canada. Here, in the land where the mighty *Tyrannosaurus rex* roared, we now honour the beaver. *T. rex* would use beavers as tennis balls—assuming dinosaurs played tennis or coexisted with beavers. Regardless, their old bones, discovered in southern Alberta's badlands, have been found in the world's richest fossil bed.

Like most young boys, I was fascinated by dinosaurs, reciting their long-winded *-saurus* names and taking extra time to look at today's tiny lizards, wondering where it all went wrong. Or, given the rise of mammals, right. Unfortunately, by the time I arrived at Dinosaur Provincial Park, I was just another jaded adult too consumed by

# ON THE BUCKET LIST: Professor Philip J. Currie

*The world's foremost dinosaur expert (think Sam Neill in Jurassic Park, who was partially based on Dr. Currie) digs into the National Bucket List:*

The Milk River Canyon north of the American border is Alberta's deepest canyon and is also in the most sparsely populated region in the southern half of the province. The unhindered view of prairie grasslands is augmented by a great bowl-like depression that slopes down toward the canyon, offering a spectacular view of the mysterious Sweetgrass Hills on the south side of the border. The badlands have produced some of the most interesting fossils from the province, including embryonic duckbilled dinosaurs within eggs and a superbly preserved skeleton of the ancestor of *Tyrannosaurus rex*!

> Professor Philip J. Currie,
> World-renowned Palaeontologist
> Founder, Royal Tyrrell Museum of Palaeontology

maturity to appreciate the fact that I had just plucked a 70-million-year-old dinosaur bone directly from the ground. The kids around me, however, went berserk.

All it takes is a little imagination. Seventy-five million years ago, the Red Deer River valley was as lush and tropical as Central America. Huge beasts roamed about, looking very much like giant lizards, or birds, or museum skeletons, depending on which theory you choose to believe in. When the dinosaurs woke up to the Worst Day Ever, and promptly died, their bones settled on the riverbed, were covered up by soft sandstone and mudstone, and were all but forgotten until the 1800s, when the fiercest creatures on earth, humans, now wore funny hats. During the last ice age, a glacier had removed the top level of dirt, exposing hundreds of bones from over forty dinosaurs, including Tyrannosauridae, Hypsilophodontidae and Ankylosauria (you know, the ones with thick ankles).

Today, this UNESCO World Heritage Site is more than just Dinosaur Central. Sure, the visitor centre and interpretation drives

ALBERTA ↑

are interesting, and you can drive a couple of hours to the Royal Tyrrell Museum of Palaeontology in Drumheller to see what the fossils look like cleaned up and bolted together. But it's the landscape itself that struck me, dare I say it, like a meteor.

The badlands are so called because the soil makes this land terrible for farming but wonderful for filming science fiction. Cracked grey earth resembling the skin of an elephant is tightly wrapped around phallic rocks called hoodoos. Rattlesnakes shake among the riverside cottonwoods, while the much smaller descendants of dinosaurs fly overhead or bask in the sun. Taking it all in, it's hard not to appreciate the scale of our planet's history, and the palaeontological riches of Alberta.

A couple of years later, I find myself extracting an articulated bone from a fossil bed cut into a steep cliff, an hour outside Grande Prairie. I am almost one thousand kilometres north of the badlands, at the site of yet another remarkable discovery. Here, among oil and gas platforms, lies one of the world's next-richest fossil beds, as palaeontologists from around the world work each summer in sun and rain to extract one fossil after another. The world's most famous dinosaur guy, Canada's own Professor Phil Currie, is spearheading the charge, complete with a $26-million namesake museum to house new-found treasures unearthed from the area.

Oil and gas beneath the earth have made Alberta Canada's richest province. Yet its earth continues to yield riches that give us profound insight into the past. Whether you're into history, museums or just unusual scenery, join the hunt for dinosaurs in Alberta. At least before a meteor comes out of nowhere, causes a deep impact, blocks out the sun, wipes out life and forces you, inconveniently, to wait another 70 million years for the opportunity.

**START HERE:** canadianbucketlist.com/dinosaur

# HELI-YOGA IN THE ROCKIES

If you place the prefix "heli" in front of any other word, the result can only sound impossibly and incredibly cool. Heli-shopping! Heli-badminton! Heli-dating! We've already covered heli-skiing in B.C., so let's get creative as we climb aboard a whirlybird to witness one of the very best views one can possibly see: the peaks, spires, glaciers, lakes and valleys of the snow-capped Rocky Mountains.

I'm Lululemoning my way into the mountains for an afternoon of Icefields Helicopter's "heli-yoga." It's the perfect blend of Canada's Western provinces: the healthy lifestyle choices of British Columbia wrapped in the big ideas and money of Alberta. I meet my hatha yoga instructor, Martha McCallum, who is also a certified hiking

guide, wildlife biologist and wellness coach. Like most yoga teachers I've encountered, she speaks with a voice as soothing as lip balm, edging me on to find my centre and connect with the earth, or in this case the mountains. She's well aware of the irony of using jet fuel for an elevating mind-body exercise, but it does bring us closer to nature without having to build any roads or destroy any shrubs. It's also a lot easier than hiking with a yoga mat.

Travel writers use the adjective *breathtaking* with far too much gusto (myself included). Breathtaking is when someone punches you in the stomach, or you're about to bungee jump off a TV tower in Macao (trust me). The view of the Rockies from a helicopter is simply awful. As in "fills one with awe," like the word was originally intended. *Awesome* is only some awe, but here we're talking full, as in "to the brim." Our pilot banks through the canyons, glides over shark-fin peaks, hovers over bighorn sheep and a lone wolf that should probably make the sheep nervous. From above, I feel like a kid who has skipped all his vegetables and gone straight to dessert. With no long hikes to the top, heli-touring is instant gratification.

We land on a site called the Wedding Knoll (what, you've never been to a heli-wedding?), where Martha safely ushers us out with mats and a picnic basket. The helicopter takes off just as smoothly as it landed, and we are all alone, 2,700 metres up, embedded in wilderness. She lays out the mats, using rocks to keep them grounded in the mountain breeze, and begins the first pose. The goal of yoga is to meditate to a point of perfect mind-body tranquility. Usually this is done in a room with polished hardwood floors, mirrors, New Age music and a dozen ladies wearing stretchy pants that flatter their buttocks. On the mountain, we still wear stretchy pants but have either far more or far fewer distractions, depending on your love for nature or for the behinds of yoga practitioners.

After the 45-minute class, we dine on Martha's homemade organic sandwiches and follow that up with a short heli-hike along the spine of the mountain. I decide that all hikes in the mountains should start at the top and then just stay that way. Our helicopter returns, and the reward for this strenuous day of exercise is another fly-by through the mountains. *Namaste!*

It is certainly not essential to combine yoga with your heli-flightseeing experience in the Rockies. Not all of us are in pursuit of mind-soul nirvana, and not all of us want to stretch into a pretzel. Seeing the Rocky Mountains from above, on the other hand, is a must. Heli-hiking, heli-poker, heli-cooking—just add the prefix *heli-* and you've got a winner, flying high on the Great Canadian Bucket List.

**START HERE:** canadianbucketlist.com/heliyoga

# BE THE COWBOY ON A RANCH VACATION

Cowboys date back to the 1700s, the name being a direct translation of the Spanish *vaquero*, a person who managed cattle by horseback. Cattle drives, averaging around three thousand head, were managed by just ten men or fewer, each with several horses, battling the elements to literally drive the meat to market. The cowboy, often poorly paid, uneducated and low on the social ladder, had many tasks to perform. These included rounding up the cattle; sorting, securing and protecting herds from thieves and wild animals; breaking in horses; and birthing and nursing sick animals.

The hazardous and strenuous nature of the work created a breed of hardened men and terrific fodder for the romance novels eagerly snapped up by urban readers fascinated by the call of the Wild West.

Despite Hollywood's portrayal, there were relatively few violent confrontations with Native Americans. Instead, most Indian chiefs were paid in cattle or cash for permission to drive cattle through their lands. Another aspect glossed over in the folklore is that, according to the U.S. census of the time, 30 percent of all cowboys were of African or Mexican ancestry. Giddy-up amigo! When railways replaced cattle drives, modern cowboys began to work on ranches and show off their skills at competitive rodeos.

Our bucket list is now singing that old eighties song: "I Wanna Be a Cowboy." Who am I to argue?

Bill Moynihan talks with a throat of gravel, as if he's been chewing on the bones of Jack Palance and needs a can of oil to wash it down. He may be seventy-five years old, but the patriarch of the 120-acre Skyline Ranch is as tough and grizzled as any bootstrapping cowboy. Located in the Porcupine Hills, Skyline offers ranch vacations where guests can assist with daily chores, including feeding the three hundred head of cattle, roping up steers and patrolling for wild animals. The area, captured beautifully in Ang Lee's *Brokeback Mountain*, sweeps up to the Rocky Mountains on the horizon. Bill's kids and grandkids are all involved in the family operation, a working ranch where you can leave your hat on and get your hands dirty.

Bill's moustache looks like an army guarding his upper lip. The former boxer, bush pilot, cop and rodeo cowboy sizes me up. I'm a regular cowpoke, as alien to life on a ranch as I am to life in the

## Speak Like a Cowboy

*Grab your bangtail from the picket line and hop in the rig, here's some genuine cowboy slang to prove you're not a city slicker (even if nobody will know what the heck you're talking about).*

**bake:** When you ride your horse too hard, you bake it.

**bangtail:** a mustang

**burn the breeze:** gallop at full speed

**chewed gravel:** got thrown from a horse

**dusted:** got thrown from a horse

**grassed:** got thrown from a horse (sense a theme?)

**greenhorn:** someone from the East who don't know diddly-squat

**hurricane deck:** what you sit in when a horse starts bucking

**outlaw:** a horse that cannot be broken

**owl head:** a horse that won't stop looking around

**rig:** a saddle

**saddle bum:** a drifter

**slicker:** a raincoat

**widow maker:** a misbehaving horse ➤

Himalayas. I select a white horse named Barry (ahem) and saddle up for my first roundup. Here's what they don't tell you about Angus cows: they're big, and they can be rather belligerent. My cutting horse, bred for sudden stops and bucking cows, isn't fazed. Bill lassos a young calf and I assist with tagging it on the ear, nervous about its 600-kilogram mom who seems endearingly protective. Next I feed heifers some grain and dispense hay from an industrial tractor. While I barely manage to heave a bale of hay to the shed, Bill walks past carrying two on each hand. When the zombies attack, I hope I'm around a guy like Bill.

Skyline guests can also go hiking, fishing, biking and horse riding in the hills, but ranch work is where the action is. Moving hay, shovelling shit, feeding the animals: farm life is physically tough and yet satisfyingly simple. You know what has to be done, and you do it.

That evening, over cold cans of Lucky Lager, I share stories with Bill and his son Reid, learning about the respect one has for the environment when one actually lives in it. "When the stars are out, you can see just about every one of them," explains Reid, feeding the firepit. The chain bonding ranching and nature is thick, and the Moynihans have a deep appreciation and respect for the animals and the land that provide their livelihood.

They also have a deep appreciation for fun. When Bill teaches me how to lasso, the only thing I succeed in lassoing is my eyeball. City slickers are always good for a laugh around the fire.

The following day, I succeed in sticking my arm deep inside a pregnant cow's vagina, verifying all is ripe for birthing. Yes, I've come a long way in a couple of days. We saddle up for a ride to the property fences, making sure nothing is damaged and looking for signs of predators. A strong, icy wind blows across the foothills.

"The biggest thing you can do in life is pass on the thing you love to somebody else," Bill tells me. He is not a man of many words, but cowboys don't have to be. I try to grunt, but it comes out like a squeak.

The word *dude* technically refers to someone who doesn't know cowboy culture but pretends otherwise. You can also refer to a dude as being "all hat and no cattle." A dude like, say, me. Yet the hospitality from these earthy folks was wonderfully warm and genuine, and the values of the modern-day cowboy seem to be alive and well. As it rides its way onto the Great Canadian Bucket List, ranch life remains as real and alluring as the cowboy myth that promotes it.

**START HERE:** canadianbucketlist.com/ranch

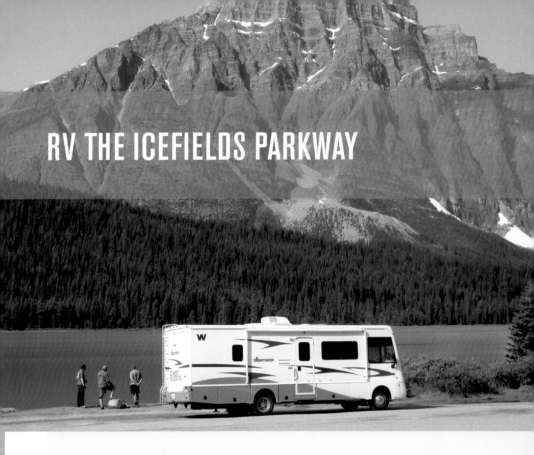

# RV THE ICEFIELDS PARKWAY

The first time I hauled a backpack around the world, I had a wonderful sensation of independence. Everything I needed was right there: clothes, toiletries, my iPod, books, cash, a sense of adventure. My daily challenge was deciding where to sleep and use the toilet. The first time I went on an RV adventure, I felt that familiar gush of independence, only the daily challenges were flushed away with the black water.

My dad, my brothers and I had rented a nine-metre Winnebago for a week's Mancation to the Rockies. We would become just one of over a million RVs on Canadian roads that summer, the others hopefully driven by people with more experience than us. With a complete kitchen, two television sets, a bedroom and a bathroom, the RV rattled and rolled its way out of Vancouver, wobbling in the wind with the aerodynamics of a cement brick. I was driving, my brothers were yelling: "Too close to the side!" "Watch the lines!" "You almost hit that car!" Ah yes, just a few hours in and I could feel our Mancation easing my stress . . . right up behind my eyeballs and straight to the back of my throat.

My dad has always been in love with mountains, but since emigrating from South Africa he'd never had the opportunity to see the Rockies. For the full effect, I steered our roadworthy beast to Highway 93—a.k.a. the Icefields Parkway—a 232-kilometre stretch of road between Lake Louise and Jasper. It is, without a doubt, one of the world's most spectacular drives, a gee-whiz postcard moment waiting for you at every turn. The visual impact of the mountains and glaciers that line the highway rivals that of the Himalayas, but boy, the Rockies are a lot easier to get to. Passing turquoise lakes and glacier-cut mountains, we craned our necks from side to side to capture the view out of the large windows, like we were watching a game of tennis. The overall effect, especially for someone who enjoys mountain beauty, can be as rich as overly cheesy fondue. "It's too much," I heard my dad reporting to my mom on his cellphone. "But in a good way."

Rock flour, crushed and carried by glaciers, makes mountain lakes glow in luminous shades of blue and green. We visit Moraine Lake on a postcard-perfect day, getting our group photo in front of one of Canada's most popular and sought-after views. By the time we reach Peyto Lake, farther up the highway, our camera batteries need refuelling from the RV's generator. The RV's height, big windows and ease of movement made it the perfect vehicle from which to gawk at the mountains, if not always to park. Thank you, Parks Canada, for the extra-long parking bays at all the major sites. Parks

## Canada's Top RV Destinations

GO RVing is an organization representing RV dealers, manufacturers and campground operators that helps to promote the freedom, flexibility and fun of the RV lifestyle. Here's a list from their Top Destinations to RV in Canada:

**BC** Ashnola River
Bella Coola

**AB** Banff National Park
Beauvais Lake Provincial Park/
Waterton Lakes National Park

**SK** Douglas Provincial Park
Duck Mountain Provincial Park

**MB** Spruce Woods Provincial Park

**ON** Algonquin Park
Bronte Creek Provincial Park

**QC** Bannick, Ville-Marie
Gaspésie

**NS** Aspy Bay, Cape Breton
Cabot Trail

**NB** Fundy National Park
Littoral Acadien

**PEI** Cavendish Sunset
Twin Shores, Darnley

**NL** Gros Morne
Twillingate

**YK** Kluane Lake
Tatchun Lake

Canada protects our wilderness, and they park Canada too!

We pop into the Athabasca Glacier, where monster customized four-by-four buses take us directly onto a six-kilometre-long ice floe in the Columbia Icefields. Out on the ice, I scoop up melted water, drinking the taste of nature at its purest.

Bookending the Parkway are two of Canada's most iconic wilderness areas: Banff and Jasper national parks. No surprise that we came across a bear chewing berries alongside the road, or huge elk stopping traffic in its tracks. During the week, we take the Banff Gondola and the

Jasper Tramway, barbecue steaks in an RV park, play a terrific round of golf at the Jasper Park Lodge, rent Harley-Davidsons to rocket up Mount Edith Cavell, and even swim in the ice-cold waters of a glacier lake. It is, in short, an epic Mancation, immersed in true Canadiana. We even manage to keep the RV in relatively good shape, although on the last night of our journey we realize that nobody had been paying too much attention to the instructions about how to empty the black water. Push a few buttons, pull a few knobs, and the next thing we know, the tube comes loose and drenches my brother and me. Truth be told, black water looks rather yellow. My dad would have wet himself laughing, but of course we'd already beaten him to it.

I've been on the Icefields Parkway several times since, yet the RV trip stands out. Travel magic is not about what you're doing, it's about whom you're doing it with. Wise words to remember when crossing off any item on the Great Canadian Bucket List.

**START HERE:** canadianbucketlist.com/icefields

ALBERTA ↑

# HIT YOUR TARGET AT THE WEST EDMONTON MALL

Yes, I'm fully aware how this looks. Here's a book listing the ultimate things to do in Canada before you die, and you just read: visit a mall. It's not even the biggest mall in the world. That honour belongs to— No, wait, someone else just built a bigger one. Yet Canadian malls are a little different. Take Montreal's Underground City. Officially called RÉSO, it's a warren of tunnels beneath twelve square kilometres of downtown Montreal, linking shops, hotels, residential buildings, schools, train and bus stations, offices and tourists searching for a glimpse of daylight. Accessed by half a million people every day in winter, RÉSO contains several malls and so cannot technically be called a solitary mall in its own right. Calgary has its four-storey CORE, beneath three city blocks and with 160 stores. "Big deal!" yawn our friends in Ontario, where Toronto's Eaton Centre has 330 stores, Brampton's Bramalea City has 342 and Mississauga's Square One a whopping 360 places of commercial worship. In British Columbia, where people can actually step out-side in winter, Burnaby's Metropolis at Metrotown trumps them all, at 450 stores, including a massive Asian supermarket.

Yes, Canadians like to shop, and by the looks of it, they like to shop at the same chain stores you'll find at just about every mall in the country. And then, suddenly, like an unexplained star burning across the retail sky, you get the phenomenon of the West Edmonton Mall. The largest mall in North America has over 800 stores, cover-ing 570,000 square metres of retail, more than double the size of Metropolis. There's parking for more than 20,000 cars, it employs over 20,000 people, receives 30 million visitors a year, and is Alberta's busiest tourist attraction.

I hear you asking: "Robin, seriously, isn't one mall just a carbon copy of the next? Stores, food court, gadget stores, teenagers in paint-on jeans, glass elevators, confusing maps?" I thought so too, until I found myself pulling the trigger of a .44 Magnum revolver, blasting a bottle-cap hole in my paper target—at the West Edmonton Mall.

How many malls are accredited as a zoo? How many malls boast the world's second-largest indoor amusement park, complete with twenty-four feature rides and a thrilling roller coaster called the Mindbender? How many malls have the world's largest indoor water park, with the world's largest indoor wave pool, 25-metre-high slides and a bungee jump tower? At this mall, you can say hello to the sea lion that swims beneath a replica of Señor Columbus's *Santa Maria*, skate on an Olympic-sized hockey rink and then transplant your-self to New Orleans, Paris or Beijing at one of three themed areas: Bourbon Street, Europa Boulevard and Chinatown. Should you get tired of walking around trying to make sense of the thoughtfully pro-vided maps, take a nap in one of the mall's two hotels.

You might expect to find such a mall in Vegas, or perhaps Dubai, which stole the Biggest Mall in the World title before relinquishing it

## Canadians Are Shopaholics

According to a report by KPMG, nine of North America's fifteen most productive malls are in Canada. Measured by their sales per square foot, these include:

**Sherway Gardens**, Toronto ($950/sq. ft.),
**Chinook Centre**, Calgary ($1,055/sq. ft.),
**Oakridge Centre**, Vancouver ($1,200/sq. ft.),
**Yorkdale Shopping Centre**, Toronto ($1,300/sq. ft.),
**Toronto Eaton Centre** ($1,320/sq. ft.) and, topping the list, beating out Caesars Palace in Vegas ($1,470/sq. ft.) as the most productive mall on the entire continent: Vancouver's Pacific Centre, at a whopping $1,580/sq. ft. ➤

to China, Malaysia and the Philippines. Asian malls dominate the list of biggest malls, but standing out like a proud beaver among the tigers is our very own West Edmonton Mall. To celebrate, I armed myself.

Flora Kupsch owns the family-friendly Wild West Shooting Centre. Flora is a multidisciplinary champion in firearms competitions and ably hands me a nine-millimetre .357 and a .44 Magnum bazooka. The Wild West sells a range of ammunition and guns, and offers various packages to clients who visit from all over the province. Where else can you pick up a bikini, do the groceries and let off a few rounds? Increasingly, many of Flora's customers are young girls, strung out on *Twilight*, aiming for Team whoever they're not into that month.

I surprised Flora, and myself, by turning out to be a pretty good shot. Is there another mall where you can walk out with lingerie for your wife and used target sheets? Exactly.

**START HERE:** canadianbucketlist.com/wem

# HIKE OR SKI INTO SKOKI LODGE

In 1931, Swiss mountain guides and members of the Banff Ski Club decided to build western Canada's first commercial ski lodge. With thousands of kilometres to choose from, they settled on a place called Skoki, selected for its scenic beauty, quality of snow, proximity to a creek and safety from avalanches. Today, one of the oldest and highest backcountry lodges in Canada is an eleven-kilometre hike from the groomed ski slopes of the Lake Louise Resort, and I'm feeling every step of it.

It's my first time on cross-country skis, slipping and sliding forth with surprising ease. A strip of material under each ski, called the skin, grips the snow as I edge my way through pine forest, over frozen

ALBERTA

## The Royal Throne

When the newly married Duke and Duchess of Cambridge needed time alone on their first royal visit to Canada, Skoki Lodge was the perfect fit: miles away from the paparazzi, relaxing, and in the bosom of the Rockies. Skoki's staff worked with royal handlers to keep the destination mum and prepare it for the future King and Queen of England (and Canada). This meant the no-running-water, no-electricity charm of Skoki would need a little polish. A helicopter brought in a modern bathroom, complete with flush toilet, bathtub and sink, painstakingly installed to the bemusement of long-time staff, who have always found other ways to make do. Everything went off splendidly, even if the royal stay was less than twenty-four hours. As for the bathroom, it was hastily demolished and cleared away. Since Skoki is a wonderful slice of rustic history, guests are directed to the outhouses, as perfectly serviceable a throne as any. ➤

lakes and across windy mountain passes. Every guest must ski, hike or snowshoe in, unless you're the Duke and Duchess of Cambridge, in which case Parks Canada will organize a helicopter. Skoki made headlines for attracting the newly wed William and Kate on their Canadian honeymoon. No electricity, no cellphone or Internet coverage, no running water, no paparazzi—Skoki provided a rustic royal break from the media frenzy. It wasn't the first royal connection either: one of the lodge's first guests was one Lady Jean, a lady-in-waiting to Queen Victoria, who visited Skoki with her travel-writer husband, Niall Rankin. While the Rankins used the outhouse like regular guests, William and Kate had a specially built bathroom constructed for their visit, which was hastily destroyed afterwards, lest regular guests get any ideas.

Skoki strives to be as authentic a backcountry experience today as it was in the 1930s. That means candles, blankets and late night stumbles to the outhouse during blizzards. It's one of the best winter adventures in North America, with an emphasis on adventure. You'll

know this as you make your way up Deception Pass, a steep uphill that keeps going, and going, and going. By the time I arrive, covered in sweat and snow from too many downhill tumbles, the fireplace is surrounded by guests enjoying hot homemade soup. The lodge accommodates up to twenty-two guests, and we each feel we deserve our place on one of the sink-in couches. Among the guests are two Norwegians, a ski club from Manitoba, a couple returning for the ninth time from the Northwest Territories, a birthday party and a couple on their second honeymoon (staying in the Honeymoon Cabin, of course). Will and Kate, who signed the guest book like everyone else, preferred the Riverside Cabin, close to the creek. I offload my gear in a cabin called Wolverine, named for the wolverine that got stuck in it and almost tore it to shreds. Although Skoki's original builders took refuge in a special bear tree, the bears, cougars and wolves that roam Banff National Park nowadays keep their distance. The most bothersome creatures appear to be pine martens, porcupines and exhausted travel writers.

Skoki itself is the launch pad for hiking and skiing trails, which most guests explore on their second day. Two-night stays are typical, giving you just about enough time to recover from the eleven-kilometre trek in order to do it all over again. Nobody can expect to lose much weight, however. The chef and staff somehow prepare gourmet meals, such as coconut-crusted Alaskan halibut, and marinated tenderloin served with candied yams, avocado Caesar salad and fresh homemade bread. That everything is packed in by snowmobile (horses in summer) and prepared using propane stoves makes it all the more impressive, and appreciated.

The discussion around the fire revolves mostly around Skoki's beauty, history and legacy. One couple sifts through the guest books until they find the last time they signed it, in 1974. Another guest plays the piano, helicoptered in sometime in the early 1980s. I read an old book about western Canadian outlaws, play with Lucy and Bill (Skokie's resident Jack Russells) and let the fresh air and exercise sink into my pores. On my final night, the moon is so full I can read without a headlamp. Miles away from anything, protected by a world of mountains, forest and snow, Skoki is the perfect escape, for royals and the rest of us.

**START HERE:** canadianbucketlist.com/skoki

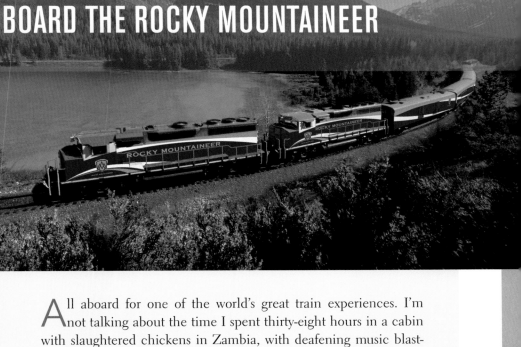

# BOARD THE ROCKY MOUNTAINEER

All aboard for one of the world's great train experiences. I'm not talking about the time I spent thirty-eight hours in a cabin with slaughtered chickens in Zambia, with deafening music blasting through the cobwebbed, distorted speakers. No, the Rocky Mountaineer is an altogether more genteel affair, smothered in five-star service, tasty libations and views of the Rockies in all their splendour. Running on four routes going both east and west, the Rocky Mountaineer is North America's largest private rail service. National Geographic called it one of the World's Greatest Trips, and *Condé Nast Traveler* listed it among the Top 5 Trains in the World. I hopped

↑

ALBERTA

on board at the station in Vancouver for a two-day journey up to Banff.

You don't sleep on the Rocky Mountaineer. The thousand-kilometre journey takes place during daylight so you can enjoy the views, with passengers staying overnight at the company's hotel in Kamloops. Guests are seated in a two-level, glass-domed coach with panoramic views, drinks service and a helpful, unnervingly cheery attendant pointing out places of interest along the way. On the way out of B.C. we pass over Hells Gate, the narrowest point of the Fraser River, and spot a bear walking across the tracks behind us. We enter the engineering marvel of the Spiral Tunnels and are halfway through a game of cards when Mount Robson, the highest mountain in the Rockies, comes into view. That deserves another Caesar.

There's an excellent gourmet meal service and optional activities such as wine tasting, to put you nicely in the groove of the rocking train. Of course, like many of life's great luxuries, the comfort comes with a price tag. The trip is ideal for Vancouver cruise shippers extending their journey, seniors or anyone looking for a little bit of romance. Recalling the time I paid ten dollars for an attendant's Snickers bar in Croatia, the only food I had in eighteen hours, I relax knowing that the Rocky Mountaineer is all about the journey, not the destination. If only all journeys were quite as civilized.

**START HERE:** canadianbucketlist.com/rockymountaineer

# SWALLOW A PRAIRIE OYSTER

Chef Aaron Scherr invites me into the restaurant kitchen and pulls out his balls. He asks me if I want to hold them, and I can't deny I'm a little curious. They are grey and slimy, acorn shaped, with the texture of sponge. They could be the brains of a chipmunk, or perhaps a forgotten, desiccated plum. But no, there's simply no getting around it. These are testicles.

Buzzards Restaurant has had its famous prairie oysters on the menu for two decades, a special addition to the menu during the Calgary Stampede. Now, a cowboy, even one fresh off the ranch, would have to look long and far to find the sea in the Prairies. The fact is, these oysters are as removed from seafood as catnip from a banjo. They do, however, bear some relation to Rocky Mountain Oysters, which you can find south of the border.

ALBERTA ↑

# A Ballsy Recipe

*Chef Aaron Scherr prepares his famous Prairie Oysters*

### The Crown Jewels

### Ingredients:

1 pair (2) prairie oysters, scrotum removed

2 oz. (60 mL) Crown Royal Canadian rye whisky

3–4 fresh strawberries, quartered or sliced,
   depending on desired presentation

1 4-oz. (125 g) portion of fresh-baked corn bread

1 oz. (30 g) gently crushed walnuts

1 tsp. (5 mL) real maple syrup

1 tbsp. (15 mL) salted butter

salt and pepper—6-to-1 ratio, to taste

### Method:

1. Prior to cooking, the oysters (balls) must be blanched and cleaned. Bring a pot of salted water to a boil and carefully place balls in water. Cook for 3–4 minutes. Remove and place in ice-water bath to stop the cooking process. After the testes have cooled, carefully remove the external membrane without damaging the ball. Gently slice into "coins."

2. Preheat a shallow sauté pan over medium temperature, add butter and, as soon as it melts, toss in coins and season with salt and pepper. This part of the cooking process is crucial: if the oysters get overcooked, they will be rubbery and undesirable, so speed is the key to success. Quickly add the strawberries and maple syrup, turn up the heat, and hit the pan with Crown. Once the flambé subsides, remove from heat and toss with walnuts.

3. On a sexy-lookin' plate, place corn bread slice as the anchor to the customer's eye, and cover with contents of pan.

4. Chef's option: Presentation is everything, so feel free to add more berries or nuts, a dollop of whipped cream, or a drizzle of heavy cream. Serve with ginger beer. ➤

In order for cattle farmers to control their stock, male calves must be castrated. Typically, this is done when they are branded. Alternatively, testicles are tied with elastic, and eventually fall to the ground to be eaten by coyotes (ah, the circle of life!). Some of the balls roll their way to Buzzards, which has thought of creative means to cook, grill and sauté them for the adventurously hungry. Each year they are given a new name and recipe. I was lucky enough to receive the Crown Jewels, to which Scherr adds Crown Royal whisky for flavour.

He hands me a testicle and a sharp knife. I make a cut right at the top and ask him if this makes it kosher. Oh, he's heard them all before, with nigh a sentence passing without a pun. "Sprinkle on nuts, will you?" I ask him if he's lost his marbles. He warns me I might get the sack, and . . . you get the idea.

I slice the organ, rich in protein, into thin coin-sized medallions. Over the stove, Aaron adds maple butter over high heat, some whisky, salt, fresh-cut strawberries and gooseberries. For all their novelty on Buzzard's otherwise terrific menu, prairie oysters receive a lot of attention. Buses of Japanese tourists might arrive specifically to sample them. During the ten-day Stampede festival, the chef cooks up over one hundred kilograms of *cajones*.

Lately, sourcing bull balls has become a bit of a problem. Few large meat packers will tackle this soft market, but Aaron has found some farms in his native Saskatchewan to come to the rescue. He even prepared some bison nuts recently, which were bigger than baseballs. Apparently they were a home run with the customers.

He serves up the Crown Jewels at the table. In my travels I have been fortunate to sample crickets (legs get stuck in the teeth), termites (taste nutty), deep-fried guinea pig (stringy chicken), fermented horse milk (acidic) and crocodile (less-stringy chicken). The bucket list demands I eat the testicles of a bull, because this is something to do in Canada. Organ meat tastes like organ meat, and since I grew up on chopped liver, it's not a taste that's unfamiliar to me. Still, I'm not ordering seconds.

I ask for two bottles of beer and pull out my favourite souvenir of all time: a genuine, 100-percent-authentic, hairy kangaroo-scrotum bottle opener, picked up in Australia. The chef thinks I might be yanking his chain, but if you're going to have a themed meal, you might as well go balls to the wall. In the end, culture determines what we find acceptable to consume and what we don't. Eating the gonads of a raging bull, which carry flavour rather well, is deemed unacceptable by the same society that will happily nosh on pig's feet, liver, rump and halibut cheeks. The bulls get the snip either way, which keeps coyotes, Japanese tourists and national bucket lists satiated.

**START HERE:** canadianbucketlist.com/balls

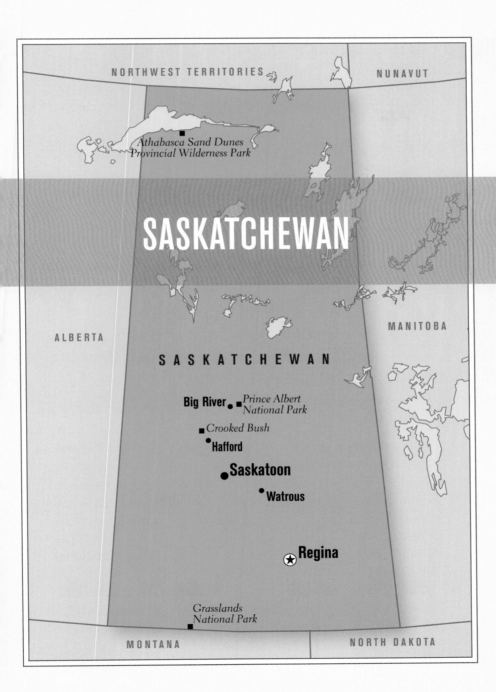

NORTHWEST TERRITORIES

NUNAVUT

Athabasca Sand Dunes
Provincial Wilderness Park

# SASKATCHEWAN

ALBERTA

MANITOBA

SASKATCHEWAN

Big River ■ Prince Albert
National Park

■ Crooked Bush

Hafford

● Saskatoon

● Watrous

⭐ Regina

Grasslands
National Park

MONTANA

NORTH DAKOTA

# SALUTE THE RCMP

The red serge is such a Canadian icon that the Mounties have trademarked it. After all, this is a police force on which others around the world are modelled. The Great Canadian Bucket List wants to understand just what the Royal Canadian Mounted Police is, who these people are and what makes them so great. I want to chase cars and shoot guns and catch bad guys. Hell, I want to be RCMP. So it's off to Regina's Depot, the very soul of the RCMP, the mother from which all cadets are given birth.

The excellent Arthur Erickson–designed Heritage Museum can answer my questions, but I want to get inside the organization's skin. So I continue driving, through the security gate, warned that I might encounter live training exercises. At the clothing facility, the Stores Person, Sean Lussier, measures me up: I am freckled, accented, with a streak of anti-authority tendencies. Mind you, he's got tattoos, piercings and a waxed moustache. Sean pulls out his pencil and tape measure. I am fitted with formal and casual wear, handed a pair of leather boots that need to be polished for twenty-five hours before they attain the appropriate sheen. He tells me new cadets tear up when they try on the red serge for the first time. I slip on the red blazer and immediately feel three inches taller.

It's off to the barber, where, from a selection of short, shorter and eight ball, I really begin to look the part. In the morning I am taking the Physical Ability Requirement Evaluation (PARE), an obstacle designed to challenge bodies and minds of incoming cadets. New cadets must complete four circuits of the course in under 4:45, plus tackle a weight mechanism. If they fail, they are given three days to give it another go. Failing that, they are released from duty, dreams and all. To graduate, the PARE must be completed within four minutes.

Cadets sleep on average just five hours a night. They will pack in the studies equivalent of a four-year degree in just twenty-six weeks. Speaking to some of them at breakfast in the canteen, I learn just how determined they are to make it, and how proud they are to be RCMP. I eat lightly before nervously making my way to the gym for the PARE test. Prior to the attempt, each cadet's blood pressure is checked as a precaution, which only succeeds in rocketing the nerves.

I am shown how to jump over this, hop over that, up the stairs, around the orange cone, on my back, on my front, again, again, again. The clock starts, and I keep an even pace. It doesn't seem too difficult at first. By the second lap, I am breathing heavily. Cadets are starting to cheer. By the third lap, my body feels ambushed. The jumps seem longer, my steps heavier. Fourth lap, the cadets are cheering, "Go Robin!" I can't let them down. If they see me fail,

## They Always Get Their Man

- The RCMP is the provincial police force for all provinces except Quebec, Ontario, and Newfoundland and Labrador. It provides additional policing services to 200 municipalities in Canada and nearly 200 First Nations communities.
- The red serge, which is worn only at civic ceremonies, celebrations and memorials, consists of a scarlet tunic with a low-neck collar and brass buttons. The pants are black riding breeches with a yellow stripe down each leg. Spurs accompany brown leather riding boots.
- The Dempster Highway (see page 323) was named after RCMP inspector William John Dempster, for his service to the North.
- Charles Dickens's son served as a member of the North-West Mounted Police, a precursor to the RCMP.
- Women first graduated as RCMP members in March 1975.
- The last RCMP dog patrol was in 1969.
- The RCMP served in the Boer War, World War I and World War II.
- Only Canadian citizens can join the RCMP.
- There are currently over 27,000 members and employees of the RCMP. ➤

they'll be discouraged, and here is a room of future peace officers, people who will save lives. I'm choking on lack of breath but continue to the weight machine, where I must thrust my body forward and pull weights in a fluid semicircle. My heart tries to rip itself out like the creature in *Alien*. Still, the cadets are cheering, and their cheering keeps me going. Suddenly I understand why home ice is so important.

I complete the task and pick up a 36-kilogram bag, carefully carrying it around a cone and returning it in complete control. The sergeant announces my time: 3:50. I collapse in exhaustion, the cadets are cheering. Already they are beginning their rotations, so I am whisked out of the gym. Who needs media in a time like this? Corporal Dan, the communications officer showing me around, is impressed. I'm coughing up intestine, tasting the iron of blood at

the back of my throat. "That's the PARE cough," says the corporal. "You'll have it for a couple days."

No time to recover. I rush off to formation marching and the daily Sergeant Major's Parade, where I am picked on by a mean-looking corporal, who makes me fully aware of his garlic-heavy diet. Cadets stand to attention as stiff as a pine forest. Then it's off to the Police Driving Unit, where Corporal Darcy Jacksteit allows me to join him for the day's exams. We play out various scenarios in his Crown Victoria, as I learn about RCMP policies and just how stressful it can be behind the wheel. After some evasive-driving procedures, I'm dropped off at a firearms unit, learning that guns are the last-ditch attempt and should always be aimed for maximum impact. Cadets will spend a minimum of fifty-two hours at the range.

Finally, I visit Sergeant B.J. Landry's Simulator Training Unit,

where high-tech cameras and simulators allow me to play out life-and-death scenarios in safety but under scrutiny. Police forces from around the world train at the Depot, sometimes employing RCMP policies. No other country has a national police force charged with performing so many roles—from policing to drug enforcement, immigration and borders to terrorism. A movie made the maxim famous: "The Mountie always gets his man." This, unfortunately, is not always the case. Yet, despite the clobbering the organization gets in the news media, its standards and traditions are of the highest calibre.

Growing up in South Africa, we were afraid of police. They were very often just as crooked as the thieves they were supposed to catch. Not so in Canada. It might not be on everyone's bucket list to put themselves through a crash course of cadet training. Yet everyone needs to visit the Heritage Museum and learn about this vital Canadian institution—to try on the red serge and see how it fits.

**START HERE:** canadianbucketlist.com/rcmp

# SUPPORT RIDER NATION

The first time I heard the word "Roughriders," I thought it was a brand of condoms. Immigrants to Canada have to face these sorts of challenges, such as how to pronounce *Saskatchewan*, or follow the puck, or learn to believe that a place called Moose Jaw actually exists. It took me some time to understand that Canadian football is different from American football, and that the most rabid fans in the CFL, if not the country, belong to Regina's own Roughriders. Indeed, when you visit Saskatchewan, you are actually visiting Rider Nation, where you'll no doubt get swept up in a frenzy of Rider Pride. This is why it's really important you don't tell anyone you once thought Roughriders was a brand of condoms. They might just stick a watermelon on your head.

It's game day for the Riders. Even though they didn't qualify for this year's Grey Cup playoffs, the fans are ready to brave sub-zero temperatures to show their enthusiastic support for the team. The Riders are far from the most successful team in the CFL (they've only won a handful of trophies in over one hundred years of chasing the ball), but fans of Canada's biggest sports franchises have a high threshold for failure. I'm throwing myself into the mix, donning the Green and

# Why the Watermelons?

Visitors to a Roughriders game will notice the colour green, lots of beer and people with watermelons on their heads. This is especially strange, because watermelons don't grow in Saskatchewan, and can be hard to find when the season extends into the cold months of September and October. Ask five fans why they're wearing watermelons and you'll get six answers, and a cold beer. Some believe it's a statement that Roughriders are so good they can wear fruity helmets for protection. Some believe it's because they're cheap to buy and fun to carve. There's a legend of some local students inventing the craze, and another that placing sticky watermelons on the head is the perfect way to cool down on a hot summer day. My research led me to someone else's research, which told of a couple of kids who went to Winnipeg to support the Riders in 2001, covered themselves in green and capped it off with a watermelon. Their antics attracted local media, which in turn attracted the marketing department of the Roughriders, who promptly encouraged the fashion, much to the delight of local watermelon suppliers. This may or may not be the winning theory, but when it comes to supporting Rider Nation, results rarely count for much anyway. ➤

White, painting my face, applying temporary Rider tattoos, putting on green bug glasses and a bright green wig. Covering it all is a thick jacket; otherwise all the swag will freeze to my skin. Initially I thought I'd overdone it, but as I walk from the Hotel Saskatchewan to Mosaic Stadium, I am snug among the faithful.

I ask some locals to explain the passion for the Riders. "Well, we haven't got a heck of a lot going on besides the Riders," explains one chap. "They're the best thing we got going!" yells another, and I begin to sense a theme. Without a hockey franchise, Saskatchewan only has one team to represent the province in the media limelight, and come snow or freezing rain, they're going to support them every yard of the way.

It's the last game of the season, and a game of meaningless consequence. The opponents are the Hamilton Tiger-Cats, who sound like characters from a Saturday morning cartoon. It's my first-ever CFL game, and a real glimpse into a Canadian sport determined to differentiate itself from the strikingly similar, much more popular version of the game just south of the border. Canadian fields are larger, the team has one extra player, there are only three downs instead of four, and the game has all sorts of strategic, tactical and rule differences. For a newbie like myself, both sports provide an opportunity to watch large armoured men slam into each other while pretty young girls with pompoms do backflips—therefore a grand day out, whatever side of the border you happen to be on. I take up my seat and immediately scream "Go Riders!" at the top of my lungs. I probably should have waited until they finished singing the national anthem.

Mosaic Stadium holds thirty thousand people and is neither covered nor heated. This is important to note should the playoffs extend into November, when Regina has recorded temperatures as low as -37°C. If you can survive watching a football game when the thermometer retreats well below zero, you deserve to support the best team in the entire universe, of any sport, period.

As the game proceeds, I do as the locals do: yell at the visitors ("Tiger-Cats, more like Pussy-Cats!"), yell at the referee ("I don't know what rules you're following, but only Riders rule!"), crack open hand warmers in my pockets and drink copious amounts of beer. This endears me to fellow fans, and I receive not one but two fluffy key chain toys of Gainer, the Riders' lovable gopher mascot. I am told Gainer pioneered the art of beating stuffed lions and tigers in the middle of a football field.

After an awful season, and against all odds, the Riders emerge triumphant, providing some consolation for Canada's most festive fans. Another season is over, but there's always next year, when the mighty Riders will charge for the Cup yet again. Time your visit to Regina to coincide with a game and you'll see why Rider Pride scores a touchdown on the Great National Bucket List.

**START HERE:** canadianbucketlist.com/riders

# FLOAT IN CANADA'S DEAD SEA

B efore you die, you really should experience the wonders of the Dead Sea. The lowest place on Earth, with waters 8.6 times saltier than the ocean, one floats without any effort, cradled by the lifeless yet legendary therapeutic waters. The Dead Sea splits Israel and Jordan in the Middle East, which is a little far to travel even by Canadian standards. So it's Saskatchewan to the rescue, with its own lake, unique in the western hemisphere, located just a ninety-minute drive southeast of Saskatoon.

Twelve thousand years ago, a receding glacier trapped a lake at the bottom of a valley. Hemmed in by the valley walls, water was prevented from seeping away by pressure caused by groundwater aquifers. Thousands of years of evaporation later, the result is Little Manitou Lake, with waters three times saltier than the ocean and laced with all sorts of wonderfully helpful minerals. As in the Dead Sea, you can float, you can heal, and you can smother yourself in goopy mud that international spas could market for small fortunes.

Having visited the Dead Sea a number of times, I admit I am skeptical. Surely, if such a lake existed, it would be on the world map, or at least North America's. Driving through the prairie, passing small towns and potash mines, I have a sinking feeling (ahem) that Little Manitou will not live up to the hype. Although few people outside the area know about it, it was immensely popular in the 1950s. "Canada's Carlsbad!" reads an enthusiastic wooden sign as I enter Watrous, the nearest town. It's sleepy and quiet, but then again, so are the towns that service the Dead Sea. I check into the Manitou Springs Hotel & Spa, my room offering a lovely view of the calm lake mirroring a big prairie sky. A few people are taking a dip, but nobody is floating on their back. Downstairs, the "rich golden colour" of the heated indoor mineral pools looks suspiciously like dirty tea, even if it is 100 percent natural.

I walk across the street to find adults sunbathing among rows of

## Top 10 Hot Springs in Canada

Watrous isn't the only place in Canada to take advantage of miracle waters. Western Canada has the right geological conditions for hot springs to flourish. Why not have a soak in:

1. Harrison Hot Springs, BC
2. Miette Hot Spring, AB
3. Ainsworth Hot Springs, BC
4. Liard Hot Springs, BC
5. Radium Hot Springs, BC
6. Banff Upper Hot Springs, AB
7. Hot Springs Cove, BC
8. Temple Garden Mineral Spa, SK
9. Nakusp Hot Springs, BC
10. Halcyon Hot Springs, BC

kids playing on the coarse sandy beach. I try to imagine Cree Indians on these same banks, discovering, to their surprise, that drinking and bathing in the water cured deathly fevers and painful rheumatism. Legend has it a group of sick men were left for dead here, only to recover thanks to the water's healing properties. When they returned to their tribe, they were initially thought to be ghosts.

Chemically, the water is rich: magnesium (helps regulate body temperature, tones skin); potassium (antibacterial); sulphate (aids nervous, blood, muscular and lymph systems); calcium (great for the skin); silica (skin tone, bone and nail growth); sulphur (for aching joints and collagen synthesis)—all of which should easily take care of the uric acid, as contributed by the small kids playing in the shallow areas. Unlike the suitably named Dead Sea, there is life in these waters: brine shrimp, bugs and sticky green weed the kids are collecting for messy wigs.

I walk to the edge, dip in my toe thermometer, lie back and expect to sink like a stone. Instead, the water is buoyant, and I find myself easily floating on my back. Admittedly, the liquid is not as supportive as the Dead Sea, but it's comfortable enough, in that one would have to work very hard to drown oneself. After applying and rinsing off the mud, I find my skin wonderfully silky and shiny, making me wonder why Dead Sea mud sells for big bucks while Manitou mud is unheard of. Watrous, there's cash to be made here! The Dead Sea undoubtedly benefits from that repetitive Trio of Important Rules: location, location, location. Manitou, on the other hand, literally means "Great Spirit" in Cree, a godly lake blessed with healing, recreational and definite bucket list qualities.

**START HERE:** canadianbucketlist.com/manitou

# VISIT A HAUNTED GROVE

Peering out the window at the landmark Delta Hotel Bessborough in Saskatoon, watching traffic cross a stone bridge over the idyllic South Saskatchewan River, I thought I'd been transplanted to Europe. A half-hour later, in my rental car, the city dissipates into a string of strip malls, homesteads, farmsteads and finally no steads at all, just endless flat fields of wheat. An ominous sky hovers above the autumn chill. My destination is a mysterious grove of deformed aspen trees that locals believe might be the freakiest trees in all of Canada. It begs investigation and provides a neat excuse to drive north into the prairie to see for myself. Crooked Bush is not on any maps. Once I drive through the small town of Hafford, I stop and ask for directions

# Canada's Top 10 Spookiest Destinations

Crooked Bush gets an extra point for being a natural phenomenon. If you're feeling brave, grab a camera and head over to:

1. **Plains of Abraham (Quebec City):** Bump into the ghost of a mutilated soldier lately?
2. **Blood Alley (Vancouver):** Butchers once poured buckets of blood onto the street, famed for murder and mayhem.
3. **Fairmont Empress (Victoria):** Old hotels are as comfortable for ghosts as for the rest of us. See also: Fort Garry Hotel, Winnipeg; Banff Springs Hotel, AB.
4. **The Five Fishermen (Halifax):** Other restaurants have ghosts, but this one was once a morgue for *Titanic* victims, who still freak the staff out.
5. **Hockey Hall of Fame (Toronto):** See the Stanley Cup and hear screams of delight—as well as those of a former bank teller who killed herself.
6. **Ghost Train (St. Louis, SK):** The beheaded victim of a train accident is allegedly behind the weird lights and noises on these phantom tracks.
7. **Old Montreal:** Two hundred years ago, two prostitutes fought over a man and one chopped the other's head off. Headless ghosts rule.
8. **Ottawa Jail Hostel:** See Spend a Night in Jail, page 142.
9. **Government House (Regina):** Strange noises, weird apparitions, muffled giggles. Government has always been kind of creepy.
10. **St. Francis Xavier University (Antigonish, NS):** Hail Mary for Mount St. Bernard College's nun ghosts, screaming in the middle of the night. ➤

at a gas station. It looks as if it could easily be the location for the hit Canadian sitcom *Corner Gas*. Fortunately, the pimply kid behind the counter knows exactly what I'm looking for. Apparently "Y'all ain't the first stranger driving these parts lookin' for trees."

He hands me a one-page sheet containing information about Crooked Bush. "The Crooked Bush is a group of wild aspen trees that . . . twist, loop, and bend into the eeriest of forests. Courage of stone is necessary to visit it at night." Fortunately, I've planned

my visit during the day, although I score extra points for making it the week of Halloween. With no help from the pamphlet's awfully confusing directions, I get lost within ten minutes of turning off the highway. When in doubt, follow those in front of you. I hope the pickup truck in question is also seeking the strange and unusual, and not, say, a tractor part. Ten minutes later, a lopsided wooden sign, written in what can best be described as witch scrawl, points right. A small clearing leads to a wooden boardwalk with a sign boldly proclaiming I've arrived at a legendary botanical mystery.

Exiting the car, hunched up against the cold, I take a few steps, stop and start yelling into the bitter wind. "Tim! Tim? Are you there?" Only director Tim Burton's warped mind could possibly have created the trees that knot themselves over the boardwalk: silver-flecked branches with black scars, tangled and twisted, like the claws of a goblin, or the dislocated legs of a giant spider. While university researchers have determined that some form of genetic mutation causes the trees, mystery still surrounds what led to the mutation in the first place, and why forests of perfectly normal, straight aspen trees surround the grove. Locals in the area have claimed to see UFOs, while others point fingers at meteorites, contaminated soil or overzealous imaginations. My favourite theory belongs to the farmer who claims to have seen an alien urinate in the area before the trees began to grow in the 1940s. This might explain another creepy forest in Poland, where pine trees are deformed at ninety-degree angles. After all, even little green men gotta go when they gotta go.

The boardwalk is not very long, and there are a few standout rock star trees that hog attention. Another couple arrive, telling me they'd heard about the trees for years. On Halloween, the Gothically inclined are known to throw creepy parties here, and they're welcome to it. There's definitely something strange in the air, an energy charged by aliens, meteors or an arboreal sense of humour. The chill is piercing my fleece, and Mrs. Esrock has run back to the car to catch up with her imagination. A few minutes later I join her for the return drive to Saskatoon, as the late afternoon sun peeks out from under the clouds, brightening up the wheat fields. The drive is straight, long and unmistakably beautiful. No verdict on whether Crooked Bush is in fact one of the most haunted spots in Canada. But for providing an excuse to drive into the prairie on a fun, hare-brained adventure, it deserves its spot on the National Bucket List.

**START HERE:** canadianbucketlist.com/crookedbush

# STAR GAZE IN A DARK SKY PRESERVE

M any years ago, human beings navigated their past, present and future by the stars. The movement of these celestial bodies determined the seasons and festivals, the direction in which to point foot, wagon or ship. Constellations gave birth to the mythology of gods, immortalized in pinpricks of light in the darkest of skies.

For those of us living in cities, it's a rare night indeed when we can observe the full glory of space. *Sky glow* is a term used for powerful urban light sources that surround a city—the street lights, building brights and stadium neon. It creates an orange haze scattered by reflections in the dust, airbrushing out the darkness of night. We don't see the Milky Way, the movement of planets and constellations, the nightly reminder of how little we know and how small our problems really are. This light pollution protects us from ourselves, a comforting blanket to warm us against the chill of insignificance. It is also an illuminated bandit that robs us of a view that is, literally, out of this world.

Fortunately, Canada is a country that leads the way in the creation of Dark Sky Preserves, areas protected from artificial light, promoting astronomy while allowing for the study of darkness's impact on wildlife. As of this writing, Canada has fifteen of the thirty-five Dark Sky Preserves that have been established worldwide, and the tightest controls to ensure they remain true refuges of night. Saskatchewan has two Dark Sky Preserves: the Cypress Hills Interprovincial Park it shares with Alberta, and the 900-square-kilometre Grasslands National Park.

Grasslands is Canada's darkest Dark Sky Preserve and has the highest rating on the Bortle Dark Sky Scale, a nine-level Richter-like measure for nocturnal darkness. Here you can see faint traces of air glow, the weak emission of planetary light, while parts of the Milky Way actually cast shadows on the ground. Parks Canada holds free stargazing events, guided by astronomers from the Royal Astronomical Society of Canada. High-powered telescopes are provided for the public. So clear are the stars that you can see the Triangulum Galaxy with the naked eye, a galaxy three million light years away. Even a pair of binoculars will serve as an able telescope. The best place to view the stars in the park's West Block is at the Belza Viewpoint, or the Two Tree Trail Access Road. McGowan's Campground and Dawson's Viewpoint are ideal in the East Block.

It took a while for my eyes to adjust, and for the sheer spectacle of the night sky to manifest itself. Satellites and shooting stars are abundant, almost overwhelming. Lying down, wrapped warm in a blanket, I have to remind myself this isn't a planetarium, that I'm

## The World's Largest Dark Sky Preserve

In 2011, Canada's largest protected area, Wood Buffalo National Park (see Wood Buffalo, page 343), submitted an application to become the world's largest Dark Sky Preserve, a title held by Canada's second-largest national park, Jasper. Clearly, no matter how big and dark you are, there's always someone bigger and darker. ➤

perfectly safe to enjoy the dark dome above me, exposed and vulnerable on the soft prairie grassland. When it's time to leave, I check the time on my cellphone and the backlight stings my retina. Rays of car beams cause me to squint. Slowly I reacquaint myself with this world of light, even as the stars above disappear in the wake of the halogen. Canada's Dark Sky Preserves are a welcome reminder that we all need to look up more.

**START HERE:** canadianbucketlist.com/darksky

# EXPLORE NORTH AMERICA'S LARGEST SAND DUNES

Twenty thousand years ago, 97 percent of Canada was covered by a thick sheet of ice. As the glaciers retreated, they left behind spectacular natural phenomena, including the Bay of Fundy, Newfoundland's Gros Morne and an area in northern Saskatchewan that looks very much as if the Sahara has relocated to the boreal forests of Canada. The Athabasca Sand Dunes blanket one hundred square kilometres on the southern edge of Lake Athabasca. They are the result of glaciers depositing bedrock into a delta, receding and exposing the remains to thousands of years of erosive wind. Local Dene nations, on the other hand, believe the dunes were created by

## Where to Find Canadian Scorpions

Athabasca's dunes may look like a desert, but for the real thing you have to head to the warmth of the west.

Forests, prairies, mountains, lakes: in Canada, a tiny desert has to fight for respect. Osoyoos, B.C., is the only recognized semi-arid desert in Canada. It has the country's lowest rainfall, highest recorded temperatures and warmest lake. Located in the South Okanagan, this desert zone is home to a hundred rare plants and three hundred rare invertebrates, and it shelters the country's only tarantulas and scorpions. Being Canadian, these fearsome critters tend to apologize for causing any inconvenience. ➤

a giant beaver, which does seem more patriotic. Winds continue to expand the dunes, by as much as 1.5 metres a year, earning Athabasca the title of the largest active sand surface in Canada—a sandpit the entire country could play in.

This is not a desert. The dunes look over a huge freshwater lake, which is fed by streams, steady rains and winter snowmelt. The water table can become high enough to foster productive nurseries for grasses, trees and shrubs, attracting birds, animals and insects. Standing at the top of a thirty-metre-high dune, gazing south, certainly plays tricks on the mind, like finding an outdoor ice hockey rink in central Saudi Arabia. Canada does have true deserts: the semi-arid Osoyoos and the soft sand in the Yukon's Carcross, recognized by Guinness as the World's Smallest Desert. Yet the size of Athabasca makes it *look* like a desert and not a freak of nature.

Athabasca Sand Dunes Provincial Wilderness Park is protected by legislation, although its way-out-there location is just as effective. The province's most remote park is only accessible via float plane and boat, and according to the official website, it contains "no communities, permanent residents, services, facilities or roads of any kind." That last bit is important, in case you expect communities of Ewoks, sky-roads and underground toilets. That being said, the Fond du Lac First Nation have a reserve adjacent to the park, and they use the dunes to hunt, trap and collect medicinal plants, as they always have.

The area is ecologically unusual and extremely fragile, containing three hundred plant species, including ten endangered plants you simply won't find anywhere else in the world. Hard-core wilderness lovers can fly in and camp in six designated camping areas, packing everything in and out so as not to disturb the natural environment in any way. Float planes deposit visitors at Canterra Lake, or you can boat into Thompson Bay. It's a day hike to the sand giants that make up the William River dune fields, through subarctic forest and plants adapted to this unique environment. Since no camping is allowed among the dunes themselves, you must return to your campsite, where you can be alone in absolute wilderness, give or take a billion bugs or two. As someone who's hiked in dunes before, I can assure you the fun wears off just as quickly as your shoes fill with sand. Still, there's something to be said for climbing a tall, kilometre-long sand dune, and something even more wonderful about doing such a thing in Canada.

**START HERE:** canadianbucketlist.com/dunes

# HORSE RIDE WITH BISON

Highway 12 slices the wheat fields north of Saskatoon, a never-ending runway as flat as a boardroom table. Our destination is Prince Albert National Park, less than three hours as the crow flies or, more accurately, plucks road kill from the highway. The speed limit on these roads is one hundred kilometres per hour, a perversely slow clip for a mid-size rental sedan, or any horseless carriage for that matter. It's memories of galloping horses keeping me awake at the wheel: the time I raced across the green plains of Mongolia; that day I cantered on a Bedouin's horse in the Jordanian desert; exploring *Lord of the Rings* locations on horseback in New Zealand; learning to ride a unicorn Lipizzaner in the training rings of Slovenia. The

SASKATCHEWAN ↑

## A Brush with Extinction

For a beast so large, it's frightening to think that North American bison almost went the way of the passenger pigeon, once among the most abundant birds on Earth, hunted to extinction in the late 1800s. It is estimated that 20 to 30 million bison once roamed the plains of America, but after decades of unchecked and wholesale slaughter, largely by fur traders, bison numbers had decreased to just over 1,000 by the late 1800s. Today, there are around 500,000 bison in North America, of which only 15,000 can be found roaming in their natural range. ➤

Great Canadian Bucket List is kicking for an equine adventure, and Sturgeon River Ranch is ready to put us back in the saddle.

We turn off Highway 55, driving twenty-six kilometres on a dirt road through the West Gate entrance of the 3,874-square-kilometre national park. Across the river are three generations of Vaadelands, a family that settled here in 1928, the same year the park was founded. Operating cattle, land and horses, Gord Vaadeland took a different route when he founded Sturgeon River Ranch as a horse riding and adventure operator, successfully integrating both his business and his family's farms with Prince Albert's star attraction: Canada's only herd of free-ranging plains bison, roaming within their historic range. Gord is waiting for us, with his trademark wide-brimmed black cowboy hat and red checkered shirt. Two bold black horses will pull our supply wagon. Along for the ride: Gord's trusty sidekicks Glen (hangdog moustache, slow prairie drawl) and Beckie (chef, bison naturalist, trail mom), and my dad, eager to believe that riding horses is like riding bicycles. It's been thirty years since he hopped in a saddle, and we're both hoping he can stay on it.

My horse is a tall brown speckled stallion named Applejack. He's got the race champion War Admiral twice in his lineage, but Gord assures me this apple has fallen miles from the tree. After years of commercial riders, Applejack is addicted to grazing on the same abundant sweetgrass attracting the bison. Still, the stallion is certainly a step up from my usual brand of trail horse, with names like Haystack or Lego, as in "always falling apart."

Saddled up, we head into a dense forest of trembling aspen and wild hazelnut bush. Gord calls this the Mantracker Trail. When the hit TV series filmed a couple of episodes in the area, Gord was the on-camera guide, while his horses tracked down the "prey." No crazy chases are expected for our overnight trip, but still, we're on a hunt: somewhere in the meadow clearings ahead are herds of wild bison, and our horses will help us find them. Wildlife viewing on horseback is ideal, explains Gord. The park's animals don't get spooked, and our horses will detect any wildlife long before we do.

As we plod along in single file, the landscape quickly proves there's so much more to the prairie than flat farmland. Jackson, Gord's feisty horse, perks his ears forward. Up ahead is a black bear, oblivious to our approach. With the wind in our favour, we ride closer and closer, until the bear suddenly realizes we're just feet away and quickly darts into the forest. Next is a lone bison bull, a tank of a beast, grazing in a meadow. We approach quietly and carefully. Having grown up in these woods, Gord knows never to corner a bison and the value of keeping your distance. "They can probably outrun your horse," he whispers. Especially Applejack, who would probably snack in the middle of a stampede.

Two hundred years ago, there were millions of bison in North America, migrating across the plains. Their meat and fur supported First Nations tribes for millennia. When European fur traders arrived, they hunted bison to the verge of extinction. In 2008, there were 450 bison roaming Prince Albert. Five years later, that number is almost halved, the result of illegal poaching, increased wolf predation and disease. While farmed bison are plentiful (their meat is a healthy alternative to beef), the genetic future of these wild bison is constantly under threat.

Riding through aspen and Jack pine forest that at times seems almost impenetrable, we arrive a few hours later at our tipis and campsite. As a licensed operator and wildlife consultant, Gord has special permission for his guests to spend the night here. Wagon unloaded, cots set up in the tipis, we sit around the fire, baking bannock on sticks in the fire to accompany Beckie's delicious wild elk stew. Gord pulls out a bottle of bourbon (a buffalo is on the label), the five of us enjoying a night of true prairie wilderness. As the fire crackles, the horses tense.

"Over here, quick!" says Glen.

Just across the river, a hundred feet away, a herd of thirty bison have wandered into a clearing to graze in the twilight. It's one of those magical, unexpected wildlife moments, when everything comes together: the people, the landscape, the weather, the animals. When it gets too dark, we sit around the fire, listening to the herd make its way upriver. Retiring to the rustic comforts of the tipi, we hear the patter of raindrops on the soft tipi walls, the howl of a wolf in the distance.

Along with its glittering lakes, fun characters, wild animals and wilder summer celebrations at Ness Creek, I fall sound asleep in little doubt that the plains of central Saskatchewan have much to offer the National Bucket List.

**START HERE:** canadianbucketlist.com/princealbert

# MEET THE FIRST NATIONS

Tyrone Tootoosis, the imposing curator and manager of cultural resources at the Wanuskewin Heritage Park, squints his eyes, looking out over the valley corridor. "When I grew up, we didn't have air conditioning . . . just a cold wife," he says.

"But I guess that made her a hot wife in winter," I reply.

"Yes, Robin, and you know, back then, Running Water was just somebody's name."

I'm laughing at the joke, but I'm laughing with gratitude too. Tyrone's humour has put me at ease as I wrap my head around the First Nations of Canada. Aboriginals? Natives? Indians? I've seen their legacy across the country, but I've come to Wanuskewin, a short drive from Saskatoon, to finally understand who these Canadians are, what they believe in and why the scars run so deep.

## Aboriginal Tourist Destinations

Learn more about Canada's First Nations at these excellent destinations:

1. Wanuskewin Heritage Park, Saskatoon, SK
2. Canadian Aboriginal Festival, Toronto, ON
3. Haida Heritage Centre, Skidegate, BC
4. Blackfoot Crossing Historical Park, Siksika First Nation, AB
5. Stampede Indian Village, Calgary, AB
6. Fort William Historical Park, Thunder Bay, ON
7. Squamish Lil'wat Cultural Centre, Whistler, BC
8. Champagne & Aishihik Da Ku Cultural Centre, Haines Junction, YK
9. Unikkaarvik Visitors Centre, Iqaluit, NU
10. Musée de Saint-Boniface, Saint-Boniface, MB

Tyrone's long black hair is braided and parted in the fashion of the Plains Cree. He's got the look of a noble actor (he's appeared onscreen), earrings, beads shaking from a waistcoat. Over a delicious pulled bison sandwich at the park's restaurant, Tyrone immediately puts things in perspective. "When people say, 'Tell us about the First Nations,' it's like arriving in Europe and saying, 'Tell us about the white man.'"

There are some 700,000 Native Canadians belonging to over 630 bands spread out across the country—bands with different languages, cultures and customs. One of the challenges for the Wanuskewin Heritage Park, a National Historic Site located on land with six thousand years of Aboriginal history, is to help visitors understand this. Another is to create a community where old wounds can heal, for all people of the Northern Plains, and forgotten

traditions can once again thrive. "We have the responsibility to tell our own story, and not necessarily through history. Aboriginal tourism is not just something to tick off, it's about discovering a comfort zone," says Tyrone. A comfort zone I didn't know existed.

We take a walk along one of the paths in the 240-hectare grounds. Tyrone explains what a powwow is: three days and three nights of dancing and singing. "If people want Indian culture, they should visit Bombay. We're the First Nations," he says proudly. Nations that communicate in a language of nature and spirits, where everything is connected to everything else. Nations that believe they have always lived on these lands — before the ice age, before Europeans arrived, before the residential schools that were cruelly implemented to annihilate their culture. Tyrone's grandfather was a "radical" and raised his family away from the Canadian government's shocking attempt to rip apart the fabric of First Nations culture. Tyrone never went to the schools, and he grew up proud.

We look at the remains of a medicine wheel as old as Stonehenge. So much oral history has been lost, nobody is quite sure what it was designed for. Back in the park's galleries, which host schools, training sessions, festivals and events, we watch a young man (and two young boys) perform a mind-boggling hoop dance. A special exhibition honours the horse,

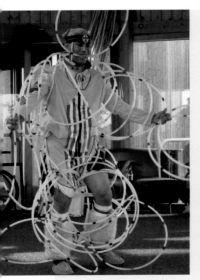

known as Mistatim, literally "big dog." Tyrone explains to me the importance of elders, the custodians of the community, and leads me to an elder named Norm McQuill. I've been encouraged to ask the difficult questions. "Why are the First Nations seemingly so down and out? How come there's so little integration? Where does all the government money go?" It's a lively discussion, and Norm's answers surprise me.

With so much pain in the past, Norm believes the First Nations must take responsibility for their own future. He rues the corruption of tribal councils, the breakdown of First Nations values. Tyrone brings over a young man who had overheard us in the gallery. "Sorry to interrupt, but this is important," he says.

The young man presents two cigarettes to his elder, according to the tabacco tradition, and begins to tell his story. He was sent away to a residential school, lost all touch with his family and culture, and is visiting from Alberta to begin the long journey home. He asks Norm if he knows of some relatives, and it turns out that Norm does indeed. In fact, Norm is a relative too. The young man trembles, his eyes riding waves of tears, the swells of happiness and disaster. It's an honour to witness a moment nobody has prepared for. An honour to glimpse into a vibrant and rich world that has so much to offer, even for just one afternoon. One doesn't have to visit Wanuskewin to embrace First Nations culture in Canada. Yet the heritage park's exhibits, history, land and personalities make it a great place to start.

**START HERE:** canadianbucketlist.com/wanuskewin

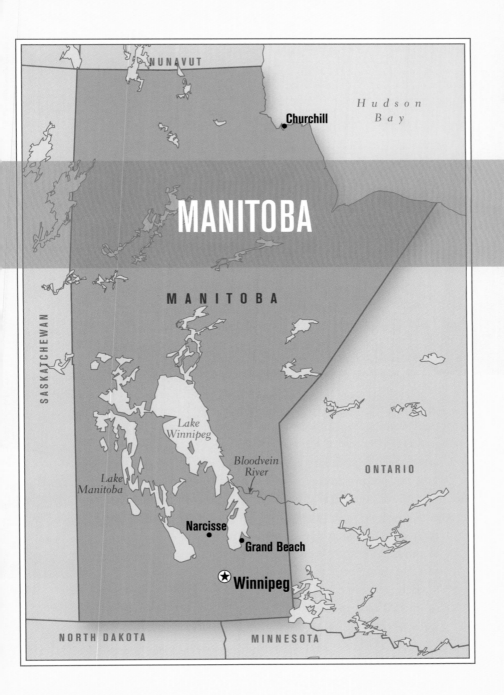

NUNAVUT

Hudson
Bay

● Churchill

MANITOBA

MANITOBA

SASKATCHEWAN

*Lake
Winnipeg*

*Bloodvein
River*

*Lake
Manitoba*

ONTARIO

■ Narcisse

● Grand Beach

★ Winnipeg

NORTH DAKOTA          MINNESOTA

# SEE POLAR BEARS FROM A TUNDRA BUGGY

POLAR BE
ALERT

STO

DON'T WALK IN THI

Standing on the outdoor viewing platform of one of Frontier North's customized Tundra Buggies, I gaze at the permafrost of northern Manitoba. Two polar bears are on their hind legs, sparring like boxers, oblivious to the fact they are providing one of the most spectacular animal encounters you can experience anywhere. I'm wearing two thermal under-layers and a layer of fleece beneath my parka, but what does it matter if my nose is an icicle? Watching the largest carnivore on Earth in its natural habitat lights a fire under your soul.

Each October and November, hungry bears along the southwest coast of Hudson Bay emerge from a state scientists call walking hibernation, reducing their metabolisms while waiting for

Melting polar ice caps are sending polar bears farther south, just as human development is pushing grizzly bears farther north. While the two species would have encountered each other in the past, there's evidence that for the first time these two different species are mating to produce hybrids: white bears with larger heads, grizzly humps and brown streaks, and brown bears with white patches, known to feast on seals. DNA testing on a pizzly shot by a hunter confirmed it was indeed a hybrid. A half-dozen wild pizzlys (also known as grolars, prizzlys or nanulak) have been spotted on Victoria Island, and as the Arctic continues to melt, scientists anticipate the numbers will grow. Since pizzly bears are not considered polar bears, they are not protected from hunters. ➤

the ice to freeze. When it does, they'll head north and break their long summer fast. Cool ocean currents in the bay freeze these waters early, making the small bayside community of Churchill the most southerly point for humans to encounter polar bears. The 900-plus bears that annually migrate through this region are joined by thousands of tourists, scientists, media and students, all excited by this unique wildlife encounter. It is not uncommon for bears to wander directly into town. Surrounded by bear traps, Churchill is closely monitored on camera, and famously has a jail for offending bears that continue to pose a problem. We're advised to stick within certain town limits, with polar bear warning signs reinforcing the message. Considering that Churchill's population shares the landscape with hundreds of hungry bears, it is remarkable there haven't been any human fatalities for decades. In fact, Churchill has become a model of how humans and wildlife can live together.

We're not ten minutes from the airport, seated in a school bus shuttle, when we spot our first bear. Fellow passengers around me explode into action: cameras, whoops, sighs, even tears. A solitary sub-adult male bear is ambling over rocks close to the bay. He stands on his hind legs like a giant meerkat, observing us with curious eyes. Although the bear has yet to feed after a long summer, there's no doubting he is a magnificent creature: shag-carpet hair the colour of a vanilla milkshake, round furry ears, a black button nose. Polar

MANITOBA ↑

bears look too cuddly to be hungry carnivores, but a loaded rifle above our driver's seat reminds us otherwise. The bears can run up to forty kilometres an hour, and with one of the best noses in the animal kingdom, can smell prey from miles away. Camouflaged against the snow, these ruthless hunters are perfectly adapted to be top of the Arctic food chain, with no natural enemies—save humans, and the rapid disappearance of their habitat.

Elated from our first sighting, we transfer to a Tundra Buggy for the ninety-minute drive to Frontier North's Tundra Buggy Lodge. The forty-passenger Buggy sits on 1.7-metre tires above a customized fire truck chassis. Heated by a propane furnace, it has anti-fog windows, an eagle-eyed driver and a handy latrine at the back (it's way too dangerous to step on the ground, and besides, good luck finding a tree on the tundra). The "road" is a rough, bouncy mud track, but all discomfort vanishes when we spot several more bears, anxiously waiting for the ice to freeze. Hundreds of photographs are taken as we observe them for a half-hour. Docking to the impressive hundred-metre-long lodge

on wheels, we settle into the bunks, kitchen and lounge for the next few days. Since the lodge is located at a particular gathering point for bears, the onboard crew don't touch ground for the entire eight-week season. The price of the excursion is steep, but nobody is complaining about sharing quarters. We're here for one reason—polar bears—and fortunately, nobody is going home disappointed.

For the next three days, we spend eight hours a day roaming the tundra and are treated to a polar bear extravaganza. Multiple male pairs spar just metres from our windows, exerting their dominance for the winter to come. Large, curious bears stand up on their hind legs against our buggy, their warm breath literally fogging up our camera lenses. A lone bear walks across a frozen lake, backlit by the low afternoon sun. It's a photographer's dream, and pure heaven for a polar bear enthusiast. Arctic foxes, hares and gyrfalcons also make an appearance, as do boxes of wine, great food, interesting presentations and wonderful company.

The bears around Churchill are among the most threatened of the estimated twenty thousand polar bears remaining in the Arctic. They're also the most accessible to reach. Frontier North's Tundra Buggy experience is without a doubt something to do before you die. Although, with melting sea ice, rising sea levels and the increasing threat to their natural habitat, you might want to act before the polar bears surrounding Churchill sadly beat you to it.

**START HERE:** canadianbucketlist.com/polarbear

MANITOBA ↑

# CRACK THE HERMETIC CODE

Things you may not know about Winnipeg:

- It was the first city in the world to introduce the 911 emergency response system.
- It consumes the most Slurpees in the world.
- Winnipeggers inspired James Bond and invented the cellphone.
- It hosted the biggest gold heist in Canadian history.
- The Manitoba Legislature is actually a mysterious temple with codes and clues that have been deciphered to reveal six thousand years of architectural magic.

A local academic named Frank Albo expects you to scratch your head at that last one. He'll also appreciate the symbolism in my choice of five, not four or six, factoids about Winnipeg. A long-time

student of the esoteric, Frank initially noticed some architectural weirdness on the sphinxes guarding the Manitoba Legislature. He decided to investigate, and ten years later he cracked a century-old code built into the imposing government building that reveals far more than anyone could possibly have imagined. Frank has since become an expert on Freemasonry, architectural symbolism and the occult. While his bestselling book *The Hermetic Code* opens the doors of perception, his evening tours personally invite you to join him at the Legislature, swallow the blue pill and follow him down the rabbit hole. Since he introduced the Hermetic Code Tour in 2009, over ten thousand people have done exactly that, and today, joining two dozen tourists, I will be one of them.

A handsome, slim, dark-haired Albo arrives fashionably late,

# Canada's Great Mysteries

The fascinating mystery of Winnipeg's Legislature has been solved, but the jury is still out on these classic Canadian mysteries.

1. **The *Mary Celeste*:** Built in Nova Scotia, a stocked, seaworthy vessel is mysteriously abandoned in the middle of the Atlantic, leaving everything intact, including the captain's logbook.

2. **Tom Thomson:** Group of Seven artist mysteriously found dead in Algonquin Park's Canoe Lake, a fishing line wrapped around his leg, and plenty of speculation about love, cash and war motives.

3. **Where is Vinland?** L'Anse aux Meadows (see L'Anse, page 299) proved that Europeans visited North America earlier than anyone had thought, but Viking sagas speak of a land rich in grapes called Vinland, which remains to be found.

4. **Shag Harbour UFOs:** In 1967, several locals (including an RCMP constable) watched four bright lights flash in the sky, dive towards the sea, hover over the water and slowly disappear, leaving an odd yellow foam in their wake. Was it a UFO, or a secret military weapon?

5. **Canadian creatures:** How do we explain dozens of sightings of Okanagan Lake's Ogopogo lake monster, the Sasquatch and the marriage of Chad Kroeger to Avril Lavigne? ➤

wearing torn jeans and well-worn boots. Given his academic prowess, everyone was expecting a bookworm. Frank's enthusiasm for the subject, and skill in bringing life to the stone, is immediately apparent. "I assure you, you will never look at architecture the same way," he tells us. "On the surface it's a house of government, but this building is a Sudoku puzzle in stone, built by grand masters and keepers of ancient secrets."

These are heady words, and Frank challenges everyone to question, to not believe. He knows how flighty these claims sound if not supported by physical evidence. It is the physical evidence, as solid as the Legislature's imposing concrete pillars, that makes this ninety-minute tour unmissable.

**FACT:** Every person involved in the construction of this building was a Freemason, as were nearly a century's worth of consecutive Manitoba premiers.

**FACT:** The Freemasons were traditionally custodians of the design of the original Temple of God, passed down through the ages under great secrecy.

**FACT:** The architect, Frank W. Simon, was a master Freemason, a professor of architecture, a man who placed nothing by ornament and designed everything with utmost thought given to the hermetic principles of numerology, astrology, geometry and alchemy.

Frank walks us outside and points to the statues overlooking the entrance. They are infused with special significance, representing two deities, Manitoba and Winnipeg, based on ancient gods, Hermes and Aphrodite. Even the pillars are measured to temple specifications. And as for the famous Golden Boy on the top? Surrounded by the four elements, it's Hermes himself, placed as the alchemic fifth essence, the quintessential symbol of enlightenment, and the hero of the architectural craft. It's heady stuff, but Frank's obvious passion, clear voice and sense of humour keep everyone fully engaged.

Inside the entrance, he points out more ancient temple similarities: guarding bison, protective amulets energized with sunlight and the repetition of the significant numbers 13, 8 and 5: 13 lights on every floor, 13 stones in the archway, 3 sets of 13 steps, 8 pointed stars. The details would require a book (hence Frank's bestseller), but symbol after symbol, fact after fact, prove that Simon's building is a Rosetta stone of mystical architecture, challenging Winnipeggers to decipher

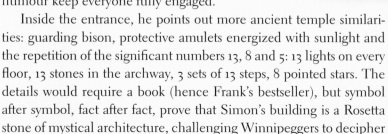

its accurate re-creation of the Biblical temple, chiselled in concrete, hidden in plain view. There is even a Holy of Holies, in this case the Lieutenant-Governor's office, off limits to outsiders, protecting a symbolic Ark of the Covenant behind purple curtains. Like the original Holy of Holies, it is accessed on just one day of the year.

Frank peppers his tour with entertaining anecdotes, such as how he convinced the premier to support his research, how members of the Assembly thought he was bonkers, and how he was accosted one night doing research in his pyjamas. When he discovered Simon's own writings about the creation of a symbolic altar, over marble with veins specifically aligned to symbolize blood, even he got a little spooked.

After shattering the traditional understanding of the Legislature's large mural, we head downstairs and stand in a circle around the Pool of the Black Star. During the day, government officials cross this star with scant regard for its intense symbolism and architectural genius. "Architecture is frozen music. You can read dimensions like notes. With the large dome visible through the 13-foot altar above your head, at this spot you're speaking in fifths, literally speaking with the power of Hermes." His voice echoes and booms through the empty building. He invites us each to stand in the star and try for ourselves. It feels as if I've entered a sound bubble; my voice deepens, swells and reverberates around me. Six thousand years of architectural mystery unfold, and my neck hairs stand up.

The great architect Frank W. Simon took his design secrets to the grave, and so the symbolism at the Legislature would have remained a complete mystery, an anomaly, another quirk in a quirky city. One man spent ten years figuring it out, and he's absolutely right: after standing in the Pool of the Black Star, you will never look at buildings the same way again.

**START HERE:** canadianbucketlist.com/hermetic

# GET CREEPY AT THE NARCISSE SNAKE DENS

I used to be petrified of snakes, a condition many a reader will relate to. Even though we are much bigger than all but the biggest of serpents, and even though most of them are completely harmless (not to mention painfully shy), they nevertheless instill terror at the very thought. Slithering, fork-tongued, sharp-fanged, poisonous killers waiting in the shadows to strike! I'm convinced our fear of these reptiles has something to do with the Bible, where the snake was picked out early as representative of a far greater evil.

In any event, I've found a way to conquer the fears that hold us back. Afraid of heights? Go skydiving. Claustrophobic? Go caving. Afraid of sharks? Jump into a cage and swim with a great white. Afraid of snakes? Adopt one as a pet. Which is what I did, in my early twenties, a metre-long North American corn snake. To be honest, I never quite got over my fear of old Aquarius the Dog, as she was named,

MANITOBA ↑

123

## Relax, This Isn't Australia

Red garter snakes are perfectly harmless. This isn't Australia, which has the Top 11 most venomous snakes in the world, and that doesn't include *Matrix* actor Hugo Weaving. Canada has twenty-four species of snake, the largest of which is Ontario's harmless black rat snake, which grows to over two metres. Vipers such as massasauga and western rattlesnakes can be nasty, but encounters are so rare you're in far more danger of getting stung by a bee. ➤

which might explain why she attacked me frequently. Corn snakes are constrictors, and although she could wrap herself tightly around my arm, she could do no more harm to me than an infant with a plastic toy. She could, however, strike for no reason, quickly, with a cold-blooded stare, sensing my fear and pouncing on it. Aquarius went missing one day, and we found her three weeks later living in my bedroom hi-fi speaker, inches from my head. After that, we named her Sony. Snakes make great pets: they're super low maintenance, value with age and scare the bejesus out of any home intruders. Strangers don't knock on doors with Beware of Snake signs.

All this to say, I was delighted to learn that 130 kilometres from Winnipeg lies the largest congregation of any vertebrate species on Earth. Twice a year, a natural phenomenon takes place that blankets the wetland region of Interlake with tens of thousands of snakes. In spring, typically late April or early May, males literally crawl over themselves in an effort to impress one female. The result is a landscape writhing and bubbling with serpents—in the crevices of their limestone dens, in the trees, on the rocks. Managed by Manitoba Conservation, a three-kilometre-long interpretive trail has been established so visitors can watch all this from the comfort of the other side of the fence. Researchers believe there are up to 150,000 snakes living in these dens, located six kilometres from the town of Narcisse, off Highway 17. To prevent the automotive slaughter of thousands of snakes, tunnels run under the roads to funnel garters away from harmful traffic. Visitors are allowed to pick up the snakes, so long as you are gentle, and release them unharmed. Red garters are quite thin and don't grow much longer than your arm.

Under a pile of one hundred male snakes might be one female, noticeably larger than the boys on her back. Rubbing their chins all over the female, the males are courting amidst stiff competition, creating what scientists call a mating ball (a similar phenomenon might be observed on the dance floors of adolescent nightclubs). The female will select only one lucky male, and then, together with the rest of the snakes, disappear into the wetlands for the summer to gorge on frogs, insects and other unlucky participants in the wetland food chain. Come autumn, the snakes return to their dens, in another brief period when you can watch this reptilian phenomenon. The snakes survive the freezing Manitoba winters by huddling up by the thousands in these limestone sinkholes, slowing their metabolisms down, turning their blood to the thickness of mayonnaise in a process known as brumation.

Come on, Esrock! Is this really something to see in Manitoba before I kick the bucket?

Look, let's not snake around the issue: this is as unique and squirmy as it gets. Plus, Canada is not Australia, cursed with many of the world's deadliest snakes. You can't pick up taipans or black tiger snakes, since they are not nearly as polite as a red garter snake. True Canadian snakes, then, involved in a truly unusual natural spectacle.

**START HERE:** canadianbucketlist.com/snakes

# WATCH ROYAL WINNIPEG BALLET IN THE PARK

I view ballet the way my wife views rugby. We both see talent at work, years of dedication by the participants, poetry of motion and the wonderful opportunity to ogle excellent specimens of the human leg. Neither of us is sure what the rules are, or the levels of difficulty, but we can sit through it, knowing we appreciate each other's company. Point being, I'm not the ideal candidate to convince you that watching the Royal Winnipeg Ballet dance their magic belongs on the National Bucket List. And yet I must, because it does.

If in doubt, simply ask yourself: how is it that a city in the Canadian Prairies boasts one of the world's most respected, sought-after and watched ballet companies? That's exactly what I asked Jeff Herd, the chief operating officer of the Royal Winnipeg Ballet.

"The long winter is an incubator for culture, and Winnipeg

## The Royal Canadian Bucket List?

There are dozens of Canadian institutions with a royal prefix, dating back to 1801, when King George III bestowed the honour on the Royal Institution for the Advancement of Learning, now known as McGill University. Queen Victoria gave us the Royal Canadian Golf Association and Royal Canadian Yacht Club; King Edward VII the Royal Lifesaving Society of Canada; King George V blessed the Royal Ottawa Sanatorium, the Royal Canadian Mounted Police and the Royal Ontario Museum; King George VI honoured Toronto's Royal Conservatory of Music and Royal Canadian Sea Cadets. Which brings us to his daughter Queen Elizabeth II, who has given over forty Canadian civilian and military institutions her royal wave of approval. ➤

has always punched above its weight when it comes to culture," he explains. He credits this to the city being a "Polyglot of the North," a fusion of cultures, with a strong European influence.

Fair enough, says I, but that could describe Toronto, Vancouver or Montreal. Perhaps the answer lies in the fact that two out of every three people who see the Royal Winnipeg Ballet do so outside Winnipeg. As a financial necessity, the RWB began touring the world in the 1950s. The result is that many people's first exposure to ballet came through this company, which pirouetted in popularity in the ensuing decades. The Winnipeg Ballet got its Royal designation in 1953, the only one of its kind in Canada, and is today the longest continuously operating ballet company in North America. Not New York. Not Chicago. Spearheaded by artistic director Arnold Spohr, who guided the RWB for three decades, its program has always leaned on the populist side—something classic, something modern and something

for guys like me. I'm not familiar with the technical genius at work, but I can appreciate something beautiful when I look at it.

So, if the Royal Winnipeg Ballet is so well received outside Winnipeg, having performed in 573 cities worldwide, why bother seeing it in its hometown?

"We're always in context in the Prairies, the colour, the light," says Jeff. "This is where we hold our world premieres and perform full sets with the Winnipeg Symphony, our home orchestra."

In hockey terms, these are the home games, with home-ice advantage. This is best illustrated in the annual free performance at the outdoor Lyric Theatre in Winnipeg's Assiniboine Park. An institution since the 1970s, the event is perfect for those who want to experience ballet in a relaxed environment. Pull up a blanket, indulge with cheese and wine from the cooler, sit back and watch one of the world's best ballet companies dazzle an appreciative audience with a diverse selection of performances. Whether you're into the *bras croisé* or just the bodies, the Royal Winnipeg Ballet presents a distinctly Canadian cultural spectacle, for wives *and* their husbands.

**START HERE:** canadianbucketlist.com/ballet

MANITOBA ↑

# VISIT A TROPICAL BEACH

As a travel journalist, I receive over a dozen press releases each day asserting the outstanding qualities of destinations, often from countries claiming to have it all. Well, as large as Canada is, we do have to face some facts. We don't have jungles or savannahs or large salt deserts, and as anyone who has been to the Caribbean will tell you, nor do we have tropical white-sandy beaches. Unless, and somewhat bizarrely, you live in southern Manitoba. Here you'll find the cocaine-powder sand of the suitably named Grand Beach on the eastern shore of Lake Winnipeg.

Less than ninety minutes' drive out of Winnipeg, I admit I have my doubts. This is the prairie, after all, and comparing a lake beach to the finest sands of Belize, Brazil and Barbados is a mighty bold statement.

↑

MANITOBA

Yet that's what Winnipeggers are apt to do. As the car makes its way along the flattest of highways and through the sleepy town of Grand Marais, I brush up on the grand history of Grand Beach.

In 1916, the Canadian Northern Railway opened a line connecting the town, and adjacent Victoria Beach, to the boom town of Winnipeg. With a boardwalk, shops and the largest dance hall in the British Empire, each summer tens of thousands flocked daily to the sunny, sandy shores of Lake Winnipeg. Eight trains a day, packed to the rafters, depositing passengers on this unlikely beach of dreams.

I pop in for breakfast with Ken and Luise Avery, who have been living in Grand Marais for thirty years, running their lovely Inn Among the Oaks B&B. With the wind blowing in a sweet fragrance from the garden, Ken fills me in on the history of the area, handing me a book with sepia photos recording a glorious yesteryear. One picture shows the beach and water so packed with people it's hard to distinguish the beach from the bodies. When the dance hall burned to the ground in 1950, and Winnipeg's boom began to dim, the railway discontinued their service and the area declined, until the province bought the land and turned it into Grand Beach Provincial Park in 1961.

Today's Grand Beach may not have the Atlantic City–like draw of its heyday, but it still attracts thousands of sun worshippers in the summer, particularly on weekends. When Winnipeggers strip off their layers of winter, they're a good-looking bunch, too. No less an authority than *Playboy* magazine named Grand Beach one of its Top 10 Beaches in the World. There's still a boardwalk, a campground, a couple of flea-market stalls, and popular hiking, biking and birdwatching trails (Grand Beach is home to several pairs of the endangered piping plover). Warm water and strong winds attract kitesurfers from around the world. "Why be pickled in salt water when you can have white sand with a freshwater lake?" laughs Ken.

I bid the Averys farewell, envious of their indoor hot tub, and drive

# Canada's Best Beaches

Yes, even a northern country can boast world-class beaches, famed for natural and rugged surroundings. Think less beach bars, more eagles.

1. Grand Beach, MB
2. Sylvan Lake, AB
3. Long Beach, BC
4. Îles de la Madeleine, QC
5. Parlee Beach, NB
6. Sandbanks Beach, ON
7. Basin Head Beach, PEI
8. Martinique Beach, NS
9. Good Spirit Lake, SK
10. Grand Bend, ON
11. Devonshire Beach, AB
12. Kelly Beach, NB
13. Wreck Beach, BC
14. Sauble Beach, ON
15. Salmon Cove Sands, NL

to the beach itself. On their advice, I head to the fourth parking lot, keeping the sand dunes, some as high as twelve metres, on my left. It's a scorching summer day, but it's early, before the crowds show up. At this point, I confess, I'm still dubious. I've been to some of the best beaches in the world, on six continents, and with no disrespect to the locals, this is a lake beach. So what if the lake is the sixth largest in North America?

Well, I should know better by now. Grand Beach lives up to its reputation. Talcum white, it squeaks when I walk, the sand as fine and white as any tropical beach I have seen. It stretches for three kilometres, cradled by lapping water and sand dunes, a pleasant breeze blowing onshore. Day trippers begin to arrive with their umbrellas, beach balls and sand buckets. Who can blame them? Canada may not have the world's best beaches, but with our slice of paradise in the Prairies, we've definitely got one that is unique.

START HERE: canadianbucketlist.com/grandbeach

# HAVE A HAPPY FOLK FESTIVAL

The Winnipeg Folk Festival is one of the world's most popular music festivals, a bold statement backed up by its enduring legacy, its global reputation and the participatory nature of the community to which it belongs. A local named Don Greig, visiting for his thirty-seventh year, puts it succinctly: "There are comfort foods, and what we have here is comfort entertainment." Bea Cherniak, on her thirty-ninth consecutive visit, typically hates crowds, but she loves the fest. "It's gotten bigger over the years, sure, but its heart is still Folk Fest."

The heart of which she speaks takes no time seducing me. As I walk around the nine stages, meeting areas, food lanes, beer tents and campgrounds, the atmosphere is enchantingly welcoming. Strangers greet each other with big smiles and a "Happy Folk Fest!" The sound of acoustic instruments—guitar, horns, strings, even piano—permeates the air. There are 2,950 volunteers donating a combined 55,000 hours of their time to make it happen, directed by just 50 full- and part-time and contract employees. Volunteers share the backstage tent with the performers, all fed by a volunteer-staffed kitchen that produces over 9,000 meals a day. Every effort is made to recycle, following a model green policy that keeps the grounds of Birds Hill Provincial Park in immaculate shape over the five-day event. Of the roughly 16,000 people who visit each day, 6,000 will be camping on-site on grounds that have turned into a destination unto themselves.

The camping atmosphere here is so fun, inviting and creative that I easily understand why some campers don't even make it to the main stages. Festival-supported animation areas allow amateur musicians to perform, while others can rest in hammocks, drum in tipis, play giant board games, dress up and join jolly daily parades. I pitch my tent with the Castle Boys, a dozen guys and girls with a reputation for throwing the wildest parties and building the most striking installations. It's difficult to tear myself away from their party and make the ten-minute walk to the main grounds. The festival also offers an RV and caravan section, along with a Quiet Camping Ground better suited for families.

Although it is much smaller in scale, the Folk Fest embodies a spirit I first discovered at Burning Man, a massive cultural event in the Nevada desert. A feeling that makes you believe in humanity and goodwill, and that everything is going to turn out just fine after all. I tell a reporter it feels like Burning Man in the Prairies and am surprised to see my quote on the front page of the *Winnipeg Free Press* the following day.

## Canada's Best Folk Festivals

Pack your blanket and umbrella, and settle in with the colourful locals and some of the world's finest musicians.

1. Winnipeg Folk Festival, MB
2. Edmonton Folk Festival, AB
3. Vancouver Folk Festival, BC
4. Folk on the Rocks, Yellowknife, NT
5. Lunenburg Folk Harbour Festival, NS
6. Miramichi Folk Song Festival, NB
7. Newfoundland & Labrador Folk Festival, NL
8. Mariposa Folk Fest, ON
9. Ness Creek Music Festival, SK
10. Dawson City Music Festival, YK

As much fun as the camping is (the limited spaces sell out quickly), performances by some of the best musicians on the planet are still the primary draw. Under the clear prairie sky, sweetened with the tang of a tangerine sunset, I watch as singer-songwriters capture the audience's attention with their songcraft, politically minded lyrics and simple charisma. The weather is smashing, and with the successful introduction of mosquito-chomping dragonflies, Manitoba's legendary summer biting insects are blessedly absent. An eight-piece Latin band kicks up the energy, the music swinging from salsa to jazz to pop to soul. With over seventy acts, the organizers ensure there is something for everyone. Unique to the Winnipeg Folk Fest, many of these artists will also collaborate through improvised workshop performances on the day stages, leading to some of the best musical experiences of the entire event.

K'naan, a Somali-born Canadian rapper-poet, rocks the crowd and wraps up the main concert, but the party continues until way after sunrise, especially atop Pope's Hill. It was built by the Catholic Church for the 1984 visit of Pope John Paul II, but I enjoyed its reincarnation as a venue for watching dreadlocked drummers beat tribal rhythms as thousands dance and drink in the new day. Not quite the spiritual communion the hill was built for, but for many it's an ecstatic religious experience nonetheless.

Canadian summers are a time for outdoor celebration. The folk festivals of Edmonton, Vancouver, Yellowknife and Regina do an incredible job allowing people of all ages and musical tastes to come together, listen, party, interact and get involved. Winnipeg, that beating heart of culture in the middle of Canada, hosts the granddaddy of them all. Leaving Birds Hill Provincial Park for the short drive back to the city, I tell the Castle Boys I'll be back, with a lot more folks in tow.

START HERE: canadianbucketlist.com/folkfest

# PADDLE A BLOODY RIVER

A 300-kilometre-long river that flows through unspoilt virgin boreal forest and is called the Bloodvein conjures up strong images of violence. Its name may refer to a bloody skirmish between local First Nations tribes, or simply to the veins that can be seen in the ancient red granite rocks and riverbed. Either way, rafting or canoeing down this remote Canadian Heritage River is an adventure that paddles (and portages) its way onto our bucket list.

Rafters take anywhere from a week to fifteen days to complete the journey, with some choosing to float plane in and out of certain lakes, carrying in all their gear as there is no road access. The Bloodvein corridor is a series of pools and drops, and as a result can be tackled in either direction, although most paddlers will go with the flow to exit at the Narrows on Lake Winnipeg, about two hundred kilometres northeast of Winnipeg. The river favours those paddlers with experience. There are over a hundred rapids, unmarked and wild enough to send you downriver on the wrong side of the canoe. Reading whitewater is a handy skill, one you'll almost certainly have developed by the final stroke.

Glaciers scoured the area during the last ice age, and due to its inaccessibility the Bloodvein was not used for trade or settlement. The result is virgin landscape, full of old-growth forest and wildlife that fulfill the promise of the Great Outdoors. Marshes, forests, lakes and the ancient rocks of the Canadian Shield host an abundance of animals, several of which are rare and endangered. Besides the usual suspects—black bears, moose, deer, otters, beavers—you're in the domain of wolverines, great grey owls, white osprey and woodland caribou. Surrounding you is some of the oldest rock on the planet, and beneath you swim trophy-size northern pike, walleye pickerel, lake trout and sturgeon. During your paddle you'll also see signs of ancient human history, archaeological sites from hunter-gatherers dating back six thousand years, and red-ochre pictographs in Artery Lake drawn between CE 900 and 1200. The Ojibwa people did use the river as a trapping area, and their descendants still live in the community of Bloodvein, at the mouth of the river, operating a lodge that greets paddlers at the end of their journey.

Paddlers will tackle the river from spring until fall, with July and August being the most popular months. That being said, you won't find that the campsites located on the spits and shores of Atikaki Provincial Wilderness Park and Ontario's adjacent Woodland Caribou Provincial Wilderness Park are crowded. There are no facilities or services, and the remoteness that has largely protected the Bloodvein from human history will continue to reserve it for those seeking a water-bound wilderness experience. Fortunately, guided tours are available to help us novices navigate the river channels, the whitewater and the challenges of a multiday canoe trip. For a name steeped in blood and battles, the Bloodvein offers just the sort of rugged adventure by which to experience the true peace of nature.

**START HERE:** canadianbucketlist.com/bloodvein

# DRINK A TOAST TO THE VOYAGEURS

With their long days and back-breaking work in an environ-ment as hospitable as a rabid python, the voyageurs paddled their way into Canadian legend as the toughest of men. Organized fur traders for the Northwest Company (a fierce competitor of the Hudson's Bay Company before being swallowed by it), these rugged French-Canadian woodsmen had reputations for hardiness, indus-triousness and a certain *joie de vivre*. Canoeing down rivers with the furs they'd trapped up north in the early nineteenth century, voya-geurs were phased out with the invention of the railway and the slowing demand for fur, but their legacy lives on with the Festival du Voyageur.

From its humble roots in 1970, the ten-day celebration has grown into the largest winter carnival in western Canada. Winnipeg's St. Boniface boasts the largest French-speaking community west of Quebec, and each February it attracts hundreds of thousands of people with its coloured lights, snow sculpture competitions, francophone performances, food stands and family activities. Fort Gibraltar, a fur trade post originally built in 1810 at the Forks—the point where the Red and Assiniboine rivers meet—has been reconstructed upriver in Voyageur Park as a living historical site, complete with costumed actors recounting tales of the daily life of the voyageur. For these men, no portage was too long, no dried pemmican

## The Heart of the Nation?

Manitobans are proud of the fact that their province is at the geographical heart of Canada—although, technically speaking, that's not the case. It does sit at the longitudinal centre of the country, but the place located directly between the most northerly and southerly points of Canada, and between the country's most easterly and westerly points, is a little town called Arviat, in the Northwest Territories. ➤

too foul and no bag of fur too heavy, even for their pittance of a living wage. Spartan living conditions at trading posts were more reminiscent of prisons.

While their role in society was phased out, the voyageurs' ability to enjoy life in any conditions has surely been passed down to their descendants, for how else to explain the festive atmosphere and out-door carnival spirit when Winnipeg's thermometer falls below "I can't feel my toes" level? No matter how cold it gets, join bundled locals for maple taffy, snow cones, flapjacks and festivities, and if the lineup gets too long, draw on the spirit of the voyageur.

**START HERE:** canadianbucketlist.com/voyageur

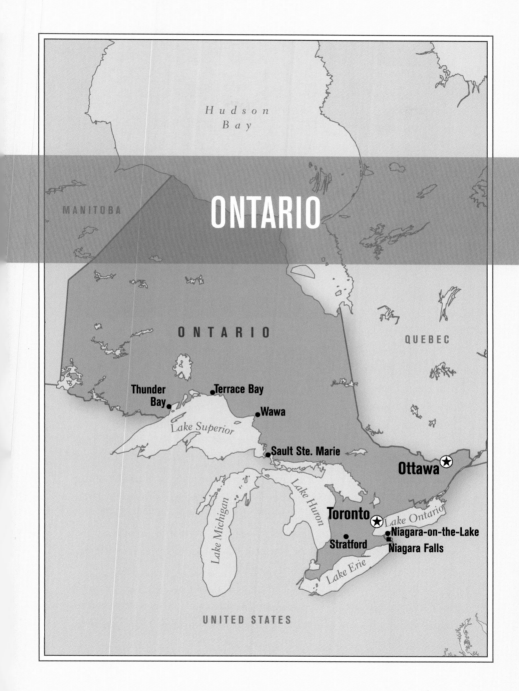

# ONTARIO

Hudson Bay

MANITOBA

ONTARIO

QUEBEC

Thunder Bay
Terrace Bay
Wawa
Lake Superior
Sault Ste. Marie
Ottawa ☆

Lake Michigan
Lake Huron
Toronto ☆
Lake Ontario
Niagara-on-the-Lake
Stratford
Niagara Falls
Lake Erie

UNITED STATES

# SPEND A NIGHT IN JAIL

On a personal list of dubious achievements, being incarcerated for something silly does have a certain appeal. Perhaps it shows that even honourable, noble lives have roguish moments. Perhaps it's because one night of prison reaffirms the benefits of freedom. Perhaps it's just something interesting to say at a dinner party, provided the words "misunderstanding," "no criminal record" and "that was an adventure!" are used in the story. Of course, the reality of prison is entirely devoid of charm. There's nothing fun about being locked away in an institutional cell, denied the joys of modern life, surrounded by people who actually deserve to be there. Still, the Great Canadian Bucket List demands adventurous transgressions, and fortunately, I found a prison cell where I could leave with my reputation, and criminal record, healthily intact.

"When they chained up the naked prisoners on the cement floor in pure darkness, were they on their backs?" This is the kind of detail that arrests my curiosity as I stand outside the "Hole" cells in

the basement of the HI-Ottawa Jail Youth Hostel. For 110 years, the thick-stoned building on Nicholas Street was known as the Carleton County Gaol, an imposing hell designed to imprison the city's most notorious offenders. Built in 1862 as a "model" British prison, the reality was far less respectable: tiny cells crammed with both men and boys (as young as five years old), reeking of excrement, the floor crawling with bugs and rats. The Gaol was eventually shut down in 1972 due to inhumane living conditions, but it reopened the following year as a refurbished youth hostel. The new owners clearly knew the lengths backpackers will go to save a buck. Today, budget travellers spend the night bunking in the original cells, drink beer in the canteen that once fed prisoners slop and wake in fear with blood-drained ghosts hovering over their beds.

Okay, I made the ghosts part up, but just barely. Ghost Walks Ottawa holds nightly prison tours in the old jail, guiding the public and hostel guests to some of the original, unrestored sections of the prison, recounting trials and tales, and revealing why this has been called one of the world's most haunted buildings. After touring the punishment cells, my Ghost Walks guide, Adriane, leads me to the eighth floor, still in its original state. The cells are punishingly small. She paints a vivid picture of life for a nineteenth-century prisoner and explains the sad, short life of Patrick J. Whelan, the man who murdered Thomas D'Arcy McGee, one of the Fathers of Confederation. Whelan met his maker at the jail during the last public execution in

# Canada's Best Hostels

*Hostels are fun, cheap, sociable and not always haunted. Corbin Fraser runs a popular blog called www.ibackpackcanada.com. I asked him to weigh in on Canada's best hostels.*

1. **Jericho Beach Youth Hostel, Vancouver, BC** Located right on the beach with some of the best views of the city, this seasonal hostel may be a little way out of town, but it's a destination unto itself.

2. **Global Backpackers, Toronto, ON** Located at King and Spadina, close to the action, Global sees a steady stream of international travellers throughout the year. The bar is always busy downstairs, staff are great, and private rooms are also available.

3. **Planet Traveler Hostel, Toronto, ON** Staying at the Planet Traveler is like renting a room in an iPod commercial. Friendly staff, a beautiful modern motif and, best of all, they're the greenest hostel in Canada.

4. **Tundra House Hostel, Churchill, MB** Open from December until October, the Tundra House Hostel is a cozy home away from home. The perfect (and cheapest) place to set up home base and explore the bears and belugas of Churchill.

5. **Samesun Backpackers, Banff, AB** My favourite hostel in the area is conveniently located near the heart of Banff. The Beaver Bar is perfect for meeting fellow travellers, and the knowledgeable staff ensures you'll see much of the area's rugged beauty, even if it's only between hangovers.

6. **Auberge de jeunesse de Montréal, Montreal, QC** Clean and friendly hostel, and the staff are only too happy to help English backpackers brush up on their French. The building is over 135 years old, but it doesn't look a day over thirty if you ask me. Free wi-fi, with a bistro and bar in the building. Close to everything, and cheap to boot!

7. **Hôtel La Ferme, Baie-Saint-Paul, QC** A high-end hostel in luxurious resort-style accommodations, Hôtel La Ferme offers Swiss-inspired dorms and hotel rooms with price ranges for everyone. This hybrid hostel/hotel/resort project was started by Daniel Gauthier, local Québécois legend, best known for co-founding Cirque du Soleil. Slightly more expensive than the average hostel, it's still considerably cheaper than a hotel.

8. **Halifax Heritage House Hostel, Halifax, NS** Stay in the heart of downtown Halifax, a stone's throw from the famous nightlife and minutes from the waterfront. Affordable rooms in a historic house with free wi-fi, comfy beds and staff who passionately call Halifax their home.

9. **HI–The Marathon Inn, Grand Manan Island, NB** The Marathon Inn offers affordable rooms on the largest island in the Bay of Fundy. Enjoy tea and a home-cooked breakfast with the owner while swapping travel stories before exploring all that Grand Manan has to offer.

10. **HI Hostel, Quebec City, Quebec City, QC** The best and most affordable way to experience the charm of Old Quebec. Daily activities, cozy common areas and a café/bar—perfect for meeting other travellers. Located in the centre of Old Quebec, within walking distance of absolutely everything. ➤

Canada. I'm led to the actual gallows, thoughtfully decorated with a hangman's rope. Five thousand people desperate for entertainment watched Whelan squirm for ten minutes. Even though Adriane has been guiding tours in the old jail for over a year, she's edgy and freaked out as we wander through Death Row. She nervously tells me about doors slamming, disembodied voices, guests reporting ghosts at the edge of their bunks. Seriously!

I bid her adieu, retire to my cell, slam the iron bars shut and make sure it's locked from the inside. Lying in my bed, I try not to think about the poor, miserable bastards who rotted away in Cell 4. It's deathly quiet, save for the snoring of someone in an adjacent cell. Although the walls are thick, the vaulted ceilings were designed to carry sound so guards could hear even the faintest of whispers. I somehow fall asleep, but wake up in a cold sweat at four a.m. Worse, I need to pee, which means I have to leave the safety of my cell and walk down the long dark hallway. At the point of bursting, I muster up the courage to rise and walk to the bathroom, but decide to film the whole thing, just in case I become the first guy to catch a ghost on camera. Relieved, I return to my cell, toss and turn for hours, and thank God, Jesus, Buddha, Allah and Elvis that I'm a free man, condemned to spend but one night in Canada's only prison hotel.

**START HERE:** canadianbucketlist.com/jail

# VISIT THE HOCKEY HALL OF FAME

"Please, for the love of God, can someone explain to me what's going on?"

It's my first week as an immigrant in Canada, and I'm staring at a TV set broadcasting twelve millionaires on ice skates. My older brother, who moved to Canada a few years before I did, has already forgotten our childhood sports of cricket, rugby and soccer, and is now wearing a Vancouver Canucks hockey vest. His conversion to Canada's national religion took less than a year, but my love for cricket bats and rugby balls will not allow me to yield quite as easily. Firstly, how can anyone take seriously a team called the Canucks? Blackhawks, Predators, Sharks, Devils, Flames—those are some badass-sounding teams. But Canucks? Canadiens? Senators? Maple Leafs? Oooh, I'm trembling. Secondly, hockey to the uninitiated is too fast to watch, too difficult to understand and too painful to listen to, especially when a guy named Don Cherry gets on his soapbox. Further, the fact that I skate like an ostrich on Rollerblades clouds my understanding of the skills and talent needed to distinguish oneself in the National Hockey League. I'm not proud of it, but when I arrived in Canada, Puck was a character from Shakespeare.

During the regular season, when it felt as if the Canucks played a game twice a day, I never quite got what all the hubbub was about . . . until I visited the Hockey Hall of Fame. Standing on the corner of Yonge and Front in downtown Toronto, the HHOF is located in what was once a Bank of Montreal office, a grand-looking building sculpted with gravity and pomp. To get inside, you have to walk through a shopping mall, which may be symbolic of the commercialization of the sport, or a practical way to control the daily crowds. And they come from far and wide, these worshippers of the vulcanized rubber puck, ready to open their wallets and drop their jaws at exhibits of the game's great knights, and stand before the Holy Grail itself: Lord Stanley's Cup.

## Canada's Official Sports

The unusual contradiction that Canada's most wildly popular sport wasn't its official national pastime was finally laid to rest in 1994. Up until that point, a game originating with Algonquin tribes along the St. Lawrence Valley was Canada's official game. In fact, lacrosse was the country's most popular sport until hockey usurped it around 1900. When politicians sought to resolve the situation, they agreed on a compromise whereby lacrosse became Canada's national summer game and hockey its national winter game. Any attempt to play either sport typically leaves me sprawled out in a bloody pulp. ➤

With sixteen different exhibits, I'm not sure where to start, so I head to the Hartland Molson Theatre to watch an introductory movie. If you edited the most stirring scenes from *Rocky*, *Hoosiers* and *The Natural* with *Gladiator* and *Braveheart*, you might approach the spirit of this sweeping, epic journey through Canada's great game. A frozen pond, wooden sticks, men with pencil-thin moustaches and the recipe for legends. The film explains the development of the game, the teams, the rules, culminating in the quest for the Stanley Cup.

I leave the theatre inspired to learn more, to meet the heroes of the game: Cyclone Taylor, Ken Dryden, Gordie Howe, Bobbie Orr, Mario Lemieux and a goal machine they call simply The Great One. After the exhibits in the NHL Zone, I wander over to the scale replica of the Canadiens' dressing room from the Montreal Forum. It's the first time I hold a stick and feel the weight of a puck in my palm. In the Dynasties exhibit, I learn about the dominance and great rivalry of the Canadiens and the Maple Leafs from the 1950s to the late 1970s, the emergence of the Oilers, and the dearth of Canadian domination ever since. In a large section called the World of Hockey, I'm amazed to see that the game extends beyond just northern countries to teams in Australia, Turkey, Mongolia and, yes, even my old South Africa. Women play hockey, kids play hockey . . . I leave the exhibits knowing the world is hockey mad, with Canadians the maddest of all.

The Great Hall of NHL trophies is approached with reverence. Here are the game's most sought-after pieces of silverware, including the original bowl donated by Governor General Lord Stanley, and the Stanley Cup itself. I'm told it's the hardest trophy to win in world sports, but fortunately, it's easy enough to stand next to and get someone to take a snapshot. Finally, I'm drawn to the interactive section of the HHOF. The Be-A-Player Zone allows me to put on some kit and play the goalie in a life-sized net. In the Slapshot Zone,

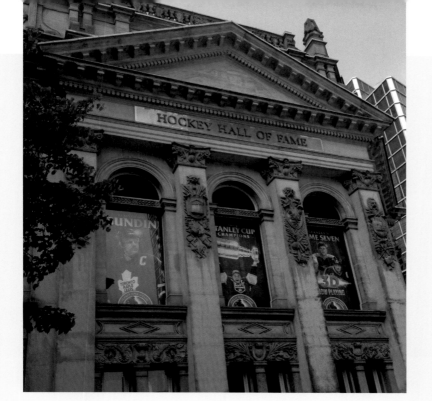

I learn that shooting is difficult enough, never mind scoring. In the Broadcast Zone, I give a live play-by-play of a recorded game, then convince a kid to play some table hockey.

By the time I leave the Hall of Fame, my conversion to Canada's national religion is complete. It's game night, and the Habs are playing the Canucks. I head over to a bar, order a pint and, for the first time, anticipate where the puck will go, understand how the rules work and thrill at just how big the hits can be. A tourist innocently wanders in front of me.

"For the love of God, move outta the way, I'm trying to watch the game!"

**START HERE:** canadianbucketlist.com/hhof

# AVOID NUCLEAR ARMAGEDDON

You haven't lived until you've seen just how close we all came to dying. About thirty kilometres outside Ottawa is a bone-chilling, fascinating and entirely unique glimpse into a time when geopolitics tightroped along a knife's edge. Two superpowers were headlocked in a Cold War, armed with atomic and hydrogen bombs capable of wiping entire cities off the map, and poisoning anyone lucky enough to survive the nuclear Armageddon. Canada recognized that the end might indeed be nigh and set to work on a top-secret military bunker that would ensure the survival of its government. Commissioned by Prime Minister John Diefenbaker, 9,300 square metres of Ontario countryside were excavated to make room for a four-storey-deep underground fortress, using 5,000 tons of steel, 25,000 cubic metres of concrete and $22 million of 1960's taxpayer dollars.

The Diefenbunker, as it became known, was a full-service facility in which 535 lucky bureaucrats would have the task of somehow

# How I Learned to Worry and Fear the Bomb

A visit to the Diefenbunker wasn't my first exposure to the highly niche world of atomic tourism. In Ukraine, I visited a former top-secret nuclear missile base and was given a tour of its underground control station by a former Soviet general who once had his finger on the button. Men like him were trained and carefully monitored to destroy the entire planet on an order. Several times in history, that order was almost given, typically as the result of a computer glitch. In Canada, Prime Minister John Diefenbaker authorized the construction of fifty Emergency Government Headquarters around the country. Smaller regional "Diefenbunkers" were built in Nanaimo (BC), Penhold (AB), Shilo (MB), Borden (ON), Valcartier (QC) and Debert (NS), along with other communication sites. While some are still active military installations, most were sold off or destroyed. ➤

rebuilding whatever was left of Canada. These appointees were selected based on their profession, not their qualifications. No family members were included, and rather naively, no psychological considerations were taken into account. A large group of mostly men would emerge weeks later into a world of ashes and radioactive zombies. These, apparently, would be the lucky ones.

Fortunately, none of this happened. Despite several near misses (you know about the Cuban Missile Crisis, and you might want to google Able Archer), the Iron Curtain smelted, the world evolved, and children no longer have to memorize how to duck and cover under a fireball. The Diefenbunker functioned as a military telecommunications base until the 1990s, at which time it was decommissioned and turned into a Cold War Museum. Due to the increasing sophistication of nuclear weapons, there simply wouldn't be time today to relocate government to the base, and at no time was the Diefenbunker used for its intended purpose. The only PM to actually visit the base was Pierre Trudeau, who promptly cut its operating budget.

Today, anyone can enter the 115-metre-long blast tunnel, cross through intimidating 36-centimetre-thick bank vault doors and explore the fully equipped world below. I'm greeted by Mike Braham, the former director of Emergency Preparedness Canada and now an enthusiastic volunteer at the museum. Mike was one of those chosen to survive in the Emergency Government Situation Centre. Shaking his head in disbelief, he reckons the real victims would have been the ones trapped inside the bunker. "With no psychological preparedness, these people would have gone nuts," he tells me.

The bunker was designed to withstand a five-megaton blast up to a couple of kilometres away. That's 250 times more powerful than Hiroshima. Its air would be triple filtered and, in theory at least, supplies would last up to thirty days. "People couldn't see beyond thirty days of nuclear war," explains Mike.

He leads me through the decontamination area and the medical and dental centres that have been transformed into excellent Cold War exhibitions. School kids might giggle at relics such as rotary phones and 1.5-metre-high computers. Adults have an entirely different reaction. "We came close, but we felt, we hoped, that common sense would prevail," says Mike.

I sit at the prime minister's desk, peering at his mounted toilet, and learn about the escape hatch, canteen and Bank of Canada vault. Today, the Diefenbunker hosts parties, spy programs for kids, even spy-era movies in a theatre. Hollywood has used its facilities, and the nearby small town of Carp has benefited from the tourism. Other bunkers around Canada have been destroyed, but much larger and still-operational facilities exist in the U.S.A. and Russia. We may live in a safer world, but as long as we possess the tools of our own destruction, the threat of Armageddon will always exist. For its unfiltered, radiation-free fresh air of much-needed perspective, the Diefenbunker is one for the bucket list.

**START HERE:** canadianbucketlist.com/diefenbunker

# ICEWINE AND DINE IN NIAGARA

Canadians didn't invent icewine, but we sure perfected it. A notable achievement, considering this sweet elixir is one of the riskiest, toughest and most labour-intensive wines to make. Healthy grapes must be frozen on the vine, hand-picked and pressed within a matter of hours, squeezing out those sweet, valuable and industry-scrutinized drops.

Niagara is Canada's largest wine region, famed for its Riesling and Chardonnay. As in B.C.'s Okanagan and Nova Scotia's Annapolis Valley, the seductive allure of life among vines has led to a boom in wineries and first-class restaurants. Niagara, blessed with ideal climatic conditions created by Lake Ontario and the Niagara Escarpment, feels like a fat grape bursting with goodness. No wonder other varietals are making their mark: Merlot, Pinot Noir, Baco Noir, Sauvignon Blanc.

My Segway rolls gently along rows of Cabernet Franc as Daniel Speck, one of three brothers behind Henry of Pelham Estate, explains the magic. Warm wind rolls off the lake and gets trapped by the Escarpment, circulating to allow grapes to reach their full potential. Among some of the healthiest vines I've ever seen, he points out the wind machines that have revolutionized wine in the

# Canada's Best Wine

After a humble start, Canadian wines now compete on the world stage for quality and taste. Natalie MacLean, editor of Canada's largest wine site (www.nataliemaclean.com) and author of *Unquenchable*, raises a glass to her Top 10:

- Benjamin Bridge Benjamin Bridge Nova 7 2010, Gaspereau Valley, NS
- Stratus White 2009, VQA, Niagara-on-the-Lake, ON
- Tawse Winery Inc. Quarry Road Riesling 2011, VQA, Niagara Escarpment, ON
- Vineland Estates Winery Chardonnay Reserve 2007, VQA, Niagara Escarpment, ON
- Le Clos Jordanne Le Grand Clos Pinot Noir 2009, VQA, Niagara Peninsula, ON
- Burrowing Owl Syrah 2009, VQA, Okanagan Valley, BC
- Jackson-Triggs Delaine Syrah 2010, VQA, Niagara Peninsula, ON
- Painted Rock Estate Winery Ltd. Red Icon 2009, VQA, Okanagan Valley, BC
- Domaine Pinnacle Sparkling Ice Cider, QC
- Inniskillin Wines Sparkling Vidal Icewine 2011, VQA, Niagara-on-the-Lake, ON ➤

region. Essentially stationary helicopter turbines, the blades suck in warm air from higher altitudes, rotating it across the vines in emergencies to prevent devastating frost. It all helps with the consistency needed to produce quality product, and to further Canada's claim as a major winemaking country.

Segways tours, offered at the estate, scoot between vines as I learn about Henry of Pelham's long history and the brothers' devotion to their craft. It makes the icewine tasting back in the dark, cool cellars all the more enjoyable. Niagara introduced the world to a Cabernet Franc icewine—light ruby-red heaven. The first drops on my tongue explode with notes of sweet strawberry jam. The Riesling is more complex, departing with a citrus aftertaste. Vidal, a sturdy grape that is the most popular icewine variety in Niagara, is a pounder, a deliriously delicious full-frontal assault of velvet.

## Karen's Ice House Slushy Recipe

Icewine is magical to share, and here's a fantastic recipe to spread the love around. Since I discovered it, it's become my go-to at dinner parties.

6 to 10 ice cubes
200 mL Vidal icewine

Blend, adding ice cubes until frothy. Toasts 8 to 10

"We need to think of icewine as a condiment, a side dish," explains Daniel. "It should be enjoyed at the start of the meal, paired with spicy and salty dishes, or just enjoyed as dessert on its own." Drinking icewine after a rich, sweet dessert can throw your appetite a life vest made of concrete. Icewine before lunch, on the other hand, is rather decadent, so I head off to Beamsville's Good Earth Restaurant and Cooking School, driving past rows of grapes basking in the sun. My wine philosophy is simple: the bottle is never as important as whom you're sharing it with—in this case, Good Earth's firecracker owner-operator, Nicolette Novak.

Having grown up on the farm before chasing adventure in the city, she moved back to open the region's first cooking school, creating an intimate space in which to pair her favourite things, food and wine. Today, her restaurant packs in locals and visitors drawn to exceptional dishes (house-smoked salmon with homegrown asparagus on flatbread, lobster and shrimp burger), with an orange-hued romantic ambience under the summer umbrellas, terrific service, smells wafting from the open-plan outdoor kitchen, and great music performed by local artists. Good Earth's wit, candour and laughs dispense with wine's traditional haughtiness, a reminder of the importance of soul on any plate, and in any glass.

After stopping off at Inniskillin, Canada's most famous icewine producer and its earliest pioneer, I pull into a small operation called Ice House, run by one of the world's most experienced icewine makers, Jamie Macfarlane. *Life is too short for cheap wine* reads a sign hanging at the door, a reminder that the cost and difficulty of making icewine justify its expense. I'm greeted by Jamie's wife, Karen, beaming with pride at her products. She pairs my tastings with wasabi peas, lime-chili chips from Australia and dark chocolate. The rich flavour of Macfarlane's icewine explodes on my tongue, revealing complex flavours, a dazzling meal for my senses. "Icewine is the sweetest kiss," muses Karen, who sealed her own wedding to Jamie with a mouthful of icewine. "It asks you: are you special enough to enjoy this?"

I leave Ice House refreshing myself with an icewine slushy, the perfect accompaniment to a hot summer day, and wonder how far I can take it. At Peller Estates, one of Niagara's largest wineries, you can take it very, very far indeed. In the award-winning, family-run estate's restaurant, I start with an icewine cosmopolitan. The meal begins: foie gras, tuna tartare spiced with Cabernet Franc icewine. Green bean salad with truffles, paired with Ice Cuvée Classic, Peller's sparkling wine, topped with icewine for sweetness. Icewine-poached lobster-stuffed ravioli, heritage beef served with quinoa and dried berries (rehydrated with icewine, of course). Each course is paired with an excellent Peller wine, building up to the finale, a glass of Signature Series Vidal Icewine. I hold the smooth liquid on my tongue, letting its acidity bloom.

Icewine's freezing origins somehow warm the soul. For its distinctly Canadian flavour—encompassing its food, wine and people—visiting Niagara's wine region is easily one for the bucket list.

**START HERE:** canadianbucketlist.com/niagara

# SKATE THE RIDEAU

I'm having coffee with some local friends in Ottawa, and one of the guys at the table starts talking about the Rideau Canal. He's not harping on the fact that it is the "best-preserved slack-water canal in North America, demonstrating the use of European technology on a large scale." We both don't know exactly what that means, but that's the quote from UNESCO's website recognizing the canal as a World Heritage Site. It's way cooler to think of this 202-kilometre-long waterway as the very reason Canada is not part of the United States, since this military-built engineering achievement allowed the British to defend the country against attacking Americans. Some historians believe that if the canal didn't exist, neither might Canada.

ONTARIO

Cooler still is the fact that every winter the Rideau turns into the world's largest outdoor skating rink. At 7.8 kilometres, the skateable section that cuts through Ottawa is equivalent to ninety Olympic-sized hockey rinks. The Rideau used to be the world's longest skateable rink, until Winnipeg took the title with its 8.54-kilometre-long Assiniboine River Trail. Now there's an upstart in Invermere, British Columbia, hoping to usurp both with its Whiteways Trail system on Lake Windermere. Ottawa's wide, Winnipeg's long. When it comes to the ego of a city, size does matter.

Back to the coffee table in Ottawa. It's a frosty -12°C outside, and the beans taste particularly good. "You know, the Rideau, it's a magical place," says my friend. "Sometimes, at midnight, I put on my speed skates, crank some music on my iPod, and I just go for it. I mean, I just skate fast and smooth, and it feels like I'm flying. Nothing beats that feeling—nothing."

He tells it the way he feels it, with deep respect and awe. His experience Axel-jumps over the historical significance of the Rideau. It spirals around the quirky fact that Ottawans skate to work, briefcases in hand. It makes my hair stand up and my heart quicken. I want to know that feeling.

That evening, I walk to Kilometre Zero, not far from the steps of Parliament. I only have one night to chase the experience, but there are some challenges to overcome. The fragrance of fresh-fried Beaver Tails wafts in the air, demanding a detour. Exquisite ice sculptures on display from the annual Winterlude Festival prove an additional distraction. I don't even have skates, but to the rescue are skate rental booths on the skateway. Everything is set, when the final two hurdles present themselves:

1. I ice-skate with the grace of a duck on skis.
2. The ice is no condition to be skated on.

Ottawa has enjoyed an unseasonably warm winter, and the result is a skateway cracked and scarred, pockmarked and as uneven as a politician's ethics. The locals know when to steer clear, but poor tourists are discovering that ice is very hard, and that an outdoor canal differs greatly from a smooth indoor skating rink. An ambulance flashes and some helpful volunteers cart off a skater. On the way, they tell me I'm mad even to think about being on the ice. The fact that I can barely stand up on ice skates (cut the immigrant a break!) isn't helping.

I close my eyes, take a deep breath and imagine myself skating at speed, under the bright stars, perhaps an artist like Ottawa's Kathleen Edwards dreamily cooing away on my headphones. Then I slip, land hard on my butt and quickly decide the only sane place for a tourist in Ottawa right now is a warm pub in the ByWard Market district. Which is exactly where I go.

So I never did quite get to skate the Rideau in all its glory. But that shouldn't stop us from adding it to the Great Canadian Bucket List.

**START HERE:** canadianbucketlist.com/rideau

# LEAN OFF THE CN TOWER EDGEWALK

Over the years, I've built a reputation as something of a thrill-seeker. Trust me, I never set out to run with bulls, jump out of planes, swing from bridges and dive with sharks. Yet one thing led to another, and a former desk-jobber morphed into the travel guy with a regular magazine column called Thrillseeker. So you're probably thinking: "Of course Esrock would choose to walk outside on one of the world's tallest free-standing structures. It's probably something he does every day." Not quite, but I have walked around the edge of Macau's 233-metre Skytower, shortly before I bungee jumped off the damn thing.

The EdgeWalk is over 100 metres higher than that, and the view over Lake Ontario and the city beats anything Macau, much less anywhere else, has to offer. To balance the Scale of Nerves, I decide to bring along the editor of this book, the wonderful but decidedly less Thrillseekerish Janice Zawerbny, and join a group of tourists ranging in age from 23 to 68. Janice is afraid of heights but feels inexplicably drawn to the EdgeWalk, the way ambitious business students and musicians from around the country are drawn to the CN Tower vortex. Piercing the sky, head and shoulders above anything else, Canada's most iconic building landmark was declared a Wonder of the Modern World by the American Society of Civil Engineers. It is a true engineering marvel, 553.33 metres at almost pure vertical, beautifully illuminated at night to become more than just an observation deck and communications tower. The CN Tower is construction as art, Canadian ingenuity at scale, a soaring symbol of Toronto and beyond. Why wouldn't you want to step outside on its rim, put your toes over the edge and place the world at your feet?

Danger? Come on, people, this is one of Canada's busiest tourist attractions. Even though we sign the customary waiver, the emphasis on safety is miles ahead of similar attractions I've encountered in Asia and New Zealand. After all, this is the world's highest full-circle, hands-free walk, and we will be walking on a 1.5-metre ledge 356 metres aboveground on the Tower's main pod.

After taking a Breathalyzer test for alcohol and drugs, we are asked to lock up all loose items—watches, earrings, wallets, necklaces—and slip on a red-rocket walksuit. Our harnesses are checked and quadruple-checked, shoes tightened (twice), glasses attached with string, hair tied up. I see a familiar nervous look in the eye of Janice. The look of: I don't know why I'm doing this, but I must do it all the same.

You can see every one of the CN Tower's 116 storeys in the elevator as you ascend the external glass-faced shaft. Suddenly the height becomes real. Suddenly the only illustrious CN Tower record I can remember is that 360, the restaurant located 351 metres up, holds the Guinness World Record for the World's Highest Wine Cellar.

In a small control centre, alongside a monitor recording wind speeds and weather, we get clipped in (twice, with additional zip ties) to a steel overhead track. You've more chance of spontaneously combusting than of slipping out of this contraption. Our affable guide, Christian, tells me that although he's undergone extensive training, his only qualification for the job was his healthy fear of heights. Empathy with clients is a natural asset.

He leads us onto the metal walkway and invites us to walk right up to the edge, our toes hanging over. Even though I know we're safer up here than the folks in the Hot Wheels–sized cars stuck in traffic below, my mind does its best to convince me that leaning over the edge of the CN Tower is not something my body should do. Fortunately, I stopped listening to myself years ago, so I follow my fellow EdgeWalkers pushing their limits and shuffle up to the edge. We applaud our efforts, swap high-fives and breathe in the sweeping view below.

As the walk continues around the Tower, we hit the windy side, with 53-kilometre-an-hour gusts of warm air instantly pickling our adrenal glands. Christian has to holler to point out landmarks. This time he encourages us to lean forward over the edge, on our tiptoes. Each challenge is ably met, so by the time the group returns to the sheltered side, facing the sea that is Lake Ontario on a day so clear I can make out the buildings at Niagara Falls, everyone is comfortable enough to lean back and smile for the photos. Arms outstretched, her heels balanced on the edge, the formerly afraid-of-heights Janice embraces the sky with a huge smile on her face. See, you don't have to be a thrill-seeker to benefit from a little edge.

**START HERE:** canadianbucketlist.com/edgewalk

Yellow Brick
Road

# MOTORBIKE AROUND LAKE SUPERIOR

Lake Superior doesn't give up her dead. The water of the world's largest lake by area is so cold, bodies sink to its depths. Mortality was on my mind as I nervously tucked into pancakes in the crowded Hoito Finnish Diner in Thunder Bay.

You have to admit, a writer getting killed in a motorcycle accident while researching a book about things to do before you die has just the sort of ironic twist you'd find in a newspaper story. Granted, I'd already walked face-first off a cliff, scuba dived wrecks and driven many a long moose-trapped highway, but the challenge ahead was particularly and personally daunting. My wife and mother were in full fret mode over my plan to research one of the great motorcycle trips of Canada: the north shore of Lake Superior. So what if I'd never been on a bike trip before? So what if my saddle hours, including my licence training, could be counted on two fingers? So what if the most powerful bike I'd ever ridden was 125 cc? And so what if a car did T-bone my scooter, breaking my knee and cracking my helmet? That accident kick-started my grand adventure, my rebirth as an adventurer!

I've faced so many limit-pushing challenges in the many years since then that I've learned the secret to getting through just about anything. Douglas Adams boldly put it in his futuristic travel book *The Hitchhiker's Guide to the Galaxy*. When Larry Lage, owner of Thunder Bay's Excalibur Motorcycle Works, hands me a jacket and gloves, he doesn't notice that under my thin-lipped smile I'm muttering my most powerful mantra:

Don't Panic.

Riding a motorcycle on the shores of mighty Lake Superior, as I was quick to discover, is one part exhilaration, one part speed, a dash of freedom, a lime wedge of danger, topped off with camaraderie and natural beauty to make a cocktail of mobile magic. No wonder this 700-kilometre stretch of the Trans-Canada from Thunder Bay to Sault Ste. Marie has such an amazing reputation with bikers. Wavy S-curves on smooth blacktop cutting through forest and rock, always close to sparkling blue lake, the north shore attracts riders from across the continent, some of whom complete the 2,100-kilometre loop around Superior on scenic roads in the United States.

Larry had loaned me his Kawasaki KWR 650 dual-sport bike, its odometer a third of the way through its second (or third) rotation. The bike is reliable and experienced, much like my biking buddy Steve Kristjanson. A semi-retired jack-of-all-trades, Steve has seen thousands of kilometres in the saddle, having ridden to the Soo and

## One Week

In the 2008 film *One Week*, Joshua Jackson plays a mild Torontonian named Ben who discovers he has terminal cancer. He promptly buys a 1973 Norton Commando motorcycle and decides to ride to Vancouver Island, a road trip so intrinsically Canadian even the Tragically Hip's Gord Downie shows up in a cameo. On his journey, Ben encounters the world's biggest nickel in Sudbury, ponders Terry Fox outside Thunder Bay and takes snaps of the world's biggest camel, tipi, hockey stick and muskie. Ben would have liked this book. ➤

back in one stretch, a 1,400-kilometre sitting. Our goal is half that in double the time, two days on the road, stopping at viewpoints and attractions along the way.

We start by paying homage to Terry Fox at his memorial just outside Thunder Bay. Here was a boy who was running across Canada, racked with cancer, on one leg. His legacy—hundreds of millions of dollars raised for cancer research—is an inspiration and further steel to arm my own courage for the incomparably lighter challenge ahead.

Still, it doesn't stop me from stalling my bike at a highway intersection, right next to Larry and his bike-instructor girlfriend Diane, who are accompanying us to the Ouimet Canyon. I expect Larry to point me right back to his shop, but he gamely encourages me instead. "Keep your head up, and look where you want to go, not at whatever you're going to hit," adds Diane, like a supportive parent. These guys live and breathe their bikes, a world apart from the annoying twits on decibel-shattering cruises, content to just parade them. I'm told the biggest danger is moose and deer, which can run out of the ditches straight into your path. Warning signs line the highway, and I spot the occasional cross in the ground commemorating those who didn't heed them. Steve hit a deer a couple of years ago going sixty, broke his knee and killed the animal. He knows he got off lightly.

Visor down, I smooth into the groove of the road. The slightest movement of my hand on the throttle has an instant effect, slowing me down, hurling me forward. We pass through the glowing ridge at Red Rocks, stopping to admire magnificent views of this sea-lake. With a surface area of 82,100 square kilometres, Lake Superior contains a whopping 10 percent of all the surface freshwater on the planet. It creates its own weather system, supports fisheries and tourism, and each winter generates waves up to 2.5 metres high, to the delight of some truly hard-core and well-insulated surfers.

After dinner in Rossport, we check out the Aguasabon River Gorge before stopping for the night in the small mill town of Terrace Bay. We ride in on a newly tarred stretch of highway candy, as smooth and black as licorice. Steve lubes the chains, checks the tires and oil, a picture of Zen with his art of motorcycle maintenance.

It's a relief to get out of my sweat-soaked biker gear, a relief that my only crash today is in the soft bed of the Imperial Motel.

Thick fog blows in ominously the following morning. Moose had crashed into my anxious dreams. Come on, Esrock, get a grip! Yes, motorcycles are more likely to lead to accidents, and having felt the wind slam against my chest at a hundred kilometres an hour, I know there's little room for error. Yet the highway is wide and forgiving, traffic relatively light, overtaking lanes frequent.

We ride into the spooky fog in staggered formation, brights on, speed down. Droplets of moisture cling to my visor, so I use my gloved hand to wipe it clean. The roar of the engine, the blur of green forest, the steam rising off lakes in the shadows: even in the fog, the adventure is . . . superior! Gradually, visibility improves, the clouds providing some welcome shelter from the unusually hot sun. I take a photo in White River, where Winnie, the bear that inspired the children's books, was born. When we reach the landmark Wawa Goose overlooking the valley, I'm still wondering what a Pooh is. The sandy beach and overlooking cliffs at Old Women's Bay are gorgeous, as is the view of the lake islands from Alona Bay.

## A Wild Goose Chase

Among the roadside attractions you'll encounter, look out for Wawa's famous Canada goose. It's the largest statue of its kind and claims to be one of Canada's most photographed landmarks. Dating back to the early 1960s, the 8.5-metre steel bird was built to encourage passing traffic on the Trans-Canada Highway to come into Wawa. Today, Wawa's goose even has its own webcam. ➤

I'm getting comfortable on the bike, accustomed to the speed, the wind, the vibration beneath me. Next time you find yourself behind a bike on the highway, watch what happens when it passes another bike going in the opposite direction. The left hand points out, wrist slightly twisted, for the friendly biker "wave." Everybody does it, like the secret handshake of some exclusive club. Everyone except three riders on Harleys, whom Steve, riding a rare Suzuki DR800, dismisses as posers anyway.

By the time we reach Batchawana Bay, stopping to enjoy a cold reward beer at Voyageurs, I feel as if I've overcome my own poser problems. Other than three deer crossing the road, the risk was benign. Whatever ghosts were haunting my nerves had been winterized in the garage. Lake Superior, with waters that never give up her dead, energized me with a rush of life.

Bike stored outside the hotel in Sault Ste. Marie, I text a biker friend back home to let him know I made it safely. He replies in seconds. "Makes you appreciate your life knowing you can die at any moment hey?"

No, it makes you appreciate life knowing you can conquer your fears.

**START HERE:** canadianbucketlist.com/superior

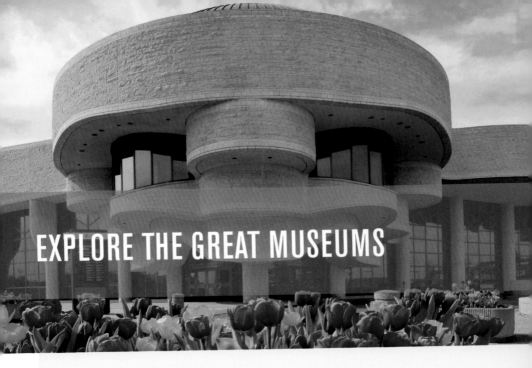

# EXPLORE THE GREAT MUSEUMS

The word *museum* sounds awfully like *mausoleum*—a place where artifacts go to die. Fortunately, Canada's great museums are anything but, having been revitalized into living temples of knowledge where one can interact with, discover and journey to far-off places, without ever leaving the building.

Let's begin our brief guided tour in Ottawa, home to a half-dozen national museums, where locals and visitors learn all about Canada and beyond. We start in the National Gallery, housing the country's largest collection of Canadian art. The brainchild of renowned Canadian architect Moshe Safdie, the Great Hall is entered via a long ramp, designed to put visitors in the right frame of mind to experience the art to come. The Great Hall uses windows and skylights to create an exceptionally light space, cleverly avoiding direct contact with the art itself while offering famous views of the Parliament Buildings. Safdie was inspired by the Library of Parliament, so much so that the Great Hall has a volume identical to that of Parliament's stone library that sits across the Ottawa River. Besides iconic works from Canadian greats throughout history, the museum also features works by Rembrandt, Van Gogh, Matisse, Monet, Picasso, Warhol and Pollock. You can't miss the gallery's distinctive glass entrance, or Louise Bourgeois's creepy spider outside.

We'll walk across the Ottawa River along the Alexandra Bridge and into Gatineau, Quebec. It takes just twenty minutes to reach the beautifully designed Canadian Museum of History, the most-visited museum in the country. Over the next few years, the former Canadian Museum of Civilization will be renovating half of its permanent space, introducing new galleries to complement old favourites. We enter through the Grand Hall, with its view of the river and Parliament Hill, under towering totem poles (the largest display in the world), to Haida artist Bill Reid's original plaster of his masterpiece *Spirit of Haida Gwaii*. It's a fitting introduction to the first level, the First People's Hall, tracing twenty thousand years of Aboriginal history in Canada. With the renovation, the former Canada Hall, Canadian Personalities Hall and Canadian Postal Museum have been combined to create the largest exhibition of Canadian history ever assembled. Unaffected by the refurbishment is the Canadian Children's Museum, where kids will continue to embed themselves in new worlds, literally getting passports as they learn how people live around the world.

Ottawa's other national museums are well worth investigating: the Museum of Nature, the Canadian Agriculture Museum, the Canadian Aviation and Space Museum, the Canadian Science and Technology Museum and the haunting Canadian War Museum, with its jarring structural angles and captivating human stories.

Still in Ontario, let's Porter (verb: to fly affordably) to Toronto and gander at T-Dot's prize museums. The Royal Ontario Museum, or

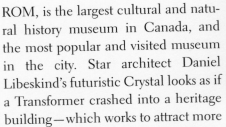

ROM, is the largest cultural and natural history museum in Canada, and the most popular and visited museum in the city. Star architect Daniel Libeskind's futuristic Crystal looks as if a Transformer crashed into a heritage building—which works to attract more than one million visitors annually to the museum's forty galleries. With over six million items, the ROM has something for everybody, and plenty left over. I love the Dinosaur Gallery, the giant totem pole and the creepy Gallery of Birds, forever flying nowhere.

Not far away, on Dundas Street, is the Art Gallery of Ontario, one of the largest gallery spaces in North America, with a collection of over eighty thousand works from the first century to the present. Residing in its Georgian manor premises since 1910, the AGO continues to host some of the world's most important art exhibitions, introducing visitors to the Old Masters, King Tut and the Pharoahs, along with priceless works from the Hermitage and India's Royal Courts.

Yes, Canada's great museums are very much alive, prized and treasured by anyone interested in culture, history, art and science. Prized and appreciated, therefore, by anyone ticking off the Great Canadian Bucket List.

**START HERE:** canadianbucketlist.com/museums

# SUPPORT THE BLUE JAYS

I'm entering the big leagues, ready to play hardball and cover my bases so I can knock this one out of the park. Although it might come out of left field, I'm going to say this right off the bat: I've never been to a baseball game, never so much as watched a baseball game on TV, and other than reading the book *Moneyball*, I can't tell the singles from the shutouts. "Say it ain't so, Joe!" but it's the truth. I grew up watching cricket, which bowls out North Americans the way baseball throws a curveball at cricket fans. Still, I can appreciate that the Toronto Blue Jays are no grandstanding bush-league team. They're the only Canadian team in the major leagues, the only other part of the World that currently qualifies for the World Series, and as such, supporting them at home deserves a spot on the Great Canadian Bucket List.

My first impression, as I enjoy the view inside the stadium from the Renaissance Hotel's Arriba Restaurant, is that these guys can throw. How their arms stay in their sockets is a mystery, as the Blue

Jays warm up for their opening match in a series against the Los Angeles Angels. The retractable roof of the Rogers Centre is open to allow the ballpark to bask in the glorious late June sun. Satiated with beer from Arriba (at considerably less than what you might pay for it in the stadium), I hop over to the stadium and take my seat in the modest crowd a dozen rows up to the left of home base. It's been decades since the Blue Jays' glory days of 1992–93, when they won back-to-back World Series, Canada's first World Series titles. Since then, at the time of writing, they hadn't made the playoffs. Poor Toronto sport fans, forever supporting their underdog hockey, basketball and baseball teams.

Still, this is the big league, and the atmosphere is festive, especially with the year's star player, Jose Bautista, smashing home runs out of the park. When he steps up to bat, the stadium simmers with anticipation, and the pitcher throws more balls than usual. I explain to my wife, poorly, that a ball is a pitch that does not qualify for a strike. She tells me I should just stick to cricket, since the only balls she can see are those being thrown, and possibly the ones on the fielder with the too-tight pants.

We watch as a foul hit ricochets into the crowd, causing a mosh pit frenzy to claim the ball. Not only is it perfectly acceptable for a whizzing baseball to scalp the inattentive fan, but it's expected that surrounding fans will trample them to hell in hopes of leaving with a souvenir. In cricket, I might add, the ball is tossed back into the field of play.

Somewhere in the middle of the game, Bautista hits a huge home run with the bases loaded, and I'm on my feet with the rest of them, cheering the four players running around the diamond. That's the moment I was looking for, right there, an instant of support and momentary triumph with the shadow of the CN Tower looming overhead. We follow the game as best we can, understanding that

it appears to be coming right down to the bottom of the ninth, in which the bases are loaded and a Blue Jays home run would sneak a victory right out from under the mitts of the Angels. Strike one. Strike two. Then, before I can fully build up my excitement, the batter hits the ball directly to an outfielder, the Blue Jays hang their heads and slump their shoulders, the Angels jump up and down, and fans begin to stream out of their seats. As the Blue Jays' newest fans, we look around and notice nobody's too hung up about it. It's the Blue Jays. They're used to this sort of thing. But it won't stop the fans from coming back—not one iota. And it won't stop those of us ticking off bucket lists either.

**START HERE:** canadianbucketlist.com/bluejays

# GIVE A STANDING OVATION IN STRATFORD

"We all hope that in your lives you have just the right amount of sitting quietly at home, and just the right amount of adventure."

—Barnaby Tucker in Thornton Wilder's *The Matchmaker*

When a small town falls on hard times, it needs to reinvent itself. Once a railway junction and manufacturing centre for locomotives, Stratford found itself in an economic pickle until a local journalist named Tom Patterson realized that a town named after Stratford-upon-Avon, sitting on its own Avon River, with a neighbouring town called Shakespeare, should have its own Shakespeare Festival. In the summer of 1953, Alec Guinness uttered the first lines of the first play (in a tent, no less), and the Stratford Shakespeare Festival was born.

By the time I visit, sixty years later, Stratford has grown to host one of the largest and most renowned theatre festivals in the world. During its lengthy April-to-November engagement, it attracts some of the

## Famous Actors Who Have
## rformed at the Festival

1. Christopher Walken (1968)
2. Peter Ustinov (1979–80)
3. Christopher Plummer (1956–2012)
4. Alec Guinness (1953)
5. William Shatner (1954–56)
6. Maggie Smith (1976–80)
7. James Mason (1954)
8. Brian Dennehy (2008, 2011)
9. Jessica Tandy (1976, 1980)
10. John Neville (1983–89)

world's best actors, directors, designers and theatre talent. The tent has been replaced by four major theatres, pioneering the thrust stage that allows the audience to surround the actors on three sides, as they would have in Shakespeare's day. Enthusiastic audiences arrive from around the world, with the theatre boom resulting in significant economic aftershocks.

Stratford boasts one of the best culinary schools in the country; an impressive selection of restaurants, hotels and theatre schools; and the third-largest costume warehouse in the world. It's a town where kids grow up knowing they can make a living in the arts—as actors, stage designers, lighting technicians or musicians. A fact acknowledged by its most recent celebrity resident, a kid who used to busk outside the Avon Theatre on Downie Street and goes by the name of Justin Bieber. The week before I arrive, Bieber humbly returned to the same spot on the same stairs, guitar in hand, to play a couple of songs. Today, as I enjoy poutine at the Downie Street Burger across the street, a violinist sends his classical notes soaring into the warm summer breeze. Spotless, small downtown Stratford hums with coffee shops, chocolatiers, boutiques, bistros and bookstores—the kind of place that leaves a whimsical impression and envy for the thirty-two thousand people who live in a small town with more culture than most major cities.

Live trumpets at the tent-inspired Festival Theatre signal that it's time for the two p.m. matinee of this year's popular farce, *The Matchmaker*. Non-Shakespearean works were introduced as early as the festival's second year, and today include musicals, comedies,

↑

ONTARIO

Broadway hits and classic works of world theatre. Thornton Wilder's *The Matchmaker* was the Broadway hit that inspired *Hello, Dolly!* and contained some of the sharpest wit and most crackling situational comedy ever seen onstage. There are several interweaving storylines, but I'm particularly drawn to the tale of two shop clerks, trapped in their work, determined, for one day at least, to have "an adventure." It all leads to love, danger, fear and shenanigans, reflected in blistering one-liners, split-second escapes and an endearing happy ending. The performances are fantastic, the stage design stupendous, and two hours later the cast graciously receives a standing ovation from the crowd. On top of the Stratford Shakespeare Festival's many accomplishments, it's this moment of appreciation that bows its way onto the Great Canadian Bucket List.

Later, I tour the fascinating costume and prop warehouse, and walk down to the Avon River. Opposite colourful artists displaying their work in the park, swans glide under the scenic arched bridge to Patterson Island. I wonder if Patterson had any notion of the impact his idea would have on the town, its people and Canada's cultural legacy. Regardless, we can all appreciate the power of reinvention and the special magic that brews when we wake up and decide to chase our own adventures.

**START HERE:** canadianbucketlist.com/shakespeare

# GET SPRAYED IN NIAGARA FALLS

Visiting the tourist zone in the town of Niagara Falls on Canada Day is a classy dream, and by *classy* I mean *tacky*, and by *dream* I mean *nightmare*. Vegas without the spectacle, the tourist zone is designed for sugar-saturated, overstimulated kids dragging along bludgeoned parents with their bruised wallets. Theme rides, water parks, lineups, burger, ice cream and hot dog joints—on a scorching July 1, it can all seem a bit much. Then I opened the drapes of the honeymooners' suite on the twenty-first floor of the Sheraton to see what had attracted all this madness in the first place.

Never underestimate the impact of seeing Niagara Falls for the first time. This from a guy who's swum in rock pools atop Victoria Falls, speedboated up the tropical canyons of South America's stunning Iguazu Falls and showered in the cascades of some of the most beautiful waterfalls on six continents. Once I got past the family holiday madness, the crowds, the crawling traffic and the fifteen-minute wait for the Sheraton's elevators, I could see Niagara Falls for what it is: Canada's most spectacular natural wonder, worthy of its draw as one of the world's great tourist attractions.

Draining Lake Erie into Lake Ontario, the American, Bridal and Horseshoe falls combine to produce the highest flow rate of any waterfall in the world, a volume of water that famously sends mist mushrooming into the sky. It's even more impressive when you consider that massive hydroelectric projects upriver redirect much of the flow before it reaches the 21- to 30-metre drop of the American Falls and the 53-metre plummet at the Horseshoe-shaped crest that separates Canada from the United States.

Given the hyper-commercialization of the town, I enjoyed simply strolling along the promenade on a warm night, watching spotlights illuminate the water, feeling the refreshing spray as I got closer to the thunderous whirlpool beneath Horseshoe Falls. Before the lake waters disappear over the edge, the Falls seem to challenge each visitor with a thought experiment: if I went over the edge, would I survive? Three people have survived after going over unprotected, including a seven-year-old boy, while others have used barrels and protective devices to increase their chances of emerging unscathed. Over the years some have succeeded, others not. Nik Wallenda's tightrope walk in 2012, the first successful attempt in over a century, becomes even more impressive at the scene of his accomplishment. Illegal as it is to attempt it, people will continue to test the might of North America's mightiest falls, on purpose and by accident.

## On the Wire

June 15, 2012, saw the first tightrope walk across Niagara Falls in 116 years. A seventh-generation tightrope walker, Nik Wallenda walked 550 metres near the base of Horseshoe Falls, watched by millions on television and huge crowds on both sides of the border. Getting permission for the stunt was no easy task, as Canadian authorities in Niagara were worried the stunt would encourage amateurs. Just a few months earlier, an unidentified man scaled a railing and jumped into Horseshoe Falls, becoming the third person to survive an unprotected fall into the Falls. ➤

The iconic experience, the must-do no matter how long the lineup, is a gorge cruise. Since 1846, the *Maid of the Mist* has soaked the passengers on its decks in the steam shower beneath Horseshoe Falls. There are several boats running every fifteen minutes on both sides of the border, taking up to six hundred passengers at a time, doing a blistering trade on the summer's busiest long weekend. Joining the Canada Day mayhem, I expected to be waiting for hours, but the lineup moved quickly and smoothly. Passengers are given blue plastic ponchos and are herded like cattle through various checkpoints before entering the boat, squeezing onto the upper and lower decks. As we motor along upriver, squeals from the kids greet the first sheet of spray. By the time we retreat from the choppy rapids several minutes later, everyone's head is soaked. From the boat, Niagara Falls looks and sounds like the wild and raging natural wonder it is.

With cash in hand, you can take Niagara Parks' Journey Behind the Falls, or take to the skies with Niagara Helicopter's nine-minute ride, or cross the canyon farther downriver in an old-fashioned air tram, or watch a 4-D movie (the extra D means you'll get sprayed with water in the theatre). That's a lot of waterfall action. I was content to enjoy the exceptional view from my hotel room and watch the nightly fireworks. Could I live without the kitsch attractions and loud, wet kids bouncing around in the elevators? Definitely. Is Niagara Falls something to see before you die? Absolutely.

In early 2012, it was announced that *Maid of the Mist* had lost its contract to print money, i.e., to be the exclusive operator of boat tours into the gorge. As of 2014, the *Maid of the Mist* will continue to run on the American side, but new vessels will run on the Canadian side, operated by Hornblower, the same company behind Statue of Liberty and Alcatraz cruises.

**START HERE:** canadianbucketlist.com/falls

ONTARIO ↑

# WATCH THE MAPLE LEAFS vs. THE HABS

The Great Canadian Bucket List does not deal in hypotheticals. It doesn't include items such as Play Hoops with Steve Nash, or Go Over Niagara Falls in a Barrel, as thrilling as they both sound. So while I'd love to list Watch Your Team Win Game Seven of the Stanley Cup Finals, the painful reality is that you might never get the opportunity to do so. Most of us will battle to find a ticket if our team actually gets to Game Seven in the first place. That being said, after an exhausting and bruising season, chances are at least two Canadian teams will make it to the annual playoffs, and you just might find yourself in the stands whooping like a crane when they do so.

I cheer for any Canadian team in the playoffs, which I understand violates several hockey codes. I'm told Montreal Canadiens fans would simply never cheer for the Toronto Maple Leafs, and the Calgary Flames would sooner be extinguished than support the slick Edmonton Oilers. Everyone east of B.C. hates the Canucks, but differences can be put aside for the Winnipeg Jets because their logo is so damn cool. All of that being said, whether you're a hockey supporter or not, the Great Canadian Bucket List demands that you

# Canada's Ultimate Hockey Matchup

Toronto and Montreal have faced each other in fifteen playoff series, the last one being in 1979. The Habs have won 8 to the Leafs' 7. Score: Canadiens 1

*Forbes* places the Toronto Maple Leafs as the NHL's Most Valuable Team. The Montreal Canadiens slot in at Number 3, behind the New York Rangers. Score: Maple Leafs 1

All-time leading scorer for the Maple Leafs is Mats Sundin (981 games, 420 goals, 987 points). All-time leading scorer for the Habs is Maurice "The Rocket" Richard (1,111 games, 626 goals, 1,091 points). Score: Canadiens 1

Number of Stanley Cups: Maple Leafs 13, Canadiens 24. Score: Canadiens 1

Final Score: In a closely contested series, I have to give it to the Winnipeg Jets. ➤

experience true hockey fever at least once, and thus I find myself at the Air Canada Centre in Toronto, watching the oldest rivalry in Canadian hockey.

I knew this was more than a game when, earlier, I stood on the subway platform in Toronto's College station. Facing me was a mural of Leafs hockey players, and against my back was a mural of Habs players. After quickly checking why the Canadiens are known as the Habs (it's short for *habitants*, the name given to French settlers in New France), I concluded that anything immortalized in subway station art must be important. Since the 1940s, these two teams have come to represent more than just hockey. Each time the skates hit the ice, a national scar gets scratched. The blue Toronto Maple Leafs are a symbol of Canada's British heritage, the English elite that have brokered the financial power among the tall buildings in Canada's biggest city. The red Habs are passionate warriors of the French-Canadian heritage, where emotions run deep and a distinct culture is celebrated. It's the yin-yang dichotomy of Canada, a cultural clash, a historical mash-up, a tale of the country's two biggest cities.

I've always believed there's a connection between the growth of commercial sport and the relatively peaceful times in which we now live. When two nations can vent their frustrations on a soccer pitch or a hockey rink, what need is there to take up axes and spill unnecessary blood? Points can be proven, boasts can be sung and losers can walk away knowing there is always a next time. Considering that many of the players are actually from the United States, Scandinavia, Russia or other parts of Canada, hockey is mostly a fan's battle anyway.

Now, if you mix red and blue together, you get purple, the right colour for the bruising matchup I expected at Air Canada Centre. I'm told there's no other game in the NHL where you'll hear so many fans cheering for the opposing team. Indeed, there's no shortage of Habs shirts walking about in hostile territory. If this were an English football game, that might be dangerous, but as it stands, I bump into two brothers wearing opposing team sweaters. "How is this possible?" I ask. They explain that they grew up in Montreal, and one brother relocated to Toronto fifteen years ago, adopting his city's team just as surely as I've adopted Canada's national sport.

The mood is festive, a little tense. I head up to the nosebleed bleachers and meet more Montreal fans, engaged in conversation with Leafs regulars the next row up. Perhaps if this were Game Seven (there go the hypotheticals again), or if the light beer wasn't so expensive, there might be some real danger.

The teams come onto the ice, the fans cheer, and Montreal proceeds to give the long-suffering Leafs a 5–0 drubbing. Months later, the Maple Leafs will have their revenge. It's all good fun until someone gets hurt, which strapping young millionaires on ice skates are very well paid to do on our behalf.

Wherever you are in Canada, cheering at a live hockey game that matters is something to do before you're sent to the Great Big Penalty Box in the Sky.

**START HERE:** canadianbucketlist.com/nhl

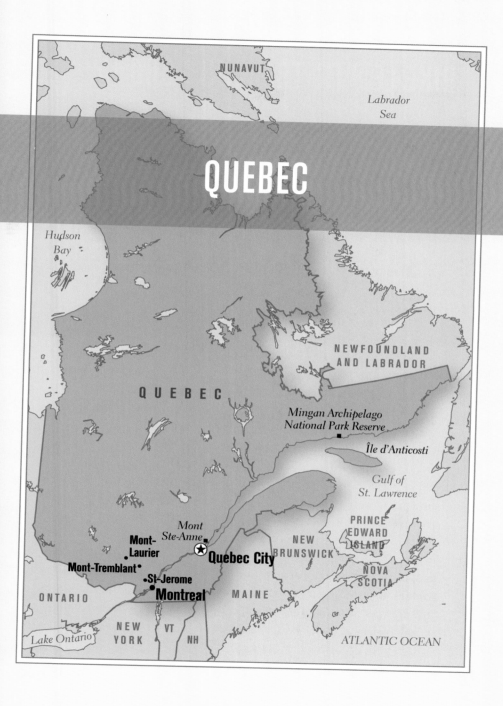

# QUEBEC

Labrador
Sea

Hudson
Bay

NUNAVUT

NEWFOUNDLAND
AND LABRADOR

QUEBEC

Mingan Archipelago
National Park Reserve

Île d'Anticosti

Gulf of
St. Lawrence

PRINCE
EDWARD
ISLAND

NEW
BRUNSWICK

NOVA
SCOTIA

Mont
Ste-Anne

Mont-
Laurier

⭐ Quebec City

Mont-Tremblant

St-Jerome

Montreal

MAINE

ONTARIO

NEW
YORK

VT

NH

Lake Ontario

ATLANTIC OCEAN

# BIKE LE P'TIT TRAIN DU NORD

Picture this: It's Monday morning. You awake in the comfortable bed of a B&B that puts the charm in charming. Pack your light bags and head downstairs for breakfast, where the owners, inevitably named Jean-Claude or Bernard or Cedric, greet you with a cup of warm coffee, fresh orange juice and the choice of a large omelette or French toast served with bananas, raspberries and custard. Figuring you're going to need the calories, you order the French toast and drown it in rich maple syrup for good measure. You leave your bags at the bottom of the stairs, walk outside and put water, snacks, cameras and sunscreen in your bicycle's saddlebags.

Across the street is the crushed gravel pathway of the longest linear park in Canada, a 230-kilometre bike trail in summer—a ski trail in winter—that runs right through the heart of the Laurentians. Bidding your host *au revoir*, and perhaps meeting some new friends loading up their bikes as well, you pedal to the trail and begin a pleasant, relaxing ride that quickly leaves the village houses behind and splits a landscape of boreal forest, bubbling brooks, rivers, wetlands and manicured golf courses. The gradient alternates between hardly uphill and lovingly downhill, so while you do work up a little sweat, you're never slogging forth with any serious effort. Passing other bikers going in the opposite direction, you greet them with a friendly *"Bonjour!"* although they're just as likely to be from Ottawa, Calgary or even Germany. There are couples, grandparents, students, kids and occasionally volunteers biking along in case anybody needs any assistance.

It doesn't take long before you meet lovely people enjoying the scenery just as much as you are, like Guy and Julie from Kitchener. You share camera duties, and leave a message scratched in the gravel for Jeff and Katie from Waterloo who can't be too far behind. The trail itself is clearly marked with mileage signs, punctuated every five to ten kilometres with toilets, a shelter or a small, century-old train station, lovingly restored. At one point a large deer springs out of the trees up ahead. Speedy chipmunks dart in and out of the dense foliage. When you pass through villages, you'll come across cafés or bistros, the kind of place where the friendly owner takes photos of your group and is so much fun that you ask him to be in the photo as well.

How much biking you decide to do that day is completely up to you — perhaps sixty kilometres, perhaps forty. Your stops are as flexible as your muscles; all you need to do is arrange with the transportation service so that your bags are waiting for you at the next B&B when you arrive. Welcomed by another B&B owner (where do they find these characters?), you lock up your bike for the night, take a warm shower and enjoy a stroll around the village. There might be a river flowing opposite your B&B, a ceramic arts festival or a quiet street with cafés and local artists.

With four days to accomplish the ride, handily divided into four sections on the easy-to-follow map, chances are you arrived at your

## Even Granddad Can Do It

In 2011, 54-year-old Winnipeg grandfather Arvid Loewin broke the world record for the fastest bicycle ride across Canada, pedalling 6,055 kilometres from Vancouver to Halifax in just 13 days, 6 hours and 13 minutes. Spending twenty hours on the saddle each day and averaging just two hours' sleep, Loewin raised hundreds of thousands of dollars for street kids in Kenya. ➤

destination early or mid-afternoon, which leaves you plenty of time to rest before a wonderful gourmet dinner, prepared by an award-winning chef. Your legs are a little tired, and your butt reminds you it's there, but you're also satisfied that you did some exercise today, which helped burn off some of that breakfast! You sleep like a baby.

It's Tuesday morning. Repeat.

Wednesday. Repeat, but your legs and butt are silent.

Thursday, much the same, until you reach Mile Zero in Saint-Jérôme, where your car awaits, parked at the hotel. This is where you were picked up four days ago and driven with your bike to Mont-Laurier, at Mile 230. The week has flown by in a green blur. Your lungs are blossoming with fresh mountain air.

This was my experience biking Quebec's fantastic Le P'tit Train du Nord. It's the beautiful outdoors, with a little exercise, adventure, culture and the chance to discover the wonders of small-town Quebec. Your bike is waiting.

**START HERE:** canadianbucketlist.com/traindunord

# DISCOVER QUEBEC CITY

"I'm from Europe," jokes comedian Eddie Izzard, "you know, where history comes from." As much history as there is in Canada, there's no denying that a couple of hundred years here—or, in the case of the West, a couple of decades there—doesn't stack up against the centuries of cobblestone that pave the old towns of Europe. *Bienvenue à* Quebec City, a UNESCO World Heritage Site, a pocket of old Europe right here in North America, where history comes from as well.

From the 221-metre-high lookout rotunda atop the Observatoire de la Capitale, I see the stone wall that surrounds the Old Town, the archway of Rue Saint-Jean allowing traffic to pass between the centuries. The fairy-tale turrets of the Château Frontenac loom over sardine-packed old brick buildings like a medieval lord's castle. I see the exact point where the mighty St. Lawrence narrows, an observation that gave birth to the name Quebec itself (which is believed to be an Algonquin word meaning "narrow passage" or "strait"). I see

## The Château Frontenac

Quebec City's most striking landmark was one of a series of hotels designed by Canadian Pacific Railway to lure tourists onto the rails, and thence into luxurious hotels. Said CPR magnate William Cornelius Van Horne: "If we can't export the scenery, we'll import the tourists!" First came the Banff Springs Hotel (1888) and Château Lake Louise (1890), then New York architect Bruce Price's magnificent Château Frontenac (1893). With its medieval turrets and distinctive copper roofs, the fairy tale–like Château offers sweeping views of the St. Lawrence River. With Quebec City now a National Historic Site, the Fairmont Hotels & Resorts group continues to host guests with luxurious old-world charm. ➤

the walls of La Citadelle, a fortress originally built in the 1600s but obtaining its distinctive star shape from British conquerors in the early 1800s. There's the Plains of Abraham, where the French and British battled for what would ultimately be the control of an entire continent. Today, Battlefields Park is a huge recreational area for sport, leisure and massive festivals in both summer and winter. The impressive Parliament Building towers as parliament buildings often do, while church steeples pierce the sky like the inverted fangs of a vampire. Devoid of billboards and neon lights, I see a view from another place and another time, reminding me of Riga, or Copenhagen, or Paris. Mirroring my experiences in those cities, I head to the streets with no map book, direction or itinerary of places to see.

Old Quebec City is small enough to walk on foot within a couple of hours, with pockets of interest lying in wait where you least expect them. I stroll down Rue Saint-Louis, which runs directly to Fairmont's grand Château Frontenac, supposedly North America's most photographed hotel. Like Banff Springs and Lake Louise, this former Canadian Pacific Railway hotel inspires feelings of princely grandness—a contrast to my own hotel, the modern Hilton, that overlooks the old city like a windowed brick. I walk past statues and churches, little shops selling bric-a-brac, Quebec mainstays such as clothing store Simons. Lunch is a quick stop at Chez Ashtons, where they make the cheese curd fresh every day to get that vital poutine squeak.

My walk deposits me in Rue du Petit-Champlain, once the city's slum, now easily among Canada's most beautiful urban walkways. It's getting a little brisk out, so I warm up on thick hot chocolate with a dash of spice at La Fudgerie. Cheese, wine, baguettes, chocolate — the city practically reeks of the good stuff. There's a crowd gathered at Place-Royale, where Samuel de Champlain founded the continent's first French settlement in 1608. A beautiful mural paints a vivid picture of the city's history since then.

Up the Funiculaire, opened in 1879 and the only one of its kind in North America, I transition to uptown, past the Dufferin Terrace Slide, where I can't help but spend a couple of bucks to race at 70 kilometres an hour on a sled. The adrenalin buzz makes climbing the 310 steps of La Promenade des Gouverneurs a cinch (the views of the St. Lawrence don't hurt either). Lost in thought, I arrive at the Musée national des Beaux-arts du Québec, where an old prison has been turned into a wing of the art gallery.

My walk is just a brief introduction, and I relish the opportunity to explore the city further. We have a little bit of Europe here too, Mr. Izzard. If you haven't already done so, it's well worth adding Quebec City to your bucket list.

Lunenburg, Nova Scotia (see page 254) and Old San Juan, Puerto Rico, are the only other two urban centres in North America designated as UNESCO World Heritage Sites.

**START HERE:** canadianbucketlist.com/quebec-city

# FIND MONTREAL'S BEST SMOKED MEAT SANDWICH

When immigrants flooded into Montreal from Europe in the early 1900s, they brought with them passionate quirks and traditional recipes. The Italians delivered their fiery tempers and coffee shops. The Greeks brought their strong family values and their souvlakis. And the Jews? They gave the city a quirky neurosis, world-class delis and bagels that have no equal.

The origin of Montreal's smoked meat sandwiches remains a topic of hot dispute. Some say the recipe is Romanian, others Lithuanian, but there's little point fighting while the food's getting cold. The Montreal smoked meat sandwich is a simple creation of edible perfection: rye bread, thinly sliced. Mustard. A pickle on the side. And the meat: expertly carved, melt-in-your-mouth steamed brisket piled so high you can build a fort with it. Choosing where to enjoy such a dish is no simple matter, and locals will let you know exactly why that is. The Great Smoked Meat Hunt has begun.

It starts at four a.m. at Dunn's, where I wash ashore this 24-hour deli after a hard night's research in the bars. Here, a brusque, whip-smart server tells me that Dunn's recipe hasn't changed in fifty years, and that, unlike some of the other shops, Dunn's is still "Jewish

## The Bucket List
## Smoked Meat Sandwich Tour

Bring a pen, a camera and one serious appetite. My conscience demands that I warn you not to try this in one day.

1. Schwartz's
2. Lesters
3. The Main
4. Ettingers
5. Smoked Meat Pete's
6. Dunn's
7. Deli Bee's
8. Snowdon Deli

owned." Not exactly, since the company now has independently owned franchises around the country. The meat arrives steaming, and melts on my tongue. At four a.m., with food this good, I don't care if Zoroaster Amazonian cross-dressers own Dunn's—the sandwich is sensational.

"Dunn's! You can't go to Dunn's for the real experience!" says the father of a Montreal friend, horrified. So he takes me to Lesters Deli in Outremont, where he advises me to order the hot smoked meat sandwich, medium fat for more flavour. Hasidic wives wheel their babies past our table as I tuck into the sandwich, kosher pickle and a plastic bottle of homemade Montreal spice at the ready. Smoked meat is smoked meat, but under the relieved gaze of a true believer, I confess that Lesters is a mouth-watering notch up from Dunn's.

"Lesters? Are you kidding me!" yells the huge ponytailed bouncer outside a nightclub. He literally grabs me by the collar and pulls me closer. His breath smells of garlic, and his skin like Montreal Old Spice. "Schwartz's. Nothing touches Schwartz's! If you don't go to Schwartz's, I'll . . ." And then he lets me go. At this point, I realize that Montrealers take their smoked meat very, very seriously.

Schwartz's has been Montreal's most famous smoked meat deli (or Charcuterie Hébraïque, as the sign outside says) since 1928. It's inspired a musical, a book and the interest of Celine Dion, who together with other investors purchased the business. Big hunks of smoked meat sit in the window outside, tempting the hungry lineups that gather around mealtimes. The service is curt, the decor basic. I order a takeout sandwich, and since I can't find anywhere to sit, I decide to cruelly eat it across the street, enshrined in food bliss while the salivating eyes of the lineup look on. Oh YES! It's nirvana for the carnivore, a foodgasm of the first order.

I returned the following day, and the next time I was in Montreal, and every time I've been in Montreal since. Schwartz's uses a secret blend of herbs and spices, marinates the meat for ten days and smokes it without preservatives. It's long resisted the urge to grow and take on the fast-food franchises, which explains why the lines are long. But the wait is worth it.

But I'm not done just yet. Across the street from Schwartz's, close to the bench where I enjoyed my first hit of their smoked meat, is the Main. The meat here is also in the window; there are also dozens of newspaper clippings about the genius of its recipe. By now I've learned about the taste benefits of ordering "old-fashioned" as opposed to the health benefits of ordering "lean." I've debated the origins and recipes of Montreal smoked meat (which writer Mordecai Richler called the "nectar of Judea") and its obvious superiority to smoked meat found in the delis of New York. Who serves the best smoked meat is beside the point. Wherever you end up will deliver the goods, a meaty dream that is infinitely better than any other meat sandwich, anywhere in the world.

**START HERE:** canadianbucketlist.com/meat

# DRINK CARIBOU WITH BONHOMME

Canada has no shortage of feisty public celebrations, but there's only space for a handful on the bucket list. They don't come any cooler than the Carnaval de Québec. Buried in my pockets, my hands were literally frozen as well. For over half a century, the world's largest winter festival has attracted millions of revellers bundled up for the snow, ice, parades, competitions, activities and parties. Much like Mardi Gras or Rio's Carnaval, the tradition dates back to the Catholic festivals preceding Lent. And like my experience at Mardi Gras and Rio's Carnaval, this translates into alcohol and dancing, with the added bonus that both keep you warm.

The Carnaval's official mascot is Bonhomme Carnaval, a jolly

QUEBEC

193

## Canada's Best Winter Festivals

A little snow and ice never hurt anyone, and it's sure not going to stop Canadians from getting outdoors and celebrating at our Top 10 Winter Parties.

1. Carnaval de Québec, Quebec City, QC
2. Winterlude, Ottawa, ON
3. Winter Festival of Lights, Niagara Falls, ON
4. Festival du Voyageur, Winnipeg, MB
5. Montreal Highlights Festival, Montreal, QC
6. Yukon Sourdough Rendezvous, Whitehorse, YK
7. Caribou Carnival, Yellowknife, NT
8. Jasper in January, Jasper, AB
9. Toonik Tyme, Iqaluit, NU
10. Telus World Ski and Snowboard Festival, Whistler, BC

snowman with an unnerving smile. He's a cross between Mickey Mouse and Elvis Presley, and his effigy is literally your entrance ticket into the Carnaval grounds in Quebec City's Battlefields Park. I'm greeted by an ice slide, kids being pulled in sleds, snow sculptures, and deep regret that I didn't add one more layer of underwear. Well, Rio can keep its wild, sweaty street parties, and New Orleans the plastic beads of Fat Tuesday. This seventeen-day Carnaval has dogsledding, snow rafts, hot tubs, human foosball and an ice palace, complete with ice discos. Over a dozen teams from around the world work through the night on snow sculptures, and all of this can be enjoyed with your cheap entrance ticket.

I head to the top of the hill for an overview. My immediate impression is that the Carnaval site is smaller than I expected, but since the temperature has plummeted to -15°C, perhaps it's wise that the crowds

stick close together anyway. Beneath the Ferris wheel, two men in costumes are leading a Zumba class from the palace stage. It's a direct challenge to winter: snow, ice, wind chill? We'll dance to Shakira!

Ice is cracking on my face as the inflatable raft bounces down a bumpy snow channel. Most activities are family friendly, but there's also a fair bit of drinking going on, mostly in the form of caribou, a hot mulled wine with added whisky. It's perfectly acceptable to buy a Bonhomme staff, twist his head off and fill up the cane with this hot liquor, a welcome and delicious anaesthetic for the cold.

There are daily events taking place during Carnaval, the most popular of which are the float parades and the ice canoe races across the St. Lawrence River. If you need proof that Canadians are a parachute short of a skydive, watch dozens of men and women paddle and run over floating chunks of ice in the St. Lawrence. Sometimes they paddle and run over each other, all for prize money that is small enough for teams to drink in one evening.

## A Recipe for Caribou

It's easy to make Quebec City's Carnaval drink of choice. Just get your hands on sherry, vodka, brandy and port. And painkillers for the next morning.

3 oz. (100 mL) vodka
3 oz. (100 mL) brandy
12½ oz. (425 mL) Canadian sherry
12½ oz. (425 mL) Canadian port
Serves 10 (or 7 lushes, 3 bangers and a partridge in a pear tree)

Since this is a celebration, I find myself sliding between the ice bars on Grande Allée, a popular evening attraction. Even though snow is piled high on the sidewalks, there's an undeniable spirit permeating the whole city. The *ceinture fléchée*, a traditional French-Canadian sash, adds colour to the waists of locals and tourists. Portraits of Bonhomme are everywhere, and while the jolly mascot initially freaked me out with his dead marshmallow eyes, by the end I'm hugging him too, joining small kids bundled up like walking pillowcases.

Canadians live in a northern country where winter is a way of life. Some people deal with it by staying home, others by moving away. Winter Carnaval is correctly revered as one of the world's unique celebrations. If you dress warmly, embrace your inner child and keep some caribou handy, you won't freeze to death crossing this one off your bucket list.

**START HERE:** canadianbucketlist.com/carnaval

# SWING A SWORD AT TAM-TAMS

During my journey, I'm often struck by how locals might take their gifts for granted. In Newfoundland, icebergs are no bigger a deal than snow-capped mountains are for British Columbians. In Montreal, the fact that thousands of people gather every Sunday in the park for a makeshift celebration as festive as any you'll find on the continent is, you know, Sunday in the park.

In the late 1970s, students began to gather at the base of the Sir George-Étienne Cartier statue in Mount Royal park, bringing their drums, blankets, bicycles and picnics. Today, all I have to do is walk up Rue Rachel towards the towering angel statue and follow the sound of the beat. *Tam-tam* is the French name for a hand drum, and these drums become the heartbeat of a spontaneous jam session that anyone can join in on—as drummer, dancer, singer or spectator. Vendors have set up blanket stores around the square selling clothing, fresh fruit and curios, with the drummers concentrated in

one corner, surrounded by a crowd of people. Two beautiful girls are dancing in the middle (much to the appreciation of the mostly male drummers), and the distinct lack of organization is part of the charm. Somehow the beat builds and climaxes, stopping for enthusiastic applause before resuming in a different direction. This goes on for hours.

Surrounding this energetic rhythm is a familiar park scene: blankets and picnics, people playing cards, doing yoga, reading, kids running about. One bench has a man playing the saxophone, another a family eating ice cream. In the city that gave the world Cirque du Soleil, it's no surprise to see locals practise their juggling, tightrope-walk between trees and polish their acrobatics. Tattoos and wild steampunk fashions mix with single yuppies, young families and seniors out for a relaxing stroll—a community nonchalantly doing what it does, so vibrantly and colourfully.

Not far from the drums, I notice a kerfuffle being kicked up in a dust storm. Here I find the medieval foam weaponry fighters, assembled with their foam swords, shields, battle-axes and blades. Evolving out of the Live Action Role Playing scene of the late 1990s, Sunday

battles have become an institution at the park, drawing kids and adults (of all ages) to chaotic dust-downs. Two fronts assemble organically, and the rules are simple: If you get hit in the chest, you're dead and must leave the field. In the arm or leg, you're immobilized. Two hits and you're dead. Battles last minutes and the hard-core regulars don't stand for cheats. Up to 150 people might gather, including a guild of rather good-looking ladies.

"We don't get an advantage from the guys, so we learn quick," says Lissette, a ten-year veteran, strapping on her knee pads. "Of course, we are known to hit harder."

Anyone can join; just go up and ask some of the regulars hanging out under the trees if you can borrow or rent a weapon. But do be careful. "With my armour, I weigh over four hundred pounds," explains Dominic, a large man holding a much larger lance. "If I fall over, a kid can get hurt." By kid, he means anyone with a penchant for swordplay on sunny afternoons.

I buy an ice cream and wander about with a certain envy in my heart. Although it's legal to drink in public spaces in Quebec, everyone seems considerate and orderly. Few cities would allow such a gathering to take place, not without mountains of red tape, permits, policing and the fear that things could get out of hand. This is just Montreal in the summer, doing what Montreal does best: celebrating life, even if you can get killed on a dusty battlefield.

**START HERE:** canadianbucketlist.com/tamtams

# SCALE A FROZEN WATERFALL

Canyoning, or canyoneering as it is known in the United States, combines aspects of hiking, climbing, rappelling and, where applicable, not drowning. The goal is to ascend or descend a canyon, through pristine wilderness like that found around Mont-Sainte-Anne, Quebec. Although relatively obscure, canyoning is a popular activity in the summer, with various routes open to all ages and fitness levels. I've slid down canyons in Costa Rica, where our guide held everyone back so he could "dispose of" a poisonous snake in our path. New Zealand, Colorado, France—the activity isn't unique in itself, but if we return to the winter ski slopes of Mont-Sainte-Anne, we can find something truly original.

Marc Tremblay's Canyoning Quebec is the only place in North America where you can attempt ice canyoning, just the sort of unique activity our bucket list is hungry for. Tall and stringy, Marc is an accomplished spelunker, the kind of guy who gets his rocks off squeaking through caverns underground. He enjoys introducing people to the joys of canyoning and is a pioneer of doing it in snow and ice. He tells me to dress warmly. Drowning is the least of my concerns.

We meet at the ticket office of Mont-Sainte-Anne, where I'm kitted out with ropes, crampons and a backpack. "The most dangerous things on this trip are crossing the highway and avoiding the snowmobiles," says Marc reassuringly. We hike over to the highway, wait for local drivers hell bent on creating roadkill and continue along a snowmobile path where Marc's assistant, Genevieve, keeps watch over a blind hill.

Once we enter the woods, we're in a magical world of snow and ice. A stream flows, barely, carving ice structures along its edges. During the summer this path will be full of hikers, but in winter it belongs to us. Farther down, Marc helps me with my crampons, shows me how to loop my figure-eight hook and ropes me up to practise my descent. "Keep your legs apart, watch out for the crampons and just ease your way down," he instructs me calmly. Child's play, which is why even children can do this. I have to watch my harness, though, which has a tendency to trap testicles, initiating a Michael Jacksonesque falsetto.

We continue downstream until we come to the edge of a forty-metre cascade. In summer, you'd descend down the same spot, showering in the flow of the waterfall. This overcast day in February, I hear water barely descending beneath a spectacular frozen formation. Nature has burned ten thousand giant, icy-white candles, and I'm about to lower myself down among the hardened wax.

Crunch! The sharp teeth of my crampons dig into the ice as I do my best to avoid breaking the frozen stalactites. Once I'm over the lip, I stop to admire the view. Limestone caves would take millennia to form these sorts of structures, but out here in winter, every day produces a different show. Goosebumps sprout like mushrooms on my neck. I eventually lower myself to the bottom, where Genevieve unhooks me. I greet her with my favourite one-syllable word: "Wow!"

I can barely recognize the waterfall when I see photos taken during the summer, but winter climes offer an entirely different adventure: an icy, exhilarating thrill that belongs on Canada's bucket list.

**START HERE:** canadianbucketlist.com/canyoning

# LAUGH, DANCE OR LISTEN AT THE GREAT MONTREAL FESTIVALS

Montreal has more festivals than there are weeks in the year. arts, children, music, history, theatre, bikes, fashion, culture—just about everything that tickles your right brain gets the treatment. Other cities—notably Edmonton, Vancouver, Toronto and Winnipeg—have no shortage of festivals either, so why does Montreal get the nod on the bucket list? Because Montreal does it bigger and sexier than anywhere else.

Take the Montreal International Jazz Festival, the world's largest jazz festival, hosting over 1,000 concerts featuring 3,000 performers from three dozen countries, attracting some two million people to the city, who visit fifteen concert venues and ten outdoor stages. Remarkably, two-thirds of these performances are completely free of charge, which means everyone has the chance to watch artists such as Prince, Norah Jones, Diana Krall, Ben Harper and Gilberto Gil perform at the huge outdoor, car-free downtown venues.

Typically scheduled at the end of June, the jazz festival's days get going at the site around eleven a.m., when various events specifically appealing to families begin. Kids can build their own instruments at workshops in the Parc Musical, while bands perform on different stages. It runs all day, until heavyweight performers take the stage, and continues as the crowd filters into the city's legendary late night

after-parties. The ten-day event transcends jazz; expect world music, rock, fusion, R&B, folk and a lineup of virtuosos, all drawn to the event like the thousands they perform for.

Come September, the hipsters gather for Pop Montreal, an indie music festival that took on special significance when local artists Arcade Fire exploded to become one of the world's biggest rock acts. From humble beginnings, the five-day festival has grown to present over 600 bands in 50 venues and has diversified with an accompanying design festival (Puces Pop), a music conference (Pop Symposium), Film Pop (for film-related music), Art Pop (visual arts) and Kids Pop. Montreal's "it" factor draws interest and artists from around the world, and while the festival was only founded in 2002, it has fast become one of the coolest cultural festivals on the continent.

Before seat-back screens allowed a measure of choice, do you remember watching dreary romantic comedies on long-haul flights, if only to alleviate the excruciating boredom? The movie (typically starring Matthew McConaughey's bare chest) would finally end, and filling up the hour would be a timeless episode of the prank series *Just for Laughs*. Suddenly, hundreds of people of ridiculously diverse backgrounds were cracking up in unison at the situations—all created, produced and executed to perfection in Montreal. Humour transcends language.

So it's fitting that every July, Montreal hosts Just for Laughs, the world's largest international comedy festival. It's more than just stand-up from the world's funniest French and English comedians. The event turns the streets of downtown Montreal into a festival, with parades, food trucks and packed pedestrian-only promenades. Meanwhile, TV execs and producers hunt for the next breakout comedy star. You may have heard of some of them: Jerry Seinfeld, Chris Rock, Tim Allen, Jay Leno, Jim Carrey. Rowan Atkinson did his first non-verbal Mr. Bean performance in front of an audience at Just for Laughs. I ask a cheerful Gilbert Rozon, who founded the event back in 1983, how Montreal has somehow become the funniest place on earth.

"In Quebec, we have a beautiful expression, 'C'est le fun!' It should be our national slogan, and it's typical about Montreal," he tells me. "Nobody can be against being happy, nobody ever said 'I laughed too much.'" Gilbert reflects on Montreal's legacy as a party town during Prohibition, how it attracted crooners from the 1930s to the 1960s, and how the current festivals uniquely close the streets and offer so many free shows.

Led by its own iconic green Bonhomme, Just for Laughs features comedy theatre, music, dance and other types of performances. North America's best stand-up stars host gala evenings, usually televised around the world. Outside the theatres, crowds flock to the pedestrian-only Ste-Catherine Street, enjoying the free spectacle under the lights in the Quartier des Spectacles, which reminds me of the Sambadromo in Rio. Call it a carnival of comedy.

"In the next thirty years, we're going to invest in beauty, and build more events around this time, so that you'll have no choice but to want to visit," says Gilbert, like a generous kid who wants to share his candy.

Later that evening, I join the long lineup to see a festival staple: the Nasty Show. Renowned for the vulgarity of its stand-ups—the show's run has featured greats such as Bill Hicks and Denis Leary— tonight's performance is a shotgun of hysterical bad taste. Before you push up daisies, visit Montreal one summer to laugh so hard the tears streak down your face.

**START HERE:** canadianbucketlist.com/festivals

# SPEND A NIGHT IN AN ICE HOTEL

Five hundred tons of ice, 15,000 tons of snow, 36 rooms and one travel writer desperately trying to avoid using the word "cool." The Hôtel de Glace, located outside Quebec City, is North America's only ice hotel. It takes fifty people about six weeks to build the hotel each winter, crafting its rooms, bar, chapel, passageways, slides and chandeliers. Lit with atmospheric non-heat-emitting LED lights, you'll get plenty of ambience if not warmth standing next to the double-glazed fireplaces. Not to fear, the romance and creative vision of the hotel will warm your heart just as surely as the interior temperature of -5°C will chill your bones.

At around nine p.m., day visitors are ushered out and the overnight guests gather in the Celsius, an adjacent, blessedly heated building, for the briefing. If you're going to spend the night in a Popsicle, the goal is not to become one in the morning. All guests are required to sit through a training session.

"The two most important things I can tell you," explains our bilingual, dreadlocked guide, "is don't go to sleep cold, and under no circumstances go to sleep wet." Put your glasses on the bedside table (made of ice) and they will soon be part of the installation. Spending the night in a hotel made of snow and ice requires a rather adventurous guest. It becomes clear that those seeking luxury and comfort will prefer your run-of-the-mill thawed hotel.

All guests are assigned lockers in the Celsius, where you'll also find bathrooms and showers. Nothing goes into your room except your pyjamas, boots and outdoor jacket. And while the builders have invented ice glasses to serve chilled vodka cocktails, they haven't invented ice plumbing, so no, there are no toilets in the ice hotel. Each bed sits on a piece of wood atop blocks of ice, with a carved ice headboard and striking sculptures in the 1.2-metre-thick walls. We are shown how to wrap ourselves in our cocoon sleeping bags, which are designed for -30°C conditions and therefore should have no problem keeping us warm at night.

Slide into the bag liner then into the bag itself, blow out the candles and turn off the glow lights with the switch cleverly built directly into your ice bed. Couples expecting a hot, passionate night in their Winter Wonderland are in for a disappointment. Exposed skin is simply not a good idea, and the sleeping bags are designed for a snug, solo fit. Although, this being Quebec, a province of passion, the designers merely ask that you get creative. How else to explain the naked life-sized couple staring at my bed? Or the hands grafted onto the headboard suggesting a night of icy consummation? Perhaps

## Your Bed for the Night

Each bed has a solid ice base, with a wooden bedspring and mattress on top, covered with blankets. Guests are provided with Arctic sleeping bags and isolating bedsheets that can keep you toasty up to -30°C. It is recommended you sleep in thermal, moisture-wicking underwear, as moisture generated by body heat will likely trap and freeze. No matter how cold it is outside, the rooms stay between -3°C and -5°C. Warm yourself up in the hot tub or sauna before you turn in, and try not to think about the bathroom in the middle of the night! ➤

there's a connection between hot thoughts and body warmth.

Before bedtime, there's plenty of time to explore the large public areas. Music thumps in the ice bar, where four hundred people can gather to drink and dance, and you never have to ask the friendly bartenders for ice in your cocktails. The chapel hosts dozens of weddings each year, with guests sitting on benches covered in deerskin while the doors are covered in fur. There's a room explaining the annual theme, sponsor exhibits, slides for adults and kids, and the fresh smell of ozone in the air.

Overnight guests are encouraged to hit the hot tubs and dry sauna before they go to sleep, warming up the body for the night ahead. I arrived after the Celsius kitchen had closed, so the attendant at the front desk, staffed twenty-four hours a day, ordered me a pizza. I half expected it to arrive in a frozen box.

Light snow is falling when I leave the hot tub, shower, put on my thermal underwear and get ready for the night ahead. Please, please, please don't let me need to pee in the middle of the night! Everything is locked up, making it exceptionally easy for guests to vacate by 8:30 a.m., staff to collect sleeping bags and the rooms to open for public viewing tours by 9:30. No housekeeping is required, other than raking the floor and straightening out the fur covers on the bed and benches.

The hotel has been built, and rebuilt each year, since 2001, and

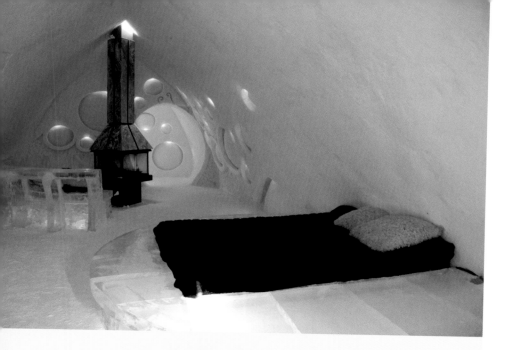

is open from the first week of January until the last week of March. Lying in the deep silence and darkness of my room, I wonder if the builders and designers are heartbroken to watch their efforts melt each spring. Or perhaps they're excited at the potential to start afresh next season? How many other hotels can literally reconfigure themselves each year? Watching the vapour of my breath, I lie awake, wide-eyed and aware of just how unique this experience is.

Ninety-nine percent of overnight guests stay just one night. Dress warmly and prepare for an adventure. One night in one of the world's most unusual hotels is all that's needed for the Great Canadian Bucket List.

**START HERE:** canadianbucketlist.com/icehotel

# ENJOY POUTINE, WITH FOIE GRAS

Canada has gifted the world gourmet treats well above its station, and any self-respecting National Bucket List should include a sample of the staples. I'm talking about ginger ale, instant mash, processed cheese, Timbits and Yukon Gold potatoes, fried in canola oil. Back bacon boosts a breakfast, Beaver Tails sweeten up cold days, and maple sugar is our apple pie (and goes great with apple pie, too).

If I were to choose a single Canadian dish that could take over the world, it would be poutine. It takes fries, a universally loved food group served from bistros to trucker bars, and simply makes them better. Poutine—healer for the hangover, sweet gravied taters for the stomach's soul. To foreigners, adding cheese curds and gravy to fries might sound as appetizing as adding clams to tomato juice, but Canadians know how a little creativity can raise the bar.

While several Québécois communities claim its invention, and the word itself has been around for ages, poutine only became popular in the late 1960s. In Quebec City, I was directed to Chez Ashton, a franchise that built its fame on the sloppy back of poutine as far back as 1972. Greasy as the greasiest spoon, one bite of their hand-cut potatoes smothered in brown gravy and the day's freshly made squeaky cheese curds was better than any poutine I've tried on the west coast. Served in a foil container it may be, but still fit for a king.

Montreal's La Banquise offers twenty-eight varieties of poutine, including La Elvis (ground beef, green peppers, mushrooms), La Kamikaze (spicy sausages, hot peppers and Tabasco) and La Obélix (smoked meat). Poutine's beauty is that you can't really go wrong with it, but for the Great Canadian Bucket List we're off to Montreal's hip Plateau neighbourhood, and a restaurant called Au Pied de Cochon. Celebrity chef Martin Picard is known for his creativity and, as Anthony Bourdain calls it, his "porky and ducky" decadence.

Seated next to me at the bar overlooking the open-concept kitchen are two guys: a bureaucrat who timed his Montreal connection to Ottawa specifically to visit the restaurant, and a bartender from Toronto who plans his trips to Montreal around available reservations. Booking is a must, at least a month ahead for large groups, a week for couples. An attractive server walks past with a cooked pig's head on a platter, with a large lobster in its mouth. Behind me, a woman is chewing on a bison rib as long as my forearm. I scan the menu: fresh seafood, handily divided into bivalve, gastropod, echinoderm, cephalopod and crustacean sections. Pickled tongue. Foie gras hamburger. Duck carpaccio. And there it is: foie gras poutine, calling me like three angels playing heavy metal on their harps.

Foie gras is, of course, a controversial food group, but wise travellers should respect local customs. David, the bureaucrat, orders Duck in a Can, which is so rich and fabulous he breaks out into a joyous sweat, calling it Heart Attack in a Can. Rare duck breast cooked with foie gras and vegetables, marinated in balsamic vinegar, opened and plopped onto mashed potatoes richer than butter. Paul the bartender orders a buckwheat pancake with bacon, mashed potatoes, foie gras

# Canada's Culinary Contribution

Poutine is not the only edible gift Canada has given the world:

1.  **Butter tarts:** The sugar-syrup-egg-and-butter delight was once a staple of pioneer cooking.
2.  **Nanaimo bars:** A chocolate-custard-wafer sandwich invented on Vancouver Island.
3.  **Tourtière:** Crispy spiced meat pie, typically served at Christmas, but delicious year-round.
4.  **Beaver Tails:** The name of Ottawa's hot sugared pastry continues to confound international tourists.
5.  **Fricot:** A hearty Acadian meat stew enjoyed when times were tough, enjoyed when they weren't.
6.  **McIntosh:** The crunchy, tart apple invented in Ontario helped Steve Jobs name his Mac, and gives Americans their finest apple pie.
7.  **Maple syrup:** Canada produces 85 percent of the world's favourite syrup, which works on everything from pancakes to salmon.
8.  **Fish and brewis:** Codfish + hard bread + salted pork fat = Newfoundland's comfort food. ➤

and maple syrup from Picard's popular sugar shack. "It's little, but it hits you hard," says Paul, twitching from the excess.

My poutine arrives smothered in a thick gravy, the chips fried in duck fat (of course), with a slab of sinful foie gras on the top. The aroma contains enough calories to feed a village in North Korea. It tastes like winning the jackpot on the first pull of a slot machine, and contains the Higgs boson particle of flavour. Another guy at the bar has ordered the same, and while he doesn't say much, his face turns the ruby shade of beet. Our friendly, attractive servers have mischievous glints in their eyes. They've seen it all before, and they'll see it all again. "Are you enjoying your meal?" they ask.

"It's . . . to die for," I answer.

**START HERE:** canadianbucketlist.com/poutine

# VIA FERRATA DU DIABLE AT MONT-TREMBLANT

Several years ago I found myself atop a holy mountain in central China, standing on two narrow wooden planks leaning against a wall of solid vertical rock. Below me was a thousand-metre drop. Trust me when I say I was ill-prepared for this experience, as many others had been before me. To prevent people inconveniently falling off and dying, Chinese authorities insist all visitors to Mount Hua pay a few bucks for a harness to clip into a static safety line running the length of the "Number One Cliffside Plank Path."

This was my introduction to the exciting world of the via ferrata (Italian for "iron road"), a fun adventure for those of us who want to climb mountains without having to risk actually climbing a mountain.

↑

QUEBEC

Popular in Europe, there are but a few via ferratas in Canada. The largest is Mount Nimbus, accessible only by helicopter near Golden, B.C. There are others near Whistler, Gatineau, Quebec City and Saguenay, but among the most popular and spectacular is the via ferrata in Quebec's largest and oldest national park, Mont-Tremblant, adjacent to the popular ski resort located 130 kilometres from Montreal.

I drive into the park on a smooth blacktop road that bends and curves through thick boreal forest, a fun roller coaster in itself. It's mid-morning when I get to the park kiosk, signing a waiver in return for a climbing harness, lanyards, helmet and carabiners. Groups are limited to eight, with the one-kilometre trail divided into three levels of difficulty. I felt bold enough to select the advanced trail, which typically takes about five hours. Sure, one kilometre is no biggie when you're walking on land, but when you have to clip and unclip your way forward against a vertical wall on iron staples with a 200-metre drop beneath your feet, well, it pays to take your time. Our guide, Valérie,

# An Alternative Climb in the Mountains

**Mount Nimbus Via Ferrata** High up in the Purcell Mountains, summer guests at CMH's Bobby Burns Lodge can snap into North America's longest via ferrata and summit the dramatic peak of Mount Nimbus. CMH recently installed the Skyladder via ferrata near their 1,600-metre-high Bugaboo Lodge.

**Whistler Via Ferrata** Located at the top of Whistler Mountain and running daily from July to September, the four-hour round trip takes you over glaciers with sweeping views of the surrounding mountains. ➤

shows us how to easily lock into the iron rungs and steel safety line, and we start off with an imposing suspension bridge over the Diable River. Apparently this is enough to make some people turn back, but here's the surefire Esrock Method for Dealing with These Things:

1. Don't Panic.
2. Trust Your Gear.
3. Remind Yourself You're in Canada, not China, and Things Usually Work in Canada.

Designed by conservationists to minimize damage to the environment but overdo the safety aspect for visitors, the line and rungs make their way along the cliff, getting more and more difficult as we progress. Slowly I get used to clipping in every few metres. Always make sure at least one of your carabiners is locked in and it's pretty much impossible to fall more than a couple of feet. I'd say the rest is literally child's play, although kids under fourteen have to turn back before reaching the advanced level.

Here things take a puckering turn as the path moves horizontally against a solid cliff face, the glorious view of the Laurentians and surrounding valley on full display. Standing on an iron rung nailed into the rock, I take my time, breathing it all in—the forest, meandering brown river, the ski slopes visible on the highest peaks. *C'est le fun!* Farther along is a "surprise," in the form of a narrow wooden beam perilously positioned in a crevice. Next is a tightrope bridge, where the braver among the group let go to just hang around in their harness, enjoying the experience of being fully exposed to the elements. Climbers know it's one thing to hike up a mountain shaded by the trees and another to ascend from the outside, hugging solid rock. If the weather isn't great, you may get lashed with wind and rain, but the view accompanies you all the way to the top.

While it's not for everyone (particularly anyone with a fear of heights, or weight or fitness issues), I will say this: In China, I recorded a little video about my experience, which has been seen over one million times on YouTube. This devilish, little-known via ferrata in Mont-Tremblant might not be as exotic, but it's just as thrilling an adventure.

**START HERE:** canadianbucketlist.com/tremblant

# THE MINGAN ARCHIPELAGO

Five hundred million years ago, a warm tropical sea covered what is today the St. Lawrence Lowlands. It would have been swell to relax on its beach, although good luck finding poutine, cheese, or even potatoes for that matter. Over the course of millions of years, fossils, sediment and seabed became compressed into rock, which was then exposed when the sea receded, ready to be carved and eroded by ice age glaciers, wind, rain, rivers and waves. Time-machine forward to the present day and you'll find the largest concentration of erosion monoliths in the country.

Almost one thousand islands and islets lay scattered east to west across 150 kilometres of Quebec coastline, moulded into overhangs, caves, arches, flowerpots and cliffs. Protected as the Mingan Archipelago National Park Reserve, the area is accessible via boat tours from the north shore of the Gulf of St. Lawrence, from towns such as Longue-Pointe-de-Mingan, Aguanish and Havre-St. Pierre.

The boats vary in terms of their size and destinations, but typically visit several of the more dramatic islands, with parks interpreters explaining the festooned cliffs, fossils, tidal pools and the area's unique geological history. It is possible to camp in the archipelago (taxi boats will shuttle you back and forth from the mainland). You can even find sandy beaches. Having experienced my personal island paradise in the Philippines and Thailand, at least I no longer have to go all the way to Asia.

Another option is a week-long kayaking trip, paddling between the rock giants, beaching on the flats at low tide. With some two hundred species of birds in the park, birdwatchers will enjoy a visit in spring, when marine birds including puffins, guillemots and kittiwakes build nesting colonies. Alternatively, the summer months bring terns, shorebirds and sea ducks migrating for food.

Highlights on the western islands are Île aux Perroquets, with its century-old lighthouse buildings, and the treeless Île Nue de Mingan, with its Arctic and subarctic microclimate. The archipelago's largest islands are located in the central sector, accessible from Havre-St. Pierre. Île Niapiskau and Île Quarry have the park's most prominent and striking monoliths, with a popular trail across the reef flats of Île du Fantôme and wild festooned cliffs farther east on Île de la Fausse Passe.

Located a ten-hour drive from Quebec City, the otherworldly landscapes of Mingan are somewhat under the radar. One more reason to add them to the Great Canadian Bucket List.

**START HERE:** canadianbucketlist.com/mingan

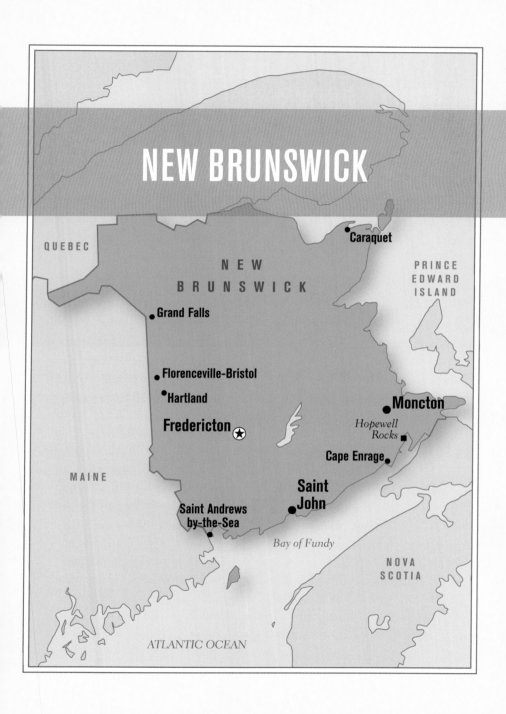

# NEW BRUNSWICK

QUEBEC

N E W
B R U N S W I C K

Caraquet

PRINCE
EDWARD
ISLAND

Grand Falls

Florenceville-Bristol

Hartland

Fredericton ★

Moncton

Hopewell
Rocks

Cape Enrage

MAINE

Saint
John

Saint Andrews
by-the-Sea

Bay of Fundy

NOVA
SCOTIA

ATLANTIC OCEAN

# WALK THE SEABED BENEATH HOPEWELL ROCKS

It's cold, it's wet, and rocks don't float my dinghy. They would have to be spectacular, like the fairy chimneys that poke the sky of Cappadocia, Turkey, or the bizarre hoodoos at the Yehliu Geopark in Taiwan, or the basalt columns that explode out of the ground in Iceland. Point is, if it's not a mind-blowing natural phenomenon, chances are I'll take a picture and do what too many tourists do in New Brunswick: floor it for the next province. This is my headspace when I arrive at the Hopewell Rocks, the most trafficked attraction in New Brunswick. I buy my ticket, walk through an informative interpretive centre and meet a guide who once again demonstrates that enthusiasm is infectious, even when it comes to rocks and tides.

Millions of years ago, a geological shift in tectonic plates produced a valley that was flooded during the last ice age, creating a shallow ocean floor for 100 million tons of water to rush in with the tides, rising up to sixteen metres on the shoreline. The Bay of

Fundy holds the distinction of having the world's biggest tides. New Brunswickers love this unique feature of their province (shared with Nova Scotia), and just about everyone I meet is compelled to describe the tidal phenomenon, which is why I've almost certainly explained it incorrectly. My guide reveals that during low tide we can literally walk on the ocean floor, among giant rock structures that have been carved and shaped by this daily flush of water. These are the Hopewell Rocks, which didn't excite my imagination until I saw them.

All my travels and experiences have tuned me into the joy of discovering something truly remarkable, something you just can't see anywhere else. We walk down a metal staircase to find huge brown monoliths, shaped and squeezed like plumber's putty. Among them are natural arches, tunnels, coves and corridors. One section feels as if I'm walking through a giant keyhole, and with green brush on top of the rocks, they do indeed look like flowerpots. The ground is muddy and spotted with seaweed, made all the more fascinating by the fact that twice a day the very spot where I'm standing will sit over a dozen metres underwater. Rocks have been christened with names such as Dinosaur, Lovers Arch, Mother-in-Law and ET. More creatively, Mi'kmaq legend holds that whales in the bay once imprisoned some people. One day they tried to escape but didn't make it to shore quickly enough and were turned to stone. Now these giant sedimentary and sandstone pillars guard the coast, staring across the bay at the shores of Nova Scotia. Shorebirds fly overhead, and our guide points out a nest to the delight of some international birdwatchers. Blue skies and sun would be great, but Fundy's damp mist and fog add to the otherworldliness of this strange landscape.

The tide comes in pretty quickly, so we return to the entrance, hopping over pools of water, grateful for our waterproof shoes. Later that day, this influx of water will result in a dramatically different experience, which is why many visitors consult online tide tables to ensure they catch both low and high tides. You can also hire kayaks and paddle between the flowerpots during high tide.

Having amazed a weary travel writer with no interest in rocks in the first place, the Hopewell Rocks are an easy addition to the Great Canadian Bucket List.

START HERE: canadianbucketlist.com/hopewell

# JET-BOAT THE REVERSING FALLS

Saint John is the largest city in New Brunswick—not to be confused with St. John's, Newfoundland, for one letter and an apostrophe doth a difference make. It's the oldest incorporated city in Canada, the centre of industry for the Maritime provinces. Sitting on the north shore of the Bay of Fundy and at the mouth of the Saint John River, it gave us Hollywood mogul Louis B. Mayer and actor Donald Sutherland. History lesson over, let's talk about New Zealand.

You see, New Zealand has become the self-proclaimed Adrenalin Destination of the World. They've pioneered commercial thrill-seeking activities such as bungee jumping, canyon swinging, sledging, zorbing, lugeing, swooping and skyjumping. I've done them all, twice, and can testify that, yes, you might soil your shorts in the name of fun. The point being: one must expect, and budget for, some pretty wild times when you visit New Zealand.

So how does the world's most thrilling jet boat ride—jet boats having been invented in New Zealand—end up in Saint John, New Brunswick? This thought stewed in my brain for exactly 3.6 seconds before pilot Harry Cox steered us into yet another Class 5 rapid.

In the 1950s, an industrious Kiwi farmer figured out a way to canvas the shallow waterways of his farm by inventing a high-powered boat that could zoom along in just inches of water. Jet boats, typically using powerful car engines, suck in water as a means of propulsion. Available around the world, today's boats can have the acceleration of an F-16 fighter jet. Jet boats can turn on a penny—called the Hamilton Turn after the inventor, William Hamilton—and stop on a dime. It's big business in New Zealand, where I've taken rides on the world's fastest commercial jet boat (100 kph in 4.5 seconds), jet-boated to *Lord of the Rings* locations and bulleted through dramatic canyons near Queenstown.

Very impressive, New Zealand, but you know what you don't have? The Bay of Fundy tides, backing up into the Saint John River, creating consistent Class 5 rapids without the hazard of rocks. You also don't have a pilot like Harry Cox, who over the course of twenty years' kayaking among this natural phenomenon has come to know every whirlpool, swell and drop.

Reversing Falls Jetboats, located at Fallsview Park, operates throughout the summer and warns its customers that, yes, you will get wet. Bring a bathing suit and towel, leave everything in the lockers and show up for the two hours of low tide, when the Reversing Falls is at its wildest. Among the thrill-seekers in this specially designed jet boat were two grannies and a fourteen-year-old girl. Yes, even you can do this!

The Bay of Fundy tide rises nearly eight metres in Saint John, and during low tide the waters of the 725-kilometre-long Saint John River empty into the bay, crashing through a narrow gorge and into

## How to Execute a Hamilton Turn

1.  Make sure you're clear of other boats, obstructions or nagging parents, and accelerate the engine to pick up serious speed.
2.  Turn the wheel sharply in either direction, making sure you're holding on tight.
3.  Cut the engine, causing the back of the boat to tilt up, spin around and blast a huge amount of water directly onto your passengers. ➤

an underwater ledge located adjacent to Fallsview Park. While you can take more genteel, scenic boat rides at other times of the day, now is the time to hop aboard Harry Cox's jet boat for what I can honestly call the ride of a lifetime. During the twenty-minute outing, the boat crests waves à la *Perfect Storm*. It slams into dips and gets spun in circles around whirlpools. Cox, laughing like the Mad Hatter, guns the boat towards the rocky bank before slamming on the brakes, knowing full well his boat can stop in a heartbeat. He executes Hamilton Turns that drench us in the cold, brackish water of the bay, but everyone (including the grannies) is too busy screaming, laughing and holding on to care. During brief pauses, Cox explains how the river and jet boat work, pointing out some seals, giggling like a maniac. Here is a man who clearly enjoys his job.

Back on land, knees shaking, I know without question that despite New Zealand's best efforts, little ol' New Brunswick offers the world's wildest jet boat ride.

**START HERE:** canadianbucketlist.com/jetboat

# ABSEIL CAPE ENRAGE

The road bends and curls on the way to Cape Enrage. By its very name, you can tell this is not the Cape of Good Hope, or Cape Cod, Cape Town or Cape Point. We're talking about fifty-metre-high cliffs that slant their eyes and glare over the Bay of Fundy. Not angry, peeved or slightly annoyed. No, these cliffs are *enraged*, with a black heart and a permanent scowl. Acadian sailors christened the cape for its exceptionally turbulent waters, boiling at half tide above a reef stretching into the bay. I arrive on a foggy summer morning, the atmosphere one of moody petulance. Maybe I woke up on the wrong side of the Maritimes, but the terrible weather is enough to make me throw myself off a cliff, and fortunately, that's exactly what I've come here to do.

Since 1838, Cape Enrage has had a lighthouse to warn ships during the thick fog and harsh winter storms—although that didn't stop ships from wrecking themselves on the reef all the same. When lighthouses were automated in the 1980s, the few battered buildings that stood at Cape Enrage were scheduled for demolition until a group of Moncton schoolteachers decided to take matters into their own hands. They've worked hard to restore the remaining buildings, creating a non-profit interpretive centre and a commercial business offering kayaking, ziplining, climbing and rappelling (or abseiling).

It's mostly run by teachers and students, and despite the ominous natural surroundings, it's full of sunny Maritime dispositions.

Today I've decided to rappel off the cliff to the bottom, where I plan to hike along the beach, mindful of falling rocks and "tidal miscalculation," which can result in something unfortunate like, say, "drowning." After I slip on a harness and sit through the safety demonstration, it's a short walk over to the platform. Here's what I've learned about rappelling off a cliff: it's a lot more fun than hiking up it. It's also imperative that the, em . . . family jewels are, how should we say, safely locked up. Fortunately, rappelling is not nearly as scary as other methods of launching oneself off a New Brunswick cliff (see page 234), partly because you don't have to look down. You don't want to look up too much either, since heavy falling rocks are your biggest danger.

I kick off from the sheer rock face and slowly descend to the bottom, stopping for a while to swivel around and gaze upon the furious view of the Bay of Fundy, with the shadowy shores of Nova Scotia in the distance. It doesn't take long before I'm on the beach, the cracked stone of fallen rocks all around me. The tide is coming in, so I don't stick around too long before climbing the much-appreciated metal staircase to the top. Here, an excellent restaurant rewards visitors with locally sourced dishes such as Raging Chowder and Lobster Tacos. By the time I leave, the sun even sneaks a smile from behind the clouds.

Quenched in both the adventure and culinary departments, I depart with the satisfaction of having tamed Cape Enrage, another item deserving of its place on the National Bucket List.

**START HERE:** canadianbucketlist.com/enrage

# BIKE IN A KILT

There are several go-to words for travel writers that make me cringe. *Charming. Spectacular. Nestled.* I say this because I use those words all the time, and so it pains me to write that St. Andrews is a charming coastal town nestled among spectacular surroundings. And yet that's the truth, and there's no getting away from it.

Canada's first seaside resort community inspires memories of youth and genteel innocence. It's a place where people politely greet one another at the candy shoppe. It doesn't take a day before I'm on a first-name basis with a half-dozen locals, drinking a cold beer on the sun-baked patio of the Red Herring. I've written many times that travel is as much about the people you meet as the places you go, and this held true when two gentlemen greeted me in kilts at the wharf upon my return from a whale-watching excursion on the Bay of Fundy. The minke, humpbacks, finbacks and endangered northern

## Canada's Small-town Gems

If you like the small-town charm of St. Andrews, you'll enjoy visiting the following:

1. Nelson, BC
2. Legal, AB
3. Forget, SK
4. Flin Flon, MB
5. Port Hope, ON
6. Hudson, QC
7. Victoria-by-the-Sea, PEI
8. Mahone Bay, NS
9. Trinity, NL
10. Dawson, YK
11. Rankin Inlet, NU
12. Fort Smith, NT

right whales gather in abundance in the bay, giving you a 95 percent chance of encountering them on a 200-horsepower Zodiac operated by Fundy Tide Runners. Today, however, belonged to the other 5 percent, so these men in kilts were just the sort of silliness I needed to cheer me up.

Offkilter Bike's Kurt Gumushel and Geoff Slater don't claim to be ambassadors for the village, or for New Brunswick in general; they just are. Kurt's dad moved to St. Andrews from Turkey to manufacture kilts, which is the sort of multicultural Timbit (Canadian for tidbit?) that makes Canada the country it is. Kurt is the local high school teacher, fitness trainer and yoga teacher, a charming rogue with a vague resemblance to George Clooney. Geoff is the artist responsible for fantastic murals you'll see in the village, and therefore much of the town's unmistakable visual character. They both ride mountain bikes in kilts, and through their bike company they share their peculiarity with tourists throughout the summer.

We bike through tall wildflowers along the coast, into a lush forest, across the rail tracks and onto beaches of pebble. All the while they regale me with stories about the town, how its 1,500 population swells in the summer months, how the famed Tudor-style Algonquin Hotel wasn't actually the inspiration for Stephen King's *The Shining* but that doesn't stop everyone from thinking so. It's easy to click with locals in New Brunswick, especially when you're riding through gorgeous scenery in kilts and the ride ends up at the Red Herring pub.

The rejuvenating drink of choice in St. Andrews is a Door Post, a local beer with an orange wedge. On the patio is Kurt's dad, along with some welcoming friends, and right then and there I decide I too would like to have grown up in St.-Andrews-By-the-Sea. How peaceful to have walked among the original heritage houses barged in from Maine during the Revolutionary War, bought candy at a nineteenth-century corner shop and practised my swing on the impossibly smooth fairways adjacent to the Algonquin. I could study marine science at the newly refurbished Huntsman Aquarium and Science Centre, and volunteer to keep the manicured Kingsbrae Gardens in tip-top shape. Who wouldn't want to live in a charming town nestled among spectacular surroundings, chomping fresh lobster rolls and slaking back Door Posts in the summer? Of course, my airbrushed dream negates those long, cold Maritime winters, which we'll conveniently overlook as we continue our journey along the Great Canadian Bucket List.

**START HERE:** canadianbucketlist.com/standrews

# APPRECIATE THE GENIUS OF DALI

Art galleries need the right environment, ambience and lighting to breathe. More life can be added with the help of a knowledgeable guide—someone to explain the nuances, the deftness of meaning, the symbolism behind the strokes. All this comes together as I stand before Salvador Dali's *Santiago El Grande* in the entrance hall of Fredericton's Beaverbrook Art Gallery.

The Beaverbrook serves as the province's official art gallery, a gift from press baron Max Aitken, a.k.a. Lord Beaverbrook. Ontario-born Aitken grew up in Newcastle, New Brunswick, and went on to become a British peer and Fleet Street's first overlord, taking the name Beaverbrook to convey his Canadian roots. As a benefactor in later life, he bestowed handsome gifts on his adopted Fredericton, including the luxury hotel that bears his name, which stands right next to the art gallery that does the same.

It is here that I meet local gallery docent and professional story-teller Joan Meade. She sizes me up quickly, in tune with my belief that art without meaning is a food without taste. I've sleepwalked through many an art museum around the world, lullabyed by the monotone voice of a bored guide on a still-life audiotape. "Here is our signature piece," says Joan. The museum's icon, taking up a sig-nificant section of its gallery allotment, is quite impossible to ignore.

Dali painted his tribute to the Apostle Saint James the Great, patron saint of Spain, for the 1958 Brussels World Fair. The four-metre by three-metre canvas depicts the saint on a noble white horse, its forelegs bucking over a liquid blue ocean, with the ascension of Christ in the top right corner. The painting, regarded as one of Dali's greats, is rife with symbolism. The bottom right corner shows a lady in a monkish robe, a portrait of Dali's wife Gala, who is often pres-ent in his works. It is said that she looks at the viewer to see how the painting is being assessed. The horse's neck muscles repeat in the sky, taking the form of angels, the hidden images that are another of Dali's trademarks.

Given the horse's pose, its penis should be quite prominent in the painting. Dali has covered it with an atomic cloud, and the purest of

## Deferring to the Genius of Dali

"There are some days when I think I'm going to die from an overdose of satisfaction." —Salvador Dali

all flowers: the jasmine. "He proclaimed that further growth of atomic power should be used for good and not for the making of bombs," explains Joan, revealing Dali's new-found interest in nuclear physics and his expression of the relationship between religion and science. Her explanation is far more interesting than my initial conclusion: that Dali covered the horse's dong with a cloud. Joan points out other symbols. The scallop shell, Santiago el Grande's religious icon, can be seen on the horse's neck, as well as a protective shell over the saint and the coastline, which resembles the land where Dali grew up.

The painting was a gift of New Brunswick–born industrialist James Dunn, one of Beaverbrook's pals, and is on permanent display in the museum. The Dunns were early supporters and friends of Dali, and they purchased the painting under the noses of the Spanish government after the World Fair. There are several other Dali works in the museum, including portraits of the Dunns themselves. Not long after James died, and keeping it all in the family, his widow married Lord Beaverbrook. Passion! Betrayal! Oil on canvas!

Joan leads me through some of the gallery's other masterpieces: the Magritte, the Turner, the haunting Lucien Freud. She knows how to tease the life out of a painting, adding fresh colour to the canvas with her words. "A pity you're not there whenever I enter an art gallery," I tell her.

"I could be, if you're buying," she says in a snap.

Art culture in Canada tends to concentrate in the major urban centres: the National Gallery in Ottawa, the Montreal Museum of Fine Art, the Art Gallery of Ontario. Here in Fredericton, up the road from the Old Garrison District and across the street from the impressive Legislature Buildings, local character fuses with world-renowned genius for an experience even non-arty types will appreciate.

**START HERE:** canadianbucketlist.com/dali

# WALK OFF A CLIFF

I am finally ready to step off a 41-metre-high cliff. While I've rappelled down gorges, caves and mountains around the world, this will be the first time I'm rappelling face first, clutching a safety rope to my belly, literally walking down a rock face. This is what one does at Open Sky Adventures, the first commercial deepelling operation on the continent. Deepelling is not bungee jumping, with its quick, what-the-hell-just-happened rush. Neither is it abseiling, where you face the wall and bounce along to the bottom. No, this is a controlled upright descent, with your eyes staring directly at sharp rocks waiting to splatter you over the riverbed. Something funny happens when I'm asked to slowly walk upright off the cliff. My mind refuses to co-operate, but my feet take the first step anyway.

The Australian army developed deepelling (also known as Aussie-style rappelling, or rap jumping) as a technique to prevent its soldiers

# For Those Who'd Prefer to Jump

Deepelling requires a special sort of thrill-seeking resolve. For those who'd prefer to just jump off a high platform and be done with it, here's Canada's Best Bungee Jumps:

1. **Whistler Bungee, Whistler, BC:** A fifty-metre plunge over a glacier-fed river into a scenic gorge.
2. **Great Canadian Bungee, Ottawa, ON:** At sixty metres, this is Canada's highest jump, alongside a limestone cliff and into a blue lagoon.
3. **Nanaimo Bungee, BC:** A 46-metre bridge jump over the Nanaimo River, adjacent to a park that offers ziplines and a high ropes course. ➤

being shot while exiting helicopters. Using one hand to control the descent, it not only allowed soldiers to see their enemies, it also kept one hand free to fire back. With practice, you can literally leap off a wall like Spiderman. That practice includes repressing your natural instinct, which will beg, bargain and plead for you to back away from the edge.

Raymond Paquet's Open Sky Adventures has been running kayak, pontoon and canoe adventures down the Saint John River for years. When Raymond came across thrill-seekers deepelling in Quebec, he thought it would be a perfect activity for the canyon he owns just a few miles outside Grand Falls. "Babies are born afraid of height," he tells me, tightening up my mountain-climbing harness. "My job is simply to help kids get rid of this fear." His youngest client was seven, his oldest eighty, so naturally he's referring to kids of all ages.

The weight of the rope tugs me forward. Raymond has my safety line and can control my fall should I release the rope by mistake. I hold it tight to my stomach, creating a natural lock. To hop down a few metres, all I have to do is release my grip. "You've done many things in the world, Robin, but I promise you'll remember this one," says Raymond behind me.

It's always the first step. Then the second. Actually, the third is just as nerve-racking. Halfway down, it occurs to me I'm walking at a ninety-degree angle down a cliff face. Sweat doesn't drip down my

forehead, it drips right off it, splashing the ground below. Bending my knees, I launch myself off the rocks and glide several metres in a single hop, like a horizontal walk in zero gravity. Less than a minute later I reach the bottom, where I tug hard on the rope, straighten myself up and land softly on my feet. Like all the best adrenalin activities, it's over too soon, and not soon enough.

Fortunately, the price of admission includes three jumps. I walk up the stairs to the viewing platform (easily the most strenuous part of the day), back along the road, and return to the wooden launch platform. Raymond is waiting there with a gleam in his eye. "Isn't that cool?" he says in his thick French-Canadian accent.

"I've never seen or done anything like it. Let's do it again!" I reply, and head back to the edge. It's still a mind killer taking that first step, but this time my jumps become higher and my grip becomes easier on the rope. I make my way down in a matter of seconds, whooping the whole way.

Deepelling has proved so popular that Open Sky also allows you to launch yourself off the walls of its 15-metre-high headquarters, and in all seasons, too. It was developed by the military, so it's not surprising that there's one enemy you can expect to face: the fear in your mind.

**START HERE:** canadianbucketlist.com/deepelling

# CROSS HARTLAND'S COVERED BRIDGE

Before you enter the world's longest covered bridge, they say you should make a wish, close your eyes, cross your fingers and hold your breath. It's no easy task making it all the way to the other side in this condition. For one thing, the bridge is 390 metres long. Secondly, if you're driving, you'll probably end up plummeting into the Saint John River beneath you. Chances are your wish isn't going to come true anyway, although many a young man in the early twentieth century still got lucky.

New Brunswick has sixty-one covered bridges, which provided a safe river covering, and an opportunistic spot to escape the invasive eyes of chaperones and parents. For this reason, covered bridges became known as Kissing Bridges, makeshift wooden darkrooms for physical romance to finally see the light. Once the horse and buggy reached the other end, scandalous passion would be left behind. I

↑

NEW BRUNSWICK

# Iconic Canadian Bridges

1. **Confederation Bridge, PEI** See page 279.

2. **Lion's Gate Bridge, Burrard Inlet, BC** Opened in 1938, Vancouver's Lion's Gate is an imposing suspension bridge connecting Vancouver to its North Shore munici-palities, guarded by imposing lion statues and servicing up to seventy thousand cars a day. The three-lane bridge is a National Historic Site.

3. **Broadway Bridge, South Saskatchewan River, SK** Saskatoon's iconic bridge connecting downtown with the east shore is the Prairies' most picturesque urban bridge, with golden arches lit up at night. When the bridge is framed in a photo-graph with the Bessborough Hotel, Saskatoon's reputation as the Paris of the Prairies is self-evident.

4. **Port Mann Bridge, Fraser River, BC** Suburban commuters to Vancouver battled daily with a bottleneck on the Port Mann Bridge. In September 2012, and $3.3 billion later, the new Port Mann opened for traffic as the world's widest long-span bridge, doubling its capacity from five to ten lanes.

5. **Pont de Québec, St. Lawrence River, QC** A National Historic Site opened in 1919, Quebec Bridge is the world's longest cantilever bridge, at 549 metres. Site of the world's worst bridge construction disaster (75 workers died in 1907), today's bridge supports road, rail and pedestrians, and is owned by the Canadian National Railway. ➤

wonder if there's a generation of New Brunswickers who still get turned on by the smell of wood, the creak of floorboards and the peculiar light that beams from the end of a tunnel.

Inside the Hartland Tunnel, my rental car robbed me of the full sensory experience, and my dad, the only other passenger in the vehicle, stole my romantic opportunity as well. Unveiled in 1901, the bridge is still the pride of Hartland, and cars line up on either side of its single-lane entries for the chance to pass through. We cross at a reasonable speed, although I'm sure farm boys slowed their horses as much as possible. Perhaps that's why the townsfolk were

so scandalized: they kept hearing "Whoa! Whoa! Whoa!" from the dark depths of the bridge. Sermons once preached the moral decay accompanying such a long covered bridge, a situation which was not helped by rumours that young men had trained their horses to stop in the middle of the bridge for the ultimate smooch spot. Sneaking a snog inside Hartland's covered bridge is a long-standing Canadian tradition. If it's just you and a family member, though, it's perfectly acceptable to grunt and say: "Cool bridge."

**START HERE:** canadianbucketlist.com/hartland

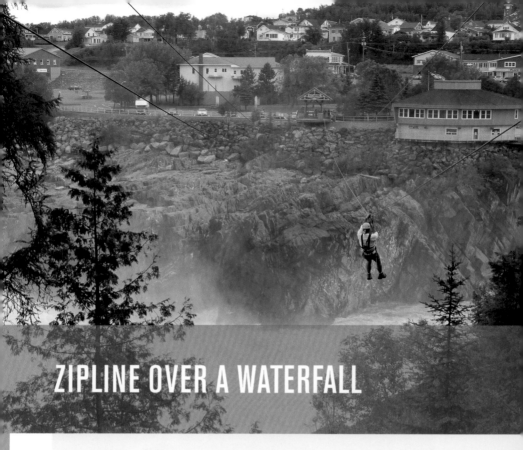

# ZIPLINE OVER A WATERFALL

Before invading just about every jungle block in Costa Rica, ziplines were a practical necessity in mountainous regions, where they were a means of transporting both goods and people. With the boom in ecotourism, enterprising operators realized tourists will pay good money for the opportunity to slide faster than monkeys through the canopy, learning about the environment as they do so. I've ziplined on four continents, and here's what I've come to realize:

1. Anyone can zipline.
2. Ziplining is only as good as the environment in which you do it.

## Canada's Longest Zipline

The country's longest, highest and fastest zipline can be found at Eagle Canyon, between Thunder Bay and Nipigon, Ontario. It's almost a kilometre long, 53 metres high, and you can hit 72 kph during your sixty-second ride. Eagle Canyon Adventures also offers Canada's longest suspension footbridge, stretching 185 metres across the canyon. ➤

Usually, the environment consists of trees, which is why this neat little operation in Grand Falls zipzags its way onto the bucket list. The town is named after the waterfalls it cradles, where the Saint John River drops twenty-three metres over a rock ledge, creating one of the largest Canadian falls east of Niagara. Eric Ouellette, a local civil engineer with some big industrial projects under his belt, saw the potential and opened Zip Zag for business. It took his team two years to build dual racing ziplines across the gorge, spanning 150 metres above the raging whitewater. He rightly believed that the only thing sweeter than a huge waterfall is ziplining through its spray on a bright, sunny day.

I collect my harness at the Malabeam Information Centre, where visitors learn about the area's history, the hydroelectric project, and how Eric and his team used 2,500 ice blocks to create the world's largest domed igloo, as certified by Guinness World Records. Clearly, here is an impressive man committed to random achievements. The only requirements for zipzaggers are that they weigh between 25 kilos and 125 kilos and are capable of walking up stairs.

Eric's wife, Christine, slips me into a harness and gives a brief demonstration, and then we walk to the launch zipline. Ziplining is perhaps the easiest of all "adrenalin" activities, requiring hardly any

physical effort, and offering the security of knowing you're safely connected to a steel rope over-engineered to take the weight of an elephant. Once I kick off, it takes only seconds to get across the canyon, which is where the real fun begins: the dual lines twenty-three metres above the waterfalls.

Grand Falls, also known as Grand Sault, is one of only two municipalities in Canada with a bilingual name. Over 80 percent of its population are completely bilingual, including all the Zip Zag guides. This is useful for American customers (the town is right on the Maine border) and Québécois customers driving in from eighty kilometres away. Regardless of whether you whoop in French or in English, once your feet leave the wooden platform, you'll find yourself gliding along at thirty to forty kilometres an hour, and with an awfully big smile on your face. A sheet of fine mist gently sprays me as I make the crossing, which is over too soon, as ziplines usually are. While the overall experience might take around an hour, the actual flying time can be counted in seconds. But believe me, those seconds count infinitely more when you're flying over a raging waterfall as opposed to a jungle canopy. There's no practical reason why anyone needs to zipline in this day and age, which is exactly why it's so much fun to do so.

**START HERE:** canadianbucketlist.com/zipline

# PAINT YOUR FACE AT TINTAMARRE

It's August 15, and the descendants of Acadia are eager to make some noise. When the church bells toll six p.m., tens of thousands of people erupt onto the streets of Caraquet dressed in costumes, making a right French-Canadian racket with whatever they can get their hands on: drums, bells, horns, buckets, whistles, voices. The annual tintamarre (literally, "clangour") tradition in Caraquet is remarkable for a number of reasons. Firstly, the population of this seaside town is just over 4,000 — so where did the other 34,000 people come from? Secondly, the tradition of celebrating Acadian culture and history with tintamarre only dates back to 1979. By the enthusiasm on display, one would think it was part of the 300-year-old Acadian heritage. Thirdly, it's just about the most fun you can have in New Brunswick, with or without the face paint.

The story of Acadia, with its origins in seventeenth- and eighteenth-century French settlement in the Maritimes, is a tumultuous one. Wars, displacement, deportation and cultural invasion—it's a wonder any culture has survived at all. In 1955, the Church organized a celebration in Moncton to commemorate the two hundredth anniversary of the Acadian Deportation, when conquering British armies dispersed the population. The racket that ensued left a lasting impression, although it wasn't until 1979 that tintamarre resurfaced as a massive street festival in the town of Caraquet. The town already boasts an Acadian Historical Village and Acadian summer festival, so it was the perfect place to celebrate the 375th anniversary of Acadia's founding. Acadia, I should point out, was a part of New France that included much of the Maritimes and parts of Maine. Acadians who resettled in Louisiana became known as cajuns.

Back to 1979, when everyone in Caraquet was invited to participate in the parade, embrace the tricolour Acadian flag and delight in a doozy of decibels. Although it was supposed to be a one-off event, a year later folks emerged from their houses with pots, pans, barrels and sticks. Soon after, costumes and face paint had been added, and visitors were flocking in from all over the province. Community leaders were already talking about holding a "traditional" tintamarre, despite the fact the tradition had barely begun to exist. Today, tintamarre has evolved into a vital expression of Acadian history, culture and pride. It has spread to other Acadian communities in New Brunswick and to parts of Quebec, a symbol of Acadian identity.

But wait a second, Robin. We're not Acadian, so why should we care?

I'll explain as I paint your face in red, white and blue, with a golden star around your right eye.

For a start, where else can you make more noise than the kids and be admired for it? Embracing the festival's joie de vivre is the kind of fun few should turn down. Unlike Fat Tuesday, this carnival makes an effort to include tourists and visitors, adding everyone into the mix, inviting participation and even home invasions. Tintamarre is the climax of the two-week-long Acadian Festival, featuring hundreds of music concerts, step-dancing, art, competitions and food. Feast on traditional Acadian fare such as *fricot à la poule*, clam pie and pulled molasses taffy. If you're historically inclined, 80 percent of the buildings in the Acadian Village are from the 1770s to the 1890s, relocated to the re-enactment village for an authentic material reference to history.

But it's the atmosphere and the smiley side of chaos that have made tintamarre one of the biggest festivals in the Atlantic provinces. Besides the party, tintamarre is an opportunity to understand and appreciate a vital cultural element that makes Canada Canada, and not, say, Australia with snow. Make some noise, together with the descendants of the Acadians: "We're here, and we're not going anywhere!"

**START HERE:** canadianbucketlist.com/tintamarre

NEW BRUNSWICK

# DRINK A POTATO SMOOTHIE

Welcome to the home of the world's favourite side dish. One-third of the world's frozen french fries are produced right here in Florenceville-Bristol, distributed by the McCain factory to 110 countries. If there were any justice, you would walk into a pub in Bangkok and order a burger with Canadian fries. Perhaps even New Brunswickan fries.

# Canada's Weirdest Roadside Attractions

Think a potato museum is unusual?

1. Vulcan Tourism and Trek Station: Vulcan (AB) cashes in on its name to tractor-beam *Star Trek* fanatics, offering over eight hundred pieces of memorabilia.

2. Gopher Hole Museum: Digging a hole in Torrington (AB) is the pinnacle of gopher taxidermy, displayed in village-life dioramas.

3. Your wishes have been granted: there is a Sardine Museum and Herring Hall of Fame, and you can peel back the tin at Grand Manan Island (NB).

4. Springhill (NS) is like a Canadian Graceland, where you can find everything you ever needed to know, and plenty you didn't, about Anne Murray at the Anne Murray Centre. ➤

Named after Florence Nightingale, this small, hyphenated town in Carlton County is home to the McCain frozen food empire, which processes around a million pounds of potatoes per hour. Fittingly, the McCain family are loyal supporters of the Potato World Museum, a quirky roadside attraction dedicated to the beauty of the world's favourite tuber. I make my way past the interpretive centre, which features customary wax models of farmers and horses. The Antique Machinery section leaves no doubt that harvesting potatoes is not nearly as easy as picking them up prewashed in plastic bags at the supermarket. In the interactive displays I learn that *potato* comes from the Amerindian word *batata*, and that potatoes were introduced to larger public appetites by sixteenth-century Spanish conquistadores in South America. Potatoes have been responsible for war, famine, heartache and heartburn. They were the first food grown in space, potato blossoms have been sported as garment decorations by royalty, there are four thousand different varieties, and . . . I could go on, but there's a smell permeating from the café and it's been a half-hour since I tucked into a bag of potato chips.

I briskly walk past the Potato Hall of Recognition, which features portraits of old white guys who have been instrumental in the development of the province's potato industry. Some of them are surnamed McCain, naturally, and I can't help but notice that some of these guys have heads shaped like potatoes too.

Potato World's Café is where things really get interesting. Ever since Thomas Jefferson introduced french fries to guests at the White House in the early 1800s, the delicious domination of the deep-fried potato has been unstoppable. Can you imagine fish and rice? Well, yes, but it's not fish 'n' chips, innit? Fries are served everywhere, from the most haughty high-end restaurants to gut-swilling dives. On the other hand, Potato World's Café creations are a true homage to the potato's flexibility. Their fries come in the following flavours: Lemon & Herb, Sweet Chili Pepper, BBQ, Tex Mex, Outbacka, Chili & Cheese, and poutine, of course. Forget the ketchup and reach for the white balsamic-cayenne mayo. Indulge your sweet tooth with potato fries and chocolate sauce, or fries rolled in cinnamon and brown sugar. And wash it all down with a strawberry, banana or wildberry potato smoothie. Yes, smoothie.

Since my visit to Florenceville-Bristol, potato chips have never tasted quite the same. No matter where I am in the world, with each bite I can close my eyes and picture the bucolic hills of New Brunswick, the old iron hoes in the museum, the flowing waters of the Saint John River and the steam billowing out of the McCain factory. Now that's a flavour worth dipping your chips into.

**START HERE:** canadianbucketlist.com/potato

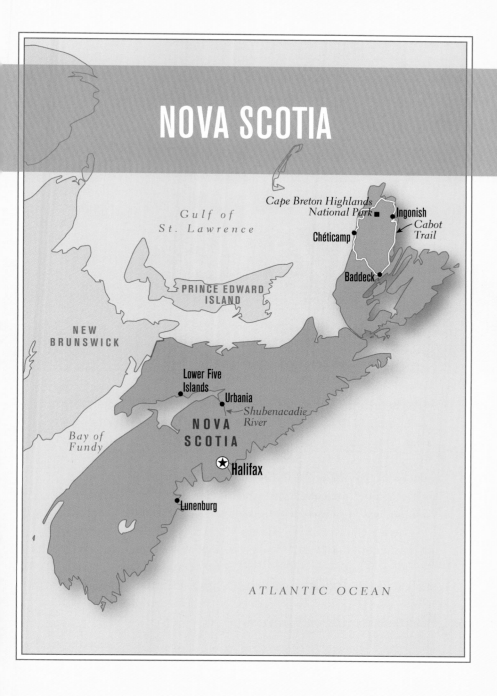

# NOVA SCOTIA

Gulf of
St. Lawrence

Cape Breton Highlands
National Park

Ingonish

Cabot
Trail

Chéticamp

Baddeck

PRINCE EDWARD
ISLAND

NEW
BRUNSWICK

Lower Five
Islands

Urbania

Shubenacadie
River

NOVA
SCOTIA

Bay of
Fundy

Halifax

Lunenburg

ATLANTIC OCEAN

# RAFT A TIDAL WAVE

When Nova Scotia's largest river, the Shubenacadie, encounters the rush of tidal water flowing in from the Bay of Fundy, *bore* is not the word that comes to mind. Yet the world's largest tides, reversing into the very rivers that feed them, are called exactly that: tidal bores. It is a true tidal wave (not to be confused with a tsunami), as the leading wave swallows sandbars and marshes in a matter of minutes, leaving a turbulent trail of waves and rapids in its wake.

There are few places in the world where you can experience this phenomenon, much less hop on a high-powered Zodiac to play in it like a theme park ride. Once a day, rafting companies along the low, shallow banks of the Shube gather clients for the incoming bore, which can bring waves as high as five metres rumbling over the muddy sandbars before harmlessly levelling out.

It's a crisp June morning when I arrive at Tidal Bore Rafting's HQ. Depending on the tide and moon cycle, the bore's size can be classified as mild, medium or extreme. I've enjoyed the thrill of Class 5 whitewater rafting before (including the world's highest commercial vertical drop in New Zealand), and so I look forward to today's extreme conditions. The 72-kilometre-long river is brackish and brown, a stream of chocolate milk running through minty green forests and farmland. I'm advised not to wear anything I care too deeply about, and handed a rainsuit, a life jacket and a pair of old shoes.

## Top 10 Canadian Whitewater Rafting Destinations

Prepare to get wet:

1.  Shubenacadie River, NS
2.  Magpie River, QC
3.  Kicking Horse River, BC
4.  Ottawa River, QC/ON
5.  Tatshenshini River, BC
6.  Fraser River, BC
7.  Kipawa River, QC
8.  Alsek River, BC/YK
9.  Athabasca River, AB
10. Thompson River, BC

Our group makes its way to the riverbank, the water running calmly about six metres below the jetty. We squish over thick mud, hop into the Zodiac and introduce ourselves. I'm with a couple from Halifax, and we're guided by a pretty young pilot named Gillian, who swaps out as a ski instructor in the river's off-season. She pilots the Zodiac upriver, and with the high-tide line clearly marked on the riverbank way above our heads, my imagination starts to run riot. I picture a massive tidal wave, twenty metres high, rushing down the valley and drowning everything in its path, like those water horses conjured by Arwen in *The Lord of the Rings*. Gillian is less concerned, pointing out the first of many bald eagles, gathered along the Shube in high concentrations to feed on sea and river fish caught in

the tides. It's why the area is home to the highest nesting concentration of bald eagles on North America's east coast.

Under their watchful eagle eyes, the Zodiac hums along with the current, passing a huge mudslide that took a few trees with it. We're a little early and so berth on a sandbar, eagerly awaiting the arrival of the bore, occupying our time by submerging our shins in sinking sand. Ten minutes later, Gillian points upriver. In the distance, a harmless white wave approaches. It seems innocent enough, not nearly as extreme as I had imagined. Gillian guns the Zodiac to meet the wave, which we ramp over and then turn back, surfing on its crest. Within minutes the wave will swallow the sandbars and begin its rise to the tide line, high on the cliffs above our heads. The Zodiac pulls out, racing farther upstream. "Are you ready, guys?"

Gillian yells. What she knows, and what we don't, is that as the high tide hits sandbars and slopes, the rush of water gets churned up like a boiling soup.

After zooting up the relatively calm side of the river, Gillian makes a hard left, and we drop in like unprepared potatoes. Bang! Ow! Wow! Whee! Bang! There's not much else we can say as the Zodiac dips and crests through the rapids, lurching feet in the air, landing hard with a thud. Keeping our mouths shut is actually a smart idea, as the Shube's muddy water drenches the boat, ready to spoon us with eager mouthfuls. The rapids are cold, invigorating and relentless. When they peter out, Gillian repeats the process, skirting the soup close to the shore before turning in for another thrill ride.

Earlier, we had passed a rock formation known as Anthony's Point, which looked like a large boot sitting far above our heads. Now it is completely submerged. We hit the soup again, and again, a concentrated and sustained dose of rapids you just can't find on traditional whitewater adventures. My knees take a beating from the drops as we get pummelled from all sides, almost losing a shipmate at one point. However, with no rocks to worry about, should you lose a man overboard, it's a relatively safe affair for the boat to find you and haul you back on board. We ride the waves until the riverbanks widen and the bore wears itself out, conveniently close to the jetty we left two hours ago. I can barely recognize its wooden steps, floating above a raging river where before they sat on metres of mud.

A hot shower later, we exchange high-fives and wide smiles, proud recipients of a true Canadian adventure you just can't find anywhere else. Despite its modern usage, the word *bore* comes from Old Norse, meaning "swell"—a word that applies both literally and figuratively to this bucket list adventure.

START HERE: canadianbucketlist.com/tidalbore

# WALK AROUND LUNENBURG

Atlantic Canada's coastline is flecked with seaside fishing villages that recall another era, an age when raw dog fishermen braved rough oceans to haul in cod that would be salted and shipped to all parts of the British Empire. The exceptionally well preserved fishing town of Lunenburg, founded in 1753, stands apart for a number of reasons. It has been designated a UNESCO World Heritage Site for being the "best surviving example of a planned British colonial settlement in North America, retaining the town's original layout and overall appearance, based on a rectangular grid pattern drawn up in the home country." I decided to visit the town to understand what that sentence means, because, let's face it, UNESCO don't make it sound very exciting.

## The Legend of the *Bluenose*

Built and launched in Lunenburg, the *Bluenose* captured the world's imagination as the fastest fishing boat on the seas, holding the International Fisherman's Trophy for seventeen years. This hulking ship was a far cry from the sleek modern vessels that race in today's sailing events; it was primarily used for fishing in some of the world's stormiest waters. Immortalized in music and books, on stamps, Nova Scotia licence plates and the Canadian ten-cent coin, history finally caught up with the old boat. It was sold as a cargo ship in the Caribbean and wrecked beyond repair on a reef in Haiti. Several replicas have been built over the years for promotional and leisure purposes, with a new replica just recently completed in Lunenburg. ➤

Driving in on a fine spring day, I'm reminded of an idyllic British seaside resort, complete with busloads of tourists. High season hasn't quite kicked in yet, but the town has tidied itself up after the long winter, eager to welcome new summer guests. My first stop is the excellent Fisheries Museum of the Atlantic, which does a great job breathing life into the legacy of east coast fishing. I learn about the birth of the industry, its lifestyle through the years, the challenges, the science, the equipment and the rum-runners who made their fortune during Prohibition. There is also an exhibition about the *Bluenose*—the Lunenburg legend honoured on the back of every Canadian dime. What strikes me most are the stories of clippers lost at sea, many with all crew on board. One fierce hurricane, the August Gale of 1927, sank several ships and claimed 184 souls. A memorial lists the names of local fishermen who never returned to shore, from the 1800s all the way up to the present day. We've come a long way from fishermen using single lines to pull in cod, getting paid in cod tongues and braving treacherous conditions.

Across the bay is High Liner Foods, one of North America's largest fish processing plants. Modern fishing has made the profession safer

but has also devastated fish stocks, and with them entire communities. All this makes the museum's exhibits seem so vital to Atlantic Canada's history. From the museum, I stroll along the waterfront, admiring the colourful paint jobs on the old wharves and wooden houses.

To get behind the charming facade, I join local guide Shelah Allen for one of her historical walking tours. Storms are threatening when we meet outside the impressive Academy building, built in 1894. The weather doesn't dampen Shelah's enthusiasm one bit, as she begins to tell me stories about the houses, what era they're from, their architecture, former inhabitants and why they're so well preserved.

"Here's my favourite house," she says, pointing to a large pink Victorian house on York Street. Built in 1888, Morash House has overhanging windows, triple bellcast roofs and a Lunenburg "bump"—large windows facing the ocean so that hopeful wives could watch for ships returning safely to port. Across the street is another old home, painted yellow. "That's actually been rebuilt pretty recently," says Shelah. The town is serious about keeping its heritage well intact. At the end of the block is the oldest Lutheran church

in Canada, reflecting the many German immigrants who made Lunenburg their home.

Each wooden home we pass has a story, until we come to the striking St. John's Anglican Church, faithfully restored after a devastating fire in 2001. An organist is playing inside, adding to the atmosphere. I learn about the many Norwegian fishermen stranded here during World War II and taken in by the locals, and the warm relations that still exist as a result. We go down King Street, past the bright green and orange wooden shops that caused a little stir when the paint dried, ending up at the Knaught–Rhuland House, one of the best-preserved eighteenth-century houses in the country, and another National Historic Site.

Shelah's one-hour tour ends at the pub, because that's just how things work in Nova Scotia. She tells me that Lunenburg is growing with an influx of entrepreneurs, and that, coupled with the town's ability to preserve and showcase its history, is making the future look pretty peachy. UNESCO's description sounds terribly square—*grid, rectangular, layout*. Rest assured, there's a warm heart waiting to greet you in Lunenburg.

START HERE: canadianbucketlist.com/lunenburg

NOVA SCOTIA ↑

# ARM A CANNON AT THE HALIFAX CITADEL

"Atten-SHUN!"

The kilted sergeant of the 78th Highlanders is doing his best to get our motley regiment into line. Granted, he's actually a paid historical re-enactor, and our regiment consists of confused tourists from Mexico, Germany and France. Call us the rank and vile. We had signed up to be soldiers for a day at Fort George, Halifax's most iconic landmark, overlooking the city atop Citadel Hill. The year is 1869, when the red-coated and kilted Scottish Highlanders manned the fort that protected the crux of British shipping interests on the Atlantic coast. We'd each been given a shilling, which crafty sergeants dropped into the pints of young men, who soon discovered they'd just signed up for a seven-year stint in Her Majesty's Army. Today we would discover what this might have been like—from barracks to guard posts—breathing fresh life into this National Historic Site.

Entrance
Entrée

In the mid-1700s, the British built a fort on the highest hill overlooking Halifax harbour. It continued to expand until the current Citadel was completed in 1856, designed to be a potent deterrent to American, French and other aggressors threatening lucrative British naval interests. With excellent sightlines, thick stone walls, powerful cannon and even a land moat, the star-shaped fortress was so successful that it never did come under attack. Unless you count tourists, penetrating the walls daily to explore this living museum and enjoy its views of the city.

Operated by Parks Canada, the Citadel gives a snapshot of life behind the walls in 1869. Historical re-enactors run through daily chores, inviting visitors to join them through the "Soldier for a Day" program and the Halifax Citadel Experience. Which is how I came to be position number five, awaiting the order to transfer a bucket of make-believe black powder to position number three, so that position number two could pretend to stoke the very real cannon and blast non-existent enemies to smithereens. While the Citadel never came under enemy fire, it did witness the tragic Halifax Explosion. In 1917, a munitions ship exploded in the harbour, flattening nearby buildings and killing some two thousand people.

Back to the present, where, according to the cannon master, we are the worst crew he's ever seen. At least he doesn't have to hear our awfulness, unlike the drum instructor, who must listen to my version of a brass shell field drum. Picture Animal, the drummer for the

Muppets. *Rat-atat-a-ratatatatata* . . . Thank you, Robin, someone else, please, anyone?

Next is the barracks, where we learn how up to twenty men would share these spartan quarters with their families, the kids sleeping under the creaking narrow bed. When winter came, even the hardiest of Highlanders had to wear pants, taking solace in the fact they were made of Mackenzie-clan tartan. Naturally, I ask a soldier if he's a true Scotsman.

"My boots are the only item beneath my kilt," he replies. Minutes later, a gust of wind causes an embarrassing Marilyn Monroe moment, and I can confirm, kilts are not nearly as becoming as white dresses.

After visiting the huge waterless moat, designed to turn attackers into sitting ducks, we learn about weapons, and watch a demonstration with a working nineteenth-century muzzle. The loud crack of black powder reminds us that these high-calibre bullets would stop an elephant, and certainly ruin the day of anyone on the receiving end. For Queen and country, the soldiers might say, pulling the trigger, feeling the breeze on their knees. Still, for all its red-coated pomp and glory, it was no fun to be in Her Majesty's Army.

Today, the Citadel continues to guard the city of Halifax like a brawny, protective grandparent. It's well worth a visit, especially now, when even the soldiers are smiling.

**START HERE:** canadianbucketlist.com/citadel

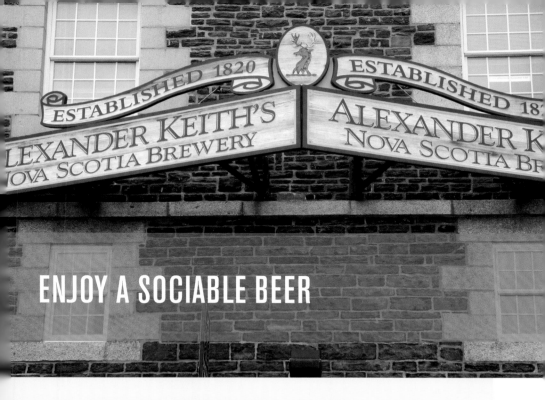

# ENJOY A SOCIABLE BEER

It is my custom, on the road, always to order the local beer. The thought of ordering Heineken in Hungary, Miller in Mexico or Corona in China may be a boon for major beer monopolies, but not for the authentic traveller. Beers taste better in the land of their brewing—except for Budweiser in the United States and Chang in Thailand, which are best enjoyed nowhere. Canada's beer, it must be said, is vastly underrated in terms of its quality. Visit Australia and you'll see how even a committed beer-drinking nation is forced to consume weak, industrial beverages such as VB, XXXX and Tooheys. Phooey!

While microbreweries have made great-tasting inroads in North America, Down Under and beyond, I'll take the mass-market Kokanee, Rickard's, Sleeman, Big Rock and Moosehead over best-selling foreign brands any day. And then there is Alexander Keith's,

# Canadian Beers to Drink Before You Die

As much as I love beer, I'm no expert. So I consulted Troy Burtch, Craft Beer Preacher, co-founder of Toronto Beer Week and author of the synergistically named Great Canadian Beer Blog. Here's Troy's Bucket List of Canadian Beer:

1. Steam Whistle Pilsner (Toronto, ON)
2. Dieu Du Ciel, Péché Mortel (Montreal, QC)
3. Blanche de Chambly, Maudite (Chambly, QC)
4. Alley Kat Brewing Co., Full Moon Pale Ale (Edmonton, AB)
5. Great Lakes Brewery, Crazy Canuck Pale Ale (Toronto, ON). Brewed in 2010 for the Ontario athletes at the Vancouver Winter Olympics and multiple award winner at the Canadian Brewing Awards.
6. Half Pints Brewing Co., Little Scrapper IPA (Winnipeg, MB)
7. Propeller Brewing Co., London Style Porter (Halifax, NS)
8. McAuslan Brewery, St. Ambroise Oatmeal Stout (Montreal, QC). A benchmark for the style and respected by beer enthusiasts in North America.
9. Spinnakers Brewpub, Mitchell's Extra Special Bitter (Victoria, BC). Sup on cask-conditioned ale at one of the oldest operating independent craft breweries in Canada.
10. Garrison Brewing Co., Spruce Beer (Halifax, NS). An annual seasonal release, Garrison goes back in time to brew a spruce beer, much as our ancestors would have done.
11. PEI Brewing Co., 1772 IPA (Charlottetown, PEI). Visit the historic Gahan House brewpub for a delicious IPA.
12. Molson Coors, Molson Canadian—because everyone has to start somewhere. A long and storied brewing past and a huge part of our social culture. Available all over Canada. ➤

purveyors of fine Nova Scotian beer since 1820. Although it's now owned by Labatt (in turn owned by Anheuser–Busch InBev, which owns just about everything else), Keith's holds a special place in the hearts of Nova Scotians. I'm told it is the largest-distributed non-specialty beer in the country, and while I'm not exactly sure what that means, it sounds as if it holds a special place in the hearts of many Canadians too.

Which explains why the Brewery Tour, held in the same brick building on Lower Water Street in which Alexander Keith created his famous Indian Pale Ale, is a popular attraction in Halifax. Historical re-enactors walk you through the history of the man, the beer and the city before depositing you one hour later in an old-fashioned tavern where you can enjoy the fruits of your labours. It's a little hokey, and I'm hesitant to say you must take this tour before you die, because, quite frankly, you might have more fun with your mates at the adjacent pub, the Stag's Head. Whatever pub you end up in in Nova Scotia, ordering a pint of Keith's will endear you to the locals, lubricate new friendships and possibly turn out to be more fun than any item on this bucket list. Probably not, but what is a beer if not its potential to lead to something more, even if it is the gutter? So raise a glass to all of Canada's beautiful beers, and say, like a true Nova Scotian, "Sociable!"

**START HERE:** canadianbucketlist.com/beer

NOVA SCOTIA ↑

# RUN A RACE OF BIBLICAL PROPORTIONS

We all know the Bible story: Moses leads the Israelites out of slavery in Egypt, chased by the resentful Pharaoh's army to the shores of the Red Sea. Here, Moses raises his staff and one of the great Biblical miracles occurs: the sea divides, allowing the Israelites to pass safely across the ocean floor. The pursuing army are swallowed by the sea, and lo, the Israelites are free . . . to wander the desert for forty years.

But that's another story. Now let's replace the Red Sea with the Bay of Fundy, which we already know has the world's highest tides. Instead of the Israelites racing for freedom, picture joggers covered up to their ankles in red mud. For the pursuing soldiers, we'll use Time itself, which relentlessly ticks forward until the bay begins to fill, drowning rocks and mud up to fifteen metres underwater. Not since Moses has there been a race against such a powerful foe, hence the name of this quirky and extreme ten-kilometre annual run along Five Islands, Nova Scotia, which is called . . . Not Since Moses!

Over a thousand competitors must race along the ocean floor—over mud, seaweed, rocks, muck and slime—to reach the finish line before high tide. These conditions make it particularly treacherous, but the well-organized event takes great pride in ensuring that no one is forced to swim to safety. Participants in the ten-kilometre run, or the less frenetic five-kilometre walk, follow a path among five islands that sit off the coast: Moose, Diamond, Egg, Pinnacle and Long. If you stop long enough to admire your surroundings (and don't slip on seaweed), you'll see eroded muddy cliffs, sandbars and distinct islands of rock—and probably a jogger knee-deep in sludge, his or her shoes lodged firmly in the mud.

The volunteer-driven event is a festive affair, culminating in live music, hot food, a poetry reading and a popular children's event. Run times typically fall between sixty and ninety minutes, with the winner clocking in at around forty-five minutes and the last runner at around two hours, by which stage the kids are already enjoying a burger and the annual Basket Run. Conditions can vary from year to year—strong winds once had competitors wading through a waist-high tidal river—and volunteer stations along the route are known to turn back slow runners. Fortunately, boats are on hand for rescues, since this is not a triathlon—yet. How great would it be to see a race on the ocean floor that starts on foot and finishes with a swim?

Not Since Moses benefits local schools, draws athletes from around the world and relies on the uncanny ability of Nova Scotians to, well, run with it. Besides the sticky terrain, runners are cautioned to expect strong winds and bring their own water (or alcohol, if that's the fuel you need). It may not be a Biblical miracle, but Not Since Moses still crosses the mud-splattered line to finish on the Great Canadian Bucket List.

**START HERE:** canadianbucketlist.com/moses

NOVA SCOTIA ↑

# EXPLORE CAPE BRETON AND THE CABOT TRAIL

" I have travelled around the globe. I have seen the Canadian and American Rockies, the Andes, the Alps and the Highlands of Scotland, but for simple beauty, Cape Breton outrivals them all."

Thus spoke Alexander Graham Bell, the distinguished gentleman who invented the telephone, the metal detector and the hydrofoil. It explains why his former Canadian residence is a National Historic Site, and why it is located in Baddeck, Cape Breton. The question is: why did Cape Breton beat out the Rockies, Andes, Highlands and Alps? Why do international travel magazines bestow titles on Cape Breton including "The Most Scenic Island in the World" (Condé Nast), "The Number One Island to Visit in continental North America" (*Travel+Leisure*) and "One of the World's Greatest Destinations" (National Geographic)? If Cape Breton casts a spell on its visitors, what lies behind its McAbracadabra?

Aye, the Scottish influence is unmistakable. Upwards of fifty thousand Highlanders found their way to Cape Breton in the early nineteenth century, bringing their Gaelic language and culture with them. Centuries later, discovering Scotland in Canada charms the kilt off most visitors, unaccustomed to the distinct Cape Breton accent they encounter in small communities dotted around the island. You will also discover some wonderfully preserved Acadian communities—Belle Côte, Terre Noire, Cap Le Moine, Grand Étang, Chéticamp—benefiting from their isolation, adapted to the distinct environmental culture of the Maritimes.

Expect fiddle romps and bagpipe blues, fresh seafood with a view of migrating whales, all hosted by notoriously friendly locals with their *Ciad Mile Failte*, literally "one hundred thousand welcomes." The sparkling emerald in the island's crown is the 948-square-kilometre Cape Breton Highlands National Park. Shaped by the Gulf of St. Lawrence on the west and the Atlantic on the east, the park consists of temperate and boreal forest containing bird species you won't find anywhere else in the country.

But it's the mountains on the elevated plateau that leave the biggest impression, rolling into the sea, a million-dollar view waiting around every corner. Some of the park's two dozen hikes take you right to the cliff edge of the headlands, the perfect place to watch the Atlantic punish the coast, her mist forming beads on your brow. The steep Highlands scenery recalls the very best vistas of Scotland, enhanced by the ruggedness, ocean and space that define the eastern coast of Canada. Best of all, the views, wildlife, culture and traditions of Cape Breton are easily accessible, primarily through "one of the world's best road trips" (Lonely Planet).

The Cabot Trail is an approximately 300-kilometre loop at the northern tip of Cape Breton, running through eight communities (Scottish, Irish and Acadian), the Margaree River and Cape Breton

## The End of Cabot's Trail

Italian explorer Giovanni Caboto, a.k.a. Jean Cabot, a.k.a. Juan Cabot, a.k.a. John Cabot, a.k.a. Zuan Chabatto, was commissioned by Henry VII of England to find a faster sailing route to Asia. In doing so, he became the first European since the Vikings to land on mainland North America, in what Canadian and U.K. historians agree was Cape Bonavista, Newfoundland. Rather skittishly, Cabot did not explore much farther than the rich offshore cod stocks. After a hero's welcome back in England, he mustered up some ships for a return voyage and was promptly never heard from again. Historians question whether he was lost at sea, settled in North America or returned to obscurity in England. ➤

Highlands National Park. Named after the Italian explorer John Cabot (a.k.a. Giovanni Caboto), the scenic highway is open year-round but draws hundreds of thousands of visitors in the summer and fall. Communities come alive for the occasion. The Acadian fishing village of Chéticamp welcomes tourists with fiddle music and traditional hooked rugs, while Ingonish, at the east entrance to the national park, touts one of Canada's most highly rated golf courses, the Stanley Thompson–designed eighteen-hole Highlands Links Golf Course.

We can all appreciate local craft stores, gourmet patio restaurants and charming inns and B&Bs, but it's the natural beauty of the Cabot Trail that takes the breath away, when the smooth, winding road enters the national park beneath the soaring Highlands that tower over the ocean.

You'll need at least three to four days to enjoy the Cabot Trail by car, motorhome or motorbike, taking in its sights, meeting its people and experiencing its history. Three or four days to agree with the opinions of nineteenth-century inventors, twenty-first century travel magazines and the National Bucket List.

START HERE: canadianbucketlist.com/capebreton

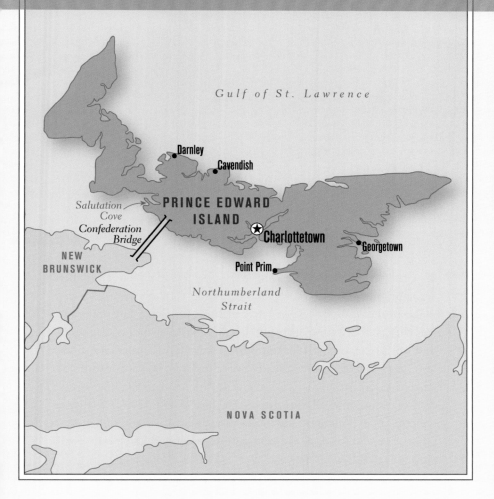

# PRINCE EDWARD ISLAND

Gulf of St. Lawrence

Darnley

Cavendish

PRINCE EDWARD
ISLAND

Salutation
Cove
Confederation
Bridge

NEW
BRUNSWICK

★ Charlottetown

Georgetown

Point Prim

Northumberland
Strait

NOVA SCOTIA

# HAUL A LOBSTER TRAP

Lobsters intimidate me. For starters, they look like miniature spider-dragon aliens, capable of slicing your neck off with one swipe of their giant claw, or latching onto your face to impregnate you with acid-dripping offspring. Just look at their undersides: surely that was the inspiration for the monsters in the *Alien* movies. Spiky legs, sharp edges and two beady eyes thinking, "If I were your size and you were mine . . ." Growing up inland, I never had lobster on the menu, and while I appreciate it is a delicacy for many, so are crickets in Thailand, worms in Venezuela and deep-fried guinea pig in Ecuador. So it is with some trepidation that I step onto Perry

Gotell's boat at four a.m., ready to experience the real working life of an east coast lobster fisherman.

It's hard work, and the season is short. Six days a week for two solid months, Perry and his first mate, Jerry Mackenzie, motor out into the bay to haul in their three hundred wooden traps and deliver a lucrative load for distributors back at the dock. Through Tranquillity Cove Adventures, anyone can join them for the experience. Blessed with a calm, clear morning, I slip on my water-proofs and get to work before we even leave the dock. A huge blue tub of mackerel must be cut up for each lobster trap. Before the sun breaches the horizon, my rubber gloves are covered in grungy, smelly fish guts. Perry is a third-generation lobster fisherman, and his traps sit at the bottom of the same waters his family have been fishing for decades.

With Perry steering the boat and keying in the GPS coordinates of the traps, Jerry takes a long pole to hook each trap's buoy, attach it to a mechanical crane and begin hauling heavy wooden crates onto the side of the boat. With dozens of lobster-fishing boats around us, the industry is heavily regulated to ensure there is no overfishing. Licences cost well into the six figures, and while a good day out can yield thousands of dollars, it's hard, relentless work with plenty of costs to go with it. Perry spends about $1,200 a week just for his bait.

But disembowelled flounder and mackerel are the least of my worries. The traps are literally crawling with huge crabs and panicky large lobsters. Both have sharp claws, protected by strong shells.

"Go ahead," says Perry. "Stick your hand in and start sorting 'em."

Lobsters with black eggs are immediately tossed back into the sea to produce new yields. Only the largest crabs are collected, to be weighed and sold; the rest also find themselves sinking back to the bottom of the Atlantic Ocean. The lobsters themselves are put in a sorting bin, from which Jerry measures their size and determines whether they are classed as premium market or standard "canned." Market lobsters have their claws banded with small blue elastics to prevent them from damaging each other. New bait is set by placing chunks of mackerel on a spike or in a vise inside each trap.

Perry locates a preferable spot and the traps are dumped overboard for another day to do their job. We repeat the above for eight hours, ticking off each of the fifty buoys and mentally counting down each of the three hundred traps. Perry's ideal is to catch old, huge and heavy lobsters, which he calls "bone crushers" for the size of their claws. At the start of the season, a typical day might net 550 kilograms of lobster, but today, towards the end, he'll be lucky to get 135 kilograms. Since fishermen are paid by weight, I can't imagine what it must be like to work four times harder than this.

Meanwhile, I'm still getting over the fear that a crab might sever an artery, or a lobster snip off a finger. "They're smaller than me and their brains are the size of a pinhead. Outthink, Outsmart, Out . . . oh, to hell with it, come here, you ugly crustacean!" Within a few hours I'm sweeping traps clear in seconds. The sunrise is spectacular, and being able to see the red cliffs of the Island helps with my sea legs, along with the added distraction of listening to Perry and Jerry's salty dog stories. Each trap presents its own challenge, its own hope of a monster haul or a better one tomorrow.

I'd spent the morning out in the elements, working with nature's bounty, conquering my fears and learning about a fascinating industry. Hard work, yes, but what an experience. "One guy, he told us fishin' lobster was on his bucket list," says Jerry, rinsing the boat. Turns out that guy wasn't alone.

**START HERE:** canadianbucketlist.com/lobster

# TONG AND SHUCK OYSTERS

I'd tasted P.E.I. long before I ever stepped foot on the Island. After all, P.E.I. mussels, oysters and lobsters are prize items on restaurant menus across North America. I looked forward to tucking into this seafood bonanza as soon as I arrived, especially oysters, that delectable bivalve long associated with decadent pleasure. Some people might argue there's nothing delicious about consuming a live, raw animal with the texture of a nasal infection. Some people need to get into the spirit of things. To help, experience the life of an oyster farmer in the field—or, more accurately, the water—through a "Tong & Shuck" activity offered by Salutation Cove's Rocky Bay Oysters.

Co-owner Erskine Lewis takes me out on a boat into the shallow waters of the cove, where oysters grow naturally in prized abundance. After demonstrating the art of tonging oysters from the sandy depth, Erskine hands me the wooden rake–like tool with stainless steel teeth. I carefully scrape the bottom, jostling the tong to loosen

## How to Shuck an Oyster

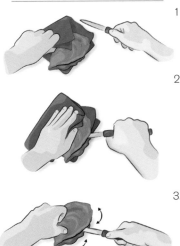

1. Rinse the oyster with fresh water, clearing away muck and mud with a steel brush. Refrigerate until ready to serve, covered with a damp towel.

2. Use a dishtowel or glove to protect yourself as you hold the oyster down on a flat surface, the pointed hinge facing you. Insert the oyster knife into the hinge, pushing it towards the bottom of the cup and giving it a slight wiggle. Twist the knife to pop the hinge.

3. To cut the muscles holding the shell together, slide the knife across the top of the shell. Separate the shell, clear away any mess, and slide the knife under the oyster flesh to detach it from the bottom shell. ➤

up oysters and hopefully bring in a decent haul. It takes a few tries before I get the hang of it, but my hauls are still a fraction of Erskine's.

We measure the size of each oyster against a simple measuring unit, returning the ones that don't make the cut. Erskine explains that the difference between choice, restaurant-grade oysters and standard, industrial oysters is simply the shape of the shell. The more round, the more sought-after, and often the less actual oyster to slurp back. Erskine rummages through my haul, selects a choice shell, shucks it right there and hands it to me. No lemon juice, no Tabasco. P.E.I. oysters are best enjoyed raw, fresh and on their own. For this is no ordinary oyster: this is the very taste of Salutation Cove, nature condensed into a food group.

In just a couple of hours, I develop a deep respect for oysters, and the amount of work it takes to grow, harvest and distribute them. The price of an oyster in a P.E.I. restaurant: $2.50. Being able to appreciate them: priceless.

It was time to put the oysters into their more familiar context, and so I enlisted the help of a top-rated local seafood restaurant, owned by the Island's oyster aficionado. John Bil is a three-time Canadian Oyster Shucking Champion, a man who believes the ocean does all the work, chefs just add heat. His Ship to Shore restaurant, located in scenic Darnley, is jammed in the summer months, and for good reason. The converted former roadhouse serves up only the freshest seafood sourced from nearby friends and colleagues.

After teaching me how to shuck an oyster and demonstrating his own renowned skill (including shucking blindfolded, behind his back), John educates me on the subtleties of oyster appreciation, and sure enough, I begin to taste the coves from which they were harvested, feeling the waves in my mouth. Dinner consists of fresh steamed mussels, fat grilled scallops and a sublime buttery-soft halibut. John recommends a sweet Château de Fargues Sauternes to round off the evening.

Why are P.E.I. oysters so revered? "Oysters are like grapes. A Sauvignon Blanc from Ontario is simply not the same as a Sauvignon Blanc from California," explains John. From which I conclude that an oyster tonged in P.E.I.'s coves is unlike an oyster from anywhere else, and its taste belongs on the National Bucket List.

**START HERE:** canadianbucketlist.com/oysters

# PLAY A ROUND OF GOLF

There are several things I look forward to doing in the autumn years of my life. I look forward to watching all these TV shows people keep talking about, so I can finally understand what kind of a creature a Snooki is, and why everyone is raving about *Mad Men*. I look forward to a long career in skydiving, weeks spent playing video games, meditation and, most of all, golf. Not all at the same time, mind you, although that would be interesting.

You see, golf demands the supreme patience, time, skill and budget reserves I don't yet possess. For those who argue the folly of whacking a little ball a long way to get it into a little cup, I say, "Four!" Yes, I spelled that correctly.

**One:** Golf gets you outside, in the fresh air, usually in beautiful surroundings.

**Two:** Golf gets you socially active, because really, it's not all that important whether you score a birdie or an eagle or any other form of bird life.

**Three:** Golf is a personal challenge, a combination of mental and physical skill that is easy to learn and impossible to master. Just ask Tiger Woods's ex-wife.

**Four:** Golf is punctuated by ice-cold beverages and ends in a clubhouse with more libations, nachos and chicken wings.

Prince Edward Island may be Canada's smallest, least-populated province, but the facts speak for themselves: At the time of writing, it claims 10 out of the Top 100 Golf Courses as rated by *Globe and Mail* readers, and 5 percent of the Top 350 Courses in North America. The Island is branded as Canada's Number One Golf Destination, and received an award from the International Association of Golf Travel Operators as the Undiscovered Golf Destination of the Year. The Island's thirty-four courses (at the time of writing) are renowned for their natural beauty, variety, design and the fact that they're mostly a half-hour drive from Charlottetown.

Take the Brudenell River Golf Club, one of the Island's most popular courses, dotted with lakes, ponds and gardens. Here I have the opportunity to learn a few tricks from LPGA pro and resident Island golf expert Anne Chouinard. Considering my experience is mostly limited to hacking the carpet off minigolf courses, Anne is impressed by my enthusiasm. She moved here from Quebec for the

# Canada's Top 10 Golf Courses

Ron MacNeill, Executive Director of P.E.I.'s Golf Association, tees up with his favourite golf courses in Canada:

1. The National, ON
2. Banff Springs, AB
3. Coppinwood, ON
4. Cape Breton Highlands, NS
5. The Links at Crowbush Cove, PEI
6. Beacon Hall, ON
7. Hamilton Golf Club, ON
8. The Devil's Paintbrush, ON
9. Dundarave, PEI
10. Weston, ON

fantastic Island lifestyle along with the world-class courses and recommends anyone with a love of the game do so as well.

We proceed to play a round, the course buttressing against a gorgeous coastline, surrounded by the tranquility of Brudenell Provincial Park. At par-three, I somehow manage to skip my golf ball twice over a water hazard and into the rough. Anne tells me Phil Mickelson did that once on purpose, which I take as a compliment. On the sixth hole, I'm pretty sure I scored a puffin, penguin and pigeon, which is definitely quite the feat. This demands further celebration back at the clubhouse, with nachos and cold beer. Despite Anne's best efforts, I have a lot to learn if I want to master this game. Before I die, there's no place I'd rather master it than on Prince Edward Island.

**START HERE:** canadianbucketlist.com/golf

# CROSS CONFEDERATION BRIDGE

At the birth pang of Canada, when the founding provinces gathered for the Charlottetown Conference, tiny Prince Edward
Island was only accessible by ferry. It may have been Canada
through and through, but it wasn't physically connected to Canada,
and winter ferry crossings could be notoriously dicey. A century later,
a debate raged about the merits of building a massive bridge to connect the Island to the New Brunswick mainland. The Islanders for a
Better Tomorrow argued for the economic benefits of building such
a bridge, in terms of both trade and tourism. Friends of the Island felt
their lifestyles were under threat and said that not enough research
had been done (or indeed could ever be done) to justify the expense.
They even tried a legal blockade, but lost when a judge ruled the
environmental assessment was adequate. Finally, it came down to a
vote in which Islanders were asked if they were in favour of replacing the ferries with an unspecified alternative. In January 1988, a
resounding 59.4 percent voted yes to the fixed link. Four years and

one billion dollars later, the 12.9-kilometre Confederation Bridge opened for traffic.

Many years later, I found myself in a car about to make this remarkable crossing. It was summer, so the fact that this is the world's longest bridge over ice-covered water didn't impress me. Nor did the pricey round-trip toll, although if there's one bridge that doesn't give you much of an option, this is it (ferry service was discontinued when the bridge opened). Once I had passed the toll on the East Bridge Approach, the fact that I was on an engineering marvel that once employed over five thousand people and boosted the province's GDP during construction by 5 percent was kind of lost on me as well. What impressed me deeply was my car cruising at eighty kilometres per hour, surrounded on either side by the cold, dark waters of the Atlantic. The architects had thoughtfully curved the bridge to ensure distracted drivers like myself would pay attention to the road, and not launch off the bridge to add motor vehicles to the marine life below. The highest curve—known as the Navigation Span—is 60 metres above seawater, which is ample height for cruise ships and tankers to pass underneath, between piers spaced 250 metres apart. For those more nervous than myself, rest easy: there are 22 surveillance cameras, 7,000 drain ports, emergency alarms, strict speed limits and a surface designed to minimize water spray. The bridge was built to last one hundred years, by which time we should be making the crossing in flying cars anyway.

Confederation Bridge is more than just a homegrown mega-industrial project, full of impressive numbers and statistics that hopefully kept you entertained. It's an umbilical cord of national pride, a symbol of democracy, and a fast, efficient way to get to a truly lovely destination.

**START HERE:** canadianbucketlist.com/confederation

# HARVEST SEA PLANTS

Writing in a pirate voice is not the same as speaking in a pirate voice, but I'm going to give it a shot anyway: "Yargh! The sea holds a rich bounty of deliciousness, yargh!"

I was hoping the wonderfully named Gilbert and Goldie Gillis would also speak in pirate, since they comb the nearby beaches for buried treasure, albeit treasure of a different sort. They greet me at their B&B, which, like many houses in P.E.I., is surrounded by lawns so immaculate one could relocate the courts of Wimbledon here. The couple are so sweet and earnest I want them to adopt me. Together they have lived here much of their lives, married in the shadow of the same Point Prim lighthouse that Gilbert's grandfather once kept, the oldest lighthouse in the province.

Get to the treasure, yargh!

## Quick Guide to Edible Sea Plants

**Dulse** Soft and chewy, distinctive taste and colour, requires no soaking or cooking, great in soups and sandwiches.

**Irish moss** Bushy red plant, traditionally boiled to release carrageen, a natural gelling agent used as a thickener in food and cosmetics.

**Sea lettuce** Leafy, dark green with distinctive flavour, good raw but can be bitter when cooked. Used in soups and salads. High in protein, iron and fibre.

**Kelp** Grouped in the same family as algae, typically used in Japanese or Chinese cooking to flavour stews and soups, or served as a pickled garnish. ➤

The Gillises have been harvesting seaweed and crafting seaweed dishes for generations, an art and hobby they now share through a program called Seaweed Secrets.

"We want to introduce people to the medicinal and nutritional value of all living sea plants," explains Gilbert, and proceeds to do so. We hop in his pickup truck and head over to beautiful Point Prim, the calm sea sparkling in the sun. It's low tide, so we scamper onto some rocks to see what's stacked on the ocean shelves. Irish moss, dulse, kelp, sea lettuce — it looks like rotten veggies, the stuff you avoid when swimming, or the gunk that might get tangled in your onboard motor. Gilbert begs to differ.

"Look at this Irish moss. It has carrageenan, which is used like gelatin," he says, picking it off a rock. The moss is rich in nutrients and can be used in all sorts of dishes. Gilbert gets excited when he spots a plant called devil's shoelace. When it dries out, it can be added to salad to add a taste not unlike crispy bacon. Then there's gracilaria, a sea plant that grows on the shells of oysters and mussels. Goldie is famous for her Wild Island Teriyaki Pickled Seaweed made from the stuff.

Back at the B&B, the Gillises have assembled an edible Sea Plant Museum in their garden barn with the aid of a botanist. I tuck into a

bag of dried sea lettuce, an alga that is high in protein, fibre, vitamins and minerals. It tastes like mouldy salt. Although sea lettuce is widely eaten around the world, traditional lettuce can feel safe for now; but then again, typical lettuce might not give you that Gillis gleam. Goldie looks radiant, her skin smooth and her hair full of body, all attributed to homemade cosmetics made of, what else, sea plants.

In the kitchen, Goldie's got some seaweed vegetable soup on the stove. None of the plants really look edible until they reach her kitchen. She gives some moss a thorough rinse and puts it in a blender. It's then whisked with sugar and vanilla, poured into a base of breadcrumbs and baked. Topped with fresh cream and home-grown rhubarb confit, the result is a custard-like tart that's as good as any I've ever tasted. Not bad for the stuff I was walking on just a couple of hours ago on the beach. We toast the sunset with a sea-plant buffet (damn, those are some fine pickles) and the fact that every day edible treasures are being washed up on the beach. Yargh to that!

**START HERE:** canadianbucketlist.com/seaplants

# MEET ANNE OF GREEN GABLES

Long, long, long before *Harry Potter* and *Twilight*, another epic children's book series crossed into the mainstream to become an international publishing phenomenon. It followed the life and misadventures of a red-headed, freckled orphan with sparkling green eyes. Set among the rolling green fields and small-town shenanigans of Prince Edward Island, Lucy Maud Montgomery's *Anne of Green Gables*, and the eight sequels that followed, immersed readers in the daily lives of early twentieth-century P.E.I. citizens. Written over a period of nearly fifteen years, the books followed Anne's evolution from scrappy kid to educated young lady to poised and upright citizen, from age eleven to her late fifties. Anne resonated around the world, with over 50 million books sold, numerous accolades for her

## Anne of Japan

Canada's best-known fictional character still resonates around the world, which is why, growing up in South Africa, I had a prepubescent crush on Megan Follows. But the adventures of the feisty orphan really hit a nerve in Japan, where she is known as *Akage no An*, literally "Anne of the Red Hair." Anne's independence strongly appealed to Japanese girls confined by society, and Prince Edward Island's natural setting appealed to their sense of fantasy. Ever since the books were first translated in the early 1950s, Anne has become a Japanese superstar. You can buy her products, watch her on TV and visit a Green Gables theme park in Ashibetsu City, Hokkaido. ➤

author and the distinction of being both a Canadian and a Japanese cultural icon. Montgomery's genius lay not only in the richness of her characters but also in her descriptions of the world in which they operated. Prince Edward Island's allure as a destination is assured with anyone who reads *Anne of Green Gables*, including school kids in Japan who continue to do so. I too was required to visit the fields of Cavendish and Avonlea as a student in South Africa. No surprise, then, that thousands of Canadian and international visitors beeline to the inspiration behind the book, along with a range of attractions honouring the Maritimes' most famous literary hero.

Green Gables Heritage Place is just part of Lucy Maud Montgomery's Cavendish National Historic Site. Visitors can explore the original farmhouse, which belonged to cousins of Montgomery's grandfather, along with the Haunted Woods and Lovers Lane that inspired places of the same names in the books. Green Gables continues to receive around 350,000 visitors a year. In the capital, July to

September sees the annual production of *Anne of Green Gables—The Musical* at the Charlottetown Festival. Adapted from the book, the musical has been running for five decades and is performed at the Confederation Centre of the Arts. A half-hour's drive away you'll find Avonlea: Village of Anne of Green Gables, a historical village that re-creates the life and times of Prince Edward Island in the early 1900s. Character actors and horses and buggies roam about the village, with visitors popping into musical kitchen parties, plays from the books, and Anne-branded chocolate factories and ice-cream parlours. If you get thirsty, grab a bottle of official Anne-branded raspberry cordial, her much-loved bright red drink.

Yes, enterprising Anne, in the form of the Anne of Green Gables Licensing Authority Inc., is not one to let a merchandising opportunity pass her by. Neither would P.E.I.'s provincial government, which owns half of the corporation, the other half owned by Montgomery's descendants. Hence the trove of Anne-branded merchandise available at the Anne of Green Gables Store, eagerly snapped up by Japanese tourists. For reasons I've been unable to dig up, the Japanese love *Anne* as much as *Alice in Wonderland*, which is why you'll probably see Japanese tourists hanging about the site of Lucy Maud Montgomery's Cavendish home, some of them in full costume.

If you don't know *Anne of Green Gables*, or have no interest in the antics of conservative, religious Maritime society, you're free to swap this item for something like, say, a visit to the sweeping Greenwich Dunes in Prince Edward Island National Park. This rare coastal dune system and its adjacent wetlands have beautiful walking trails, and a long white wooden boardwalk that glows with life at sunset. But when it comes to realizing a fantasy world, kudos to P.E.I.'s Anne attractions for living up to our imaginations.

**START HERE:** canadianbucketlist.com/gables

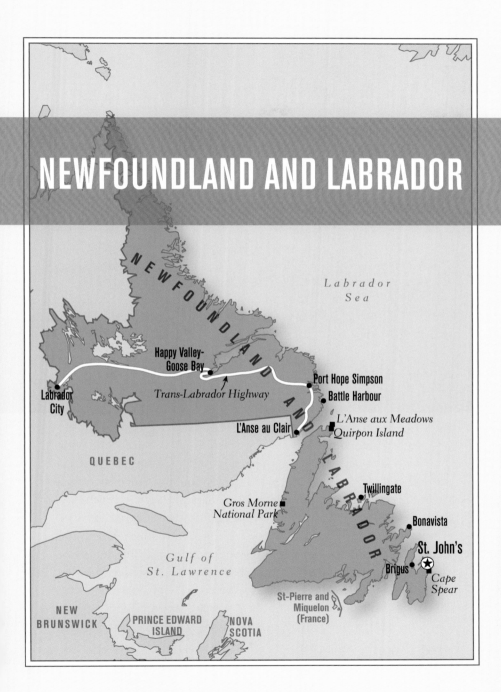

# NEWFOUNDLAND AND LABRADOR

*Labrador Sea*

NEWFOUNDLAND AND LABRADOR

Happy Valley-
Goose Bay

*Trans-Labrador Highway*

Port Hope Simpson

Battle Harbour

Labrador
City

*L'Anse aux Meadows*
*Quirpon Island*

L'Anse au Clair

QUEBEC

Twillingate

*Gros Morne*
*National Park*

Bonavista

St. John's

*Gulf of*
*St. Lawrence*

Brigus

*Cape*
*Spear*

NEW
BRUNSWICK

PRINCE EDWARD
ISLAND

NOVA
SCOTIA

St-Pierre and
Miquelon
(France)

# WATCH THE SUN RISE ON A CONTINENT

Having arrived late the previous evening in St. John's, and with just four pitiful hours of sleep, I awake with a fool's determination to witness the first sunrise in North America. Just twenty-five minutes' drive away from my hotel is Cape Spear, the most easterly point in Canada and, notwithstanding the technicalities of Greenland, the most easterly point of North America. When you have but one morning in St. John's, you have to make it count.

Sunrises are more glorious than sunsets, because you have to work much harder to witness them. No "relax with a glass of wine" moments here, but just as sunsets seal the day, early morning egg-yolk sunrises bring with them the promise of unlimited potential. Excited

# Wind, Rain and Fog

Don't be too upset if your sunset is also draped in fog. With 121 foggy days a year, St. John's is Canada's foggiest city, not to mention the windiest. Take comfort that the wind blows away the fog (along with the occasional household pet). ➤

by this thought, I pull back the curtains at the Murray Premises to see fog so thick you could float a sumo wrestler on it. St. John's is famous for this atmospheric fog, which is great if your life is a film noir mystery but rather inconvenient for sunrise hunters.

Fortified with strong coffee and hope, I hop in the car and direct the GPS towards Cape Spear. The roads at this time of day are desolate. Lonely metal clangs on the big fishing ships along Marine Drive. I follow directions to Water Street and turn left onto Blackhead Road as the car's headlights reflect back at me in the fog. There's a dirty light in the air, as if the sun is feeling ill and doesn't want to get out of bed. The car passes wooden houses, dispersed farther and farther apart, and just as I begin to relax into the ambience of driving inside a cloud, I catch a movement in the trees up ahead. A large moose jumps out in front of me, causing me to brake hard and wake up everyone within miles with a panicked thumping on my horn. Seriously, Moose, you've got the whole province to roam about in, why throw the tourist a surprise party at dawn?

I'd been warned about moose on the roads in Newfoundland, which appear to toy with cars on purpose, like spiteful teenagers

annoying authority. The moose vanishes into the brush, leaving me a shot of early morning adrenalin more powerful than any espresso. Minutes later I arrive at the Cape Spear National Historic Site, the parking lot deserted. Clearly, I'm the only person optimistic enough to believe in a foggy sunrise. The wind is howling, the air is wet, I'm cursing luck, weather and moose, when I stop dead in my tracks. The full power of the North Atlantic, crashing into the rocks of a major continent, can have that effect.

Punishing waves as high as buildings smash into the coast, as I gaze upon nature's never-ending battle of unstoppable fluid meeting immovable solid. Feeling vulnerable and puny, I notice a warning sign, flattened on the ground up ahead. Walking along the coast, wisely sticking to the trails, I listen to the waves, feeling the atmosphere. There are no icebergs and whales this morning. No, on this morning it's just the Atlantic—the mightiest of all oceans—and one humbled writer, greeting her waves before anyone else on an entire continent. An experience well worth getting up in the morning for.

**START HERE:** canadianbucketlist.com/capespear

# MAKE AN ICEBERG COCKTAIL

More than just the proverbial tip of an overused metaphor, let us salute the iceberg. Sinkers of unsinkable boats, stalking the oceans in search of prey for ironic disasters, icebergs are one of nature's finest works of art—transient, temporary and just terrific in a vodka martini. There's a certain panache in mixing millennia-old pure crystal water melted from a roaming iceberg into any beverage. Take St. John's brewery Quidi Vidi's Iceberg beer. The label on its distinctive blue bottle reads: "Made with pure 25,000-year-old iceberg water." If you can apply freshness to beer, it certainly is one of the freshest beers I've ever tasted. The blue bottle further enhances

ICEBERG
WATER

the feeling you're actually drinking mineral water, until four bottles later you realize you're very drunk.

Thousands of years' worth of heavy, compressed snow break off from glaciers or ice shelves to form icebergs, and Newfoundland's Iceberg Alley is one of the best places in the world to see them—from land, boat or kayak. Spring and early summer are the best viewing season, and so I find myself in the windswept seaside town of Twillingate, where iceberg tourism battles to save its ailing fishing industry. To fortify myself for the adventure ahead, I visit Auk Island Winery, which makes locally sourced wild berry wines. Four of their products are made with iceberg water, and the general manager, Danny Bath, assures me he can taste the difference. Inside their winery, a 6,000-litre tank holds the iceberg water, and if you think that's a lot, you underestimate just how big these ice giants can be. A ship once recorded a 500,000-ton iceberg, while a small 30-ton berg can provide a year's worth of fresh water for half a million people. You do, however, need a government licence to commercially harvest icebergs, more to protect consumers than for environmental reasons. Icebergs therefore don't need to be saved, just avoided should you happen to be captain of, say, a luxury cruise ship. Danny talks

## Real Iceberg Vodka?

Canada produces a popular, world-class vodka made with the water of 10,000-year-old icebergs blended with Ontario sweet corn. Manufactured by the Newfoundland and Labrador Liquor Board, Iceberg vodka has won numerous international awards. The makers claim that iceberg water is seven thousand times purer than tap water, which eliminates the need for water purification. ➤

about the icebergs that visit Twillingate as if they were relatives visiting from Florida. "This one, he was a third of a mile long, I tell you, he was here for five weeks!"

Thirst slaked, I feast on palm-sized fresh mussels at J&J Fishmarket (their fresh seafood platter deserves its own entry on the bucket list) and decide to enlist the help of local skipper Jim Gillard. Since the winds are strong and the rain hard, every operator in town has cancelled their iceberg tours. The friendly folks at the Anchor Inn suggest I call the Skipper, and he agrees to take me out on his seven-metre Seabreeze speedboat named *Galactic Mariner*. To find the Skipper, all I have to do is drive down Gillard Lane and look for a large observatory.

Skipper Jim was born and raised in Twillingate, a former meteorological technician for the navy and lifelong fisherman in these waters. He's also an astronomer with a mind-blowing homemade observatory complete with revolving dome (powered by Ski-Doo rails) and a thirty-centimetre LX200 Schmidt-Cassegrain telescope. Here's a guy with salt water in his blood and his head in the stars.

We don waterproofs and head out into the bay, rain stinging my eyes. Skipper Jim must have eye shields, for he's comfortably in his element. He talks about his navy days, fishing, the oceans, his kids, grandkids, whales and icebergs. Skipper Jim's bucket list is telling: finish the shed, lay down the lobster traps, enjoy the stars. Here's a man who has everything he needs, right where he needs it. It takes about ten minutes before we see our target.

"Ninety percent of the iceberg sits under the water," says the Skipper, with that distinctive Newfoundland accent. Icebergs change every day, calving and cracking, with erosion forming distinctive shapes as the ocean and shores gradually wear them down. Our "guest" today is about twenty metres high, with smooth lines,

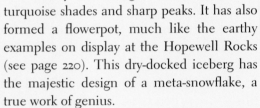

turquoise shades and sharp peaks. It has also formed a flowerpot, much like the earthy examples on display at the Hopewell Rocks (see page 220). This dry-docked iceberg has the majestic design of a meta-snowflake, a true work of genius.

The Skipper keeps his distance. We can hear the ice cracking, which could cause a lower section to roll over and take our boat with it. He pulls up alongside a floating piece of ice and we haul a chunk on board. It is dense, white and concrete heavy, unlike clear normal ice, thanks to the rain that has fallen into cracks. I take a knife and stab the top, the ice shattering into large pieces. The seas might be rough and the rain relentless, but I've come a long way to do this, and by golly you can't let a little weather stand in the way. Not in Canada.

I put the iceberg in a glass and pour some vodka on it. Calving a chunk of iceberg to make a cocktail is something to do before you die, I assure you. The vodka I used: Newfoundland's own Iceberg vodka, made, of course, with authentic iceberg water.

**START HERE:** canadianbucketlist.com/icebergcocktail

# GET THE CONTINENTAL DRIFT

Arriving at the Gros Morne National Park Discovery Centre, I am ushered into a modern theatre to watch an introductory film about the region. There follow sweeping helicopter shots of epic landscapes straight out of *Lord of the Rings*, with attractive couples hiking on the edge of emerald green cliffs. Cut to a scene that could have been shot in the fjords of Norway, with park interpreters and locals explaining in earnest voice-overs how this land has spirit, and once you experience it, that spirit will stay with you forever.

I'm always a little nervous about these introductory videos. They often set the bar too high, especially when I peer outside the window to see the now-familiar fog and rain. Why is the weather always perfect in these videos?

I walk around the centre, reading exhibits, learning about the geological wonderland of eastern Canada's second-largest park, a UNESCO World Heritage Site, where plate tectonics were first

proven as fact. The park is 1,805 square kilometres in size, encompassing large mountains, forests, shoreline, freshwater fjords and bog, and yet I find myself in a small pickle. Despite my name, I'm simply not that into rocks. Tell me that 500 million years ago the earth's plates collided, forcing its mantle to split through its crust, resulting in Gros Morne's unique Tablelands, and all I see is a mountain of stone. Then I meet Cedric and Munju, two of the park's interpreters. We take a short drive to the Tablelands, and stroll along its distinctly barren landscape. Cedric picks up a stone, and his French-Canadian accent drools with excitement.

"Each rock has a story, Robin, and the more we know, the more its story comes out." He begins to explain the basics of Gros Morne's importance in the world of science, its sheer uniqueness in our planet's time and space. Picking up a piece of rust-red serpentinite, he shows me how age-old minerals have been deposited on one side like

the scales of a snake. Much like a battle plan, he uses rocks to demonstrate how the continents are continuously in flux. As he does so, the clouds begin to lift and the Tablelands loom above us in their glory, a moon mountain on earth. There's not much time, so we jump in the car and drive to Trout River, a cliché of a small Newfoundland fishing town.

"It's always worth driving through here," says Munju, "just to say hello to the characters." A man is barbecuing fat sausages inside his smoky garage, rain be damned. Gros Morne surrounds several fishing enclaves, where communities live as they have done for centuries. This is not Disneyland, and these are not re-enactors. The hard reality of the Atlantic fishing industry is on display, unusually located within a national park, and as fascinating to a "far away" like myself as the scenic beauty. Cedric takes us to a viewpoint over Trout River, the wind whipping up whitecaps across a freshwater lake. The ruggedness of the mountains and glacier-cut valleys is something to behold. We drop him off to return to his pregnant wife, and Munju invites me for some wine at her place, overlooking the inlet at Woody Point. She's just returned from Halifax after a seven-year hiatus and can't believe her magnificent view for the summer. Some friends arrive, and we head off to the Loft for tasty moose pie. It becomes clear that Gros Morne is more than just a park, it's a community; and yes, that community definitely has a spirit.

I bid my new friends adieu to make the drive to Rocky Point for the night. Since moose were introduced to the park, they have become quite a handful, especially for motorists. Earlier I had passed a sign on the Trans-Canada Highway that read, rather disturbingly: *660 Moose Collisions*. Around the park I'm advised to watch the ditches and pay attention, especially since I'm driving at dusk, when the moose are especially active. After my close encounter in St. John's (see page 289), there's little doubt that moose through the windshield would not be as delicious as moose in a pastry.

After a week of rain, the sun at last breaks through for a glorious morning. Newfoundland has finally upgraded from a black-and-white TV to full-colour 3-D. It's a perfect day for the park's signature experience, a two-hour boat cruise up the Western Brook Pond. After I enjoy a relaxing half-hour walk over boardwalk and wild bog, the boat floats up this freshwater fjord between towering 600-metre peaks and cascading waterfalls. The natural beauty rightly stuns everyone on board.

Yet it's not the Western Brook, nor the Tablelands, nor the great company in Woody Point I'll remember most. It's stopping off at Broom Point, walking ten minutes on Steve's Trail through a tree tunnel, and emerging to a panoramic view of the aquamarine coast, black mountains and white beach all to myself. Damn it, that promotional film was right: there is a spirit to this place, and I'll never forget it.

**START HERE:** canadianbucketlist.com/grosmorne

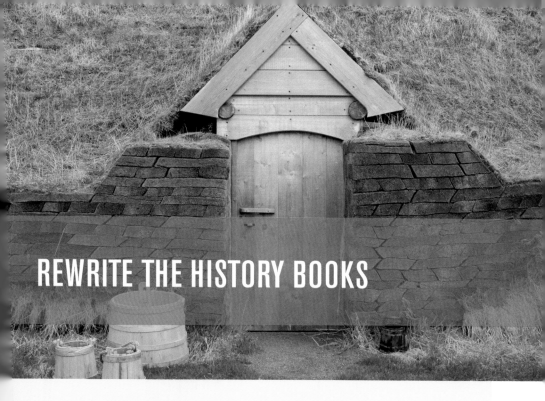

# REWRITE THE HISTORY BOOKS

History is written by the victors, conquering their version of events into hard fact. Yet every once in a while the rug gets pulled out from under us, and we're forced to re-evaluate the past. For example: Every kid in America knows that Christopher Columbus was the first European to discover the New World, in 1492. Well, thanks to a couple of tenacious Norwegians and a little outpost on the northern tip of Newfoundland, the textbooks have been revised.

The Icelandic Sagas, dating back to the tenth and eleventh centuries, told stories of "Vinland," a land of wild grapes, located in the west beyond Iceland and Greenland. The sagas told how Vinland was visited and settled by Vikings, although there was never any proof to back this up. Some theories suggest that, prior to Columbus, the Chinese traded with indigenous Americans, and even that Irish seamen traded on the American coast. A lack

of physical evidence sinks as many theories as the Atlantic sinks boats. The fact that there exists a Central and South American demigod who sailed in from the ocean—tall, white, red-headed and -bearded—certainly suggests European influence in the Americas in ages past. Yet without proof, the historical record of Columbus held true.

In the 1960s, Norwegian adventurer Helge Ingstad and his archaeologist wife Anne Stine Ingstad combed the eastern coast of North America searching for physical evidence of Norse settlement. After many red herrings along a coast rich with cod, they happened upon a small, isolated fishing community called L'Anse aux Meadows. When they described to locals what they were looking for, they were surprised to be led to a series of raised mounds. The locals had attributed them to indigenous people, and the kids who played on them called

them the Indian Camps. Over the next eight years, the Ingstads' excavations uncovered undeniable proof that this was in fact a Norse settlement dating back to CE 1,000—almost five hundred years before Columbus. Working in often brutal weather conditions, they discovered eight complete house sites and the remains of a ninth. Parks Canada took over in the 1970s, and when UNESCO awarded

its first World Heritage Site to Canada in 1978, the archaeological and historical significance of L'Anse aux Meadows won the day.

"Ya know, you definitely have some Viking in ya," says the colourful site interpreter, Clayton Colborne. (My blue eyes and red-tinged beard certainly suggest some interesting breeding in my European Jewish heritage.) Clayton was born and raised in the tiny community of L'Anse aux Meadows (population 25) and used to play on the archaeological site as a kid. Today, his bearded, bright-eyed face adorns the Parks Canada pamphlet inside their modern Visitor Centre.

It's a grey, foggy day, but the drive here from Gros Morne National Park was pretty enough, dotted with fishing communities. The landscape looks like tundra, but Clayton tells me that's only because all the trees close to the road have been cut down. Homes still need a good supply of wood to make it through the long hard winter, and the nearest tree usually does the trick. Despite the solid tourism traffic, Clayton reckons the actual town of L'Anse aux Meadows—dating back to the mid-nineteenth century, when the French ruled the shoreline—will probably disappear. All the young folk have moved on.

After learning about Norse migration and other information from the Visitor Centre's exhibits, we walk along a wooden boardwalk into the field, passing beneath a striking sculpture called *The Meeting of Two Worlds*. "Full circle, ya know," explains Clayton. "When the Norse arrived and interacted with the locals, it was the first time two branches of humanity met in 100,000 years!"

All that remains of the excavations themselves are mounds, grassed over like burial plots. The Ingstads discovered many artifacts

# Was L'Anse aux Meadows Vinland?

The latest archaeological evidence suggests that Vikings travelled south from L'Anse aux Meadows to the St. Lawrence River and into New Brunswick. Vinland, according to the Norse saga, was a country where wild grapes flourished, and New Brunswick is the northern limit for such grape varieties. Nobody knows why the Norse returned to their shipping base at L'Anse aux Meadows, packed up and sailed away to Greenland, never to return. ➤

confirming Norse settlement, including a bone knitting needle, a bronze fastening pin and nails made of a type of iron common in the British Isles. Farther along, Parks Canada has reconstructed a Norse hall, hut and house out of sod, as they would have looked one thousand years ago. A re-enactor shares tales around a fire inside, and it isn't hard to imagine the cold, brutal conditions these early settlers had to endure. Perhaps this explains why the settlement was abandoned after a decade's use, the houses burned down. The Norse left, never to return. Perhaps this was only a way station en route to a larger, yet-to-be-discovered community, the Vinland so named because of the wild grapes that grew there. Perhaps it was abandoned because of a hostile relationship with the Natives, since we can agree Vikings were not the most peace-loving of people.

It's a mystery that remains to be solved. In any event, the only known evidence of European settlement in North America aged into obscurity until a Spaniard arrived hundreds of years later and reintroduced Europe to the "New World." In addition to experiencing the beauty of a stark landscape, and my new understanding of life from another millennia, I depart L'Anse aux Meadows enriched with Clayton's stories, and the satisfying feeling that a tiny Canadian village has proudly rewritten North American history.

**START HERE:** canadianbucketlist.com/lanse

# SLEEP IN A LIGHTHOUSE

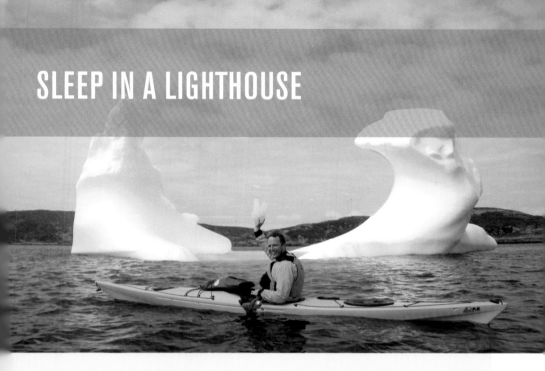

Paddling along the shoreline, Ed English gives me a lesson about Atlantic storms. "I went over to the west coast and watched a storm blow in from the Pacific. They told me it was pretty bad, an eight or nine. Well, we kayak in those kind of waves."

Clearly, Ed is not your average hotelier, and his four-star Quirpon Lighthouse Inn is not your average hotel. Built in 1922 on the northernmost tip of Newfoundland, the lighthouse overlooks a natural passageway that creates a feeding ground for marine life. Migrating roughly three thousand kilometres south from Greenland, they're joined by floating hills of solid ice. This is the start of the province's Iceberg Alley, and one of the best places to see these natural marvels drifting on their slow, melting death march.

It's early June—peak iceberg season—as our kayaks skirt the seven-kilometre-long Quirpon Island. Ed bought the lighthouse in 1998, sight unseen, when it was put up for tender by the government.

Despite wild weather and other challenges, he's turned it into a hotel that sleeps twenty-five guests in eleven rooms, from May to October. Quirpon (pronounced *kar-poon*) has since received rave reviews, especially in international media. "Right now there's a couple from France, Japan, the U.S. . . . Sometimes I don't see Canadian guests until mid-July."

Seagulls are flying above us as the sun tiptoes into view from behind the clouds. We round another corner along the coast and there it is: a single dry-docked iceberg, boxed into the coast like a Viking helmet trapped at the end of a bowling alley. Its two icy peaks tower over us, the middle eroded to reflect water in a bright shade of blue. This mountain of compacted ice looks supernaturally out of place, ten thousand years of frozen water so pure that there's simply no trace of contaminants.

"Keep your distance, Robin. Towers like that crack off all the time, and besides the wave, you don't know how huge this is beneath us."

Icebergs come in all shapes and sizes—tabular, domed, pinnacled, wedged, dry-docked and blocky—and watching them evolve from day to day is part of the fun. Yet Ed advises me never to turn my back on the ice, shape-shifting as it melts and smashes its way to oblivion on the rocks below. Kayakers should face forward, just in case.

We circle a couple of times, picking up some "bergie bits," small chunks floating in the water. My hands are numb from the cold, so we turn back to the harbour, taking advantage of the favourable wind and current.

Out of our wetsuits, we hop aboard the hotel's Zodiac to see if we can spot some whales. It's still early season, so it's unlikely, but it will give me a better look at the lighthouse from the sea, along with pairs of puffins clumsily flapping about us. It's calm as a lap pool when we leave, but within minutes we're cresting over three-metre swells. The water is choppy above the Labrador Current, the cold ocean current that flows south from the Arctic. With the icebergs come the whales—humpbacks, orcas and other species. The bergs herd the fish into the island's coast, allowing guests to watch whales feed literally right below their feet.

Quirpon Island is rocky, mossy and barren, the lighthouse exposed like a palace guard defending the coast from attacking storms. When storms arrive, guests huddle up in excitement in the dining house, perhaps with hot chocolate and some bakeapple pie. Lighthouses are built to survive hurricane-force gales and monster waves, but the inn's location does present some challenges. Just last week, the wooden dock was smashed against the shore and is currently being repaired. As Ed points out the heliport, the Zodiac hits a swell and tilts upwards at a 45-degree angle. We both pretend not to notice.

It's too early in the season and the wind is picking up, so he gratefully turns the Zodiac back to the small, protected harbour. Jacques Cartier and James Cook charted these very waters, and just up the road is L'Anse aux Meadows, where the continent's first visitors settled. With its history, wildlife and adventure, Quirpon Island provides welcome shelter in the darkest of storms.

**START HERE:** canadianbucketlist.com/quirpon

# GET SCREECHED IN

When Newfoundlanders heard I would be visiting the province for the first time, they didn't ask me if I would explore Gros Morne or track icebergs. They wanted to know if I would be getting screeched in. The fact that this tradition was born out of the St. John's bars on George Street, ready to charge you twelve bucks for the ceremony and certificate, is beside the point. To become an honorary Newfoundlander (not a Newfie, for that term is derogatory, unless you're a Newfie, in which case it's not), one must get screeched in.

Within a half-hour of my arrival in St. John's, I am at Trapper John's, a block from my hotel, just in time for the barkeep to begin

## Deed I Is!

Since I assume you'll be "spirited" long before you decide it's a good idea to kiss a puffin's arse, practise the following line to endear yourself to your Newfoundland hosts.

**When they ask you:** "Is ye an honorary Newfoundlander?"

**Reply, with gusto:** "Deed I is me ol' cock, and long may your big jib draw!" ➤

the ceremony. Christian's, another bar in a city that likes its possessive apostrophes, apparently has a more authentic ritual, but they don't do it on Mondays, and this is Monday night. Thus I enter a mostly empty Trapper John's, where a couple from the U.K. and a student's mom are signed up for the evening's Screeching. To get screeched in, one must listen to the barkeep's bluster, drink a shot of screech and then kiss a cod on the mouth—or, in the case of Trapper John's, the behind of a fluffy toy puffin. The screech in question is a type of cheap rum that hearkens back to days of yore when the same barrel might carry both rum and molasses. The sediment that remained would be fermented and mixed with grain alcohol to create a drink designed to blind a telescope. *Screech* was a term used for any moonshine, but it is now marketed as rum and consumed with great pride by locals—and by honorary locals, for that matter. It is so named because of the sound one makes after consuming it, or the sound in the flap of the sails on a boat, or whatever you're told by the local who will claim to know these things.

We line up at the bar and the bartender begins his story, which I struggle to understand. It is my first real exposure to the distinctive Newfoundland accent, which rolls like an English barrel, made of

Canadian wood, down a Scottish hill. Something about the origins of the rum, aye aye this, ya ya that. We are then asked the following question: "Is ye an honorary Newfoundlander?" To which we must reply, with enthusiasm: "Deed I is me ol' cock, and long may your big jib draw!"

I shoot back the drink expecting a harsh burn down my throat, and am relieved to find it absent. Back in my university days, I indulged in Stroh rum, which at the time was 80 percent alcohol and could strip the innocence off a club of Girl Scouts. I've also had the misfortune to shoot straight absinthe in Denmark, raki in Albania and 125-year-old moonshine in Georgia. Screech, by comparison, is palatable.

The toy puffin, representative of the province's official bird, has seen many lips, which the bartender goes to great pains to remind us. At this point I tell him about the far more intimidating Sour Toe Cocktail (see page 320), which kinda punches a hole in his sails. He must hate travel writers. Still, I gamely kiss the butt of the fluffy puffin, receive a certificate, and that is that. A highlight of Newfoundland it was not, but at least I can tell Newfoundlanders that, yes, I have been screeched in. Despite the potential for hokiness, every province should have an honorary ritual for visitors. Undeniably, it makes you feel welcome.

**START HERE:** canadianbucketlist.com/screech

# DRIVE THE TRANS-LABRADOR HIGHWAY

Cartwright 373
Port Hope Simpson 392
L'Anse-au-Loup 579

"Escaping it all" is an expression many of us can relate to. It implies that we're locked away in a prison, behind restrictive high walls we have somehow constructed ourselves. Escape also denotes serious effort, an effort that is rewarded with invigorated freedom. Still, can this explain why anyone would drive 1,185 kilometres in almost complete isolation on potholed gravel roads renowned for shredding the very soul of an automobile?

The handy *Trans-Labrador Highway Guide*, provided by Labrador's Economic Development Board, has the answer on its front page: "For the adventure of driving through one of the last frontiers in North America. It is on our bucket list as the ultimate road trip." The TLH is the only road that crosses Canada's vast eastern mainland. The province was once known simply as Newfoundland, until Labrador distinguished itself in 2001 with a three-letter bridge. And rightly so: Labrador is as large as Japan! It also has just over 26,000 inhabitants, as opposed to Japan's 128 million. That's a lot of space, a remoteness that calls out to drivers from around the world,

driving modern cars but seeking old-world challenges. One must be resourceful, as capable of dealing with mechanical faults as with persistent bloodsucking insects, bone-soaking rain and moose hell-bent on auto-suicide.

To reach the TLH, you must either drive north from Baie-Comeau, Quebec, or cross the Strait of Belle Isle by ferry from Newfoundland. Either way, you'll be leaving your cellphone behind and relying on the kindness of strangers (which is legendary in these parts), free loaner satellite phones available at hotels and communities staggered hundreds of kilometres apart. "Be sure to pack water, toilet paper and BUG SPRAY for the drive!" says the summer guide, emphasizing the bug spray as opposed to, say, life-sustaining water.

For the most part the road is narrow with soft shoulders, dusty in the sun but sticky with mud in the rain. Passing trucks are known to machine-gun windscreens with sharp rocks and loose gravel. Carrying a spare tire, preferably two, is essential. Portions of the road are, however, being paved, bringing "civilization creep," rued by some locals and visitors, although no doubt appreciated by their vehicles. That being said, reports from American and European drivers describe the road from Happy Valley-Goose Bay towards Port Hope Simpson as invoking pure road-trip nirvana—a meandering marvel of packed gravel where, for four hundred kilometres, you feel like the last great driver on Earth.

## Canada's Top 10 Road Trips

ROUTE 510 S
DRIVER ALERT
NEXT SERVICES
392 km
CHECK FUEL

It's a long, arduous road. One-pump gas stations, campgrounds, B&Bs, simple hotels, restaurants and convenience stores provide refuge in small mining towns. The huge hydroelectric dam near Churchill Falls is a welcome roadside attraction in the interior, while the coastal road offers sweeping views of the Atlantic and the icebergs, whales and seabirds that call it home. The guide suggests a 22-hour total driving time (reflecting the condition of the road), give or take a few hours per day for bad weather, construction stops and wildlife viewing. Incredibly, the highway remains open during the winter. The upside is you won't need a head net and bug jacket every time you venture outdoors. The downside is the frozen, slippery roads and temperatures that can dip to -50°C. Still, expect to encounter large herds of caribou and warm communities living under the glow of the northern lights.

Whatever the season, TLH veterans speak fondly of the pristine landscape, the locals encountered along the way, the fellow travellers enjoying the camaraderie. For allowing us to escape it all and enjoy a true adventure in Canada's eastern frontier, the Trans-Labrador is another road trip that drives itself onto the Great Canadian Bucket List.

START HERE: canadianbucketlist.com/tlh

NEWFOUNDLAND AND LABRADOR ↑

# DISCOVER THE THREE B'S

Newfoundland and Labrador has no shortage of charming fishing towns, with wooden houses brightly painted against lush green cliffs, sweeping views of the Atlantic and, if the commercials are anything to go by, unsupervised red-headed kids running about. While there are many wonderful places to visit, the bucket list focuses on the three Bs: Bonavista, Brigus and Battle Harbour.

Giovanni Caboto was an Italian explorer, sailing his fifty-ton, three-mast ship under a British flag. In 1497, he spotted North America after two months of sailing west on the Atlantic, famously declaring, *"O buena vista!"* Thus began the long history of an important fishing town, which once swelled to twenty thousand souls relying heavily on the Atlantic cod industry. Today, the town and rocky shoreline

# What's with the Pink, White and Green?

You might notice a pink, white and green flag flapping outside houses in St. John's. The Newfoundland tricolour is *not* the official flag of the province. It was created in the 1880s as the flag of a Roman Catholic group in St. John's, drawing on Irish influences, with the pink (or rose) strip possibly protesting against English Protestantism. The flag was controversially taken up by politicians and rabble-rousers, and gained in popularity in a British dominion that once debated whether or not to join Canada. More recently, there was a movement in St. John's to petition for the tricolour to gain official flag status, but a poll suggested the majority of Newfoundlanders were not tickled pink with the idea. ➤

of Bonavista (population 5,000) is a historic landmark, site of John Cabot's first landing (Giovanni has been anglicized, much like my real name, Roberto Esrockavinni). Bonavista is known for its heritage buildings, museums and famously welcoming locals. Wander down Church Road, with its narrow side streets, watch for whales and icebergs from the lighthouse, explore the wharves and piers, learn about the salt fish trade and hop aboard a full-scale replica of the *Matthew*, Cabot's ship that started it all.

Closer to St. John's is Brigus, a traditional English fishing village with a name derived from the word "brickhouse." This should give you some indication of the Scottish/Irish-influenced accent in this part of the world. Brigus dates back to 1612, when the town attracted English, Irish and Welsh settlers. For a small town, it produced many famous Arctic sea captains in its day, such as Captain Bob Bartlett, whose former home is now the Hawthorne Cottage National Historic Site. Along with other Bartlett family heroes—John, Sam, Robert, Arthur, Isaac and William—Brigus captains were the first to reach the North Pole, sailing with Admiral Robert Peary, undertaking miracle rescues and lighting the path for the shipping legacy of the Canadian Maritimes. Other Brigus attractions include the festive annual Blueberry Festival, Landfall's Kent College, year-round performances at St. George's Anglican Church, Ye Olde Stone Barn Museum, and the Tunnel, where early engineers used steel spikes

and gunpowder to blast 24-metre-long holes in solid rock to provide easy access to Abram Bartlett's wharf. You may be in a rush to see Newfoundland, but Brigus wants you to stop, breathe, walk the narrow streets, admire the harbour and chat with the locals.

Getting to Battle Harbour is not quite as easy, but that could be said about getting almost anywhere in Labrador. For two hundred years, Battle Harbour was the salt fish capital of the region, an economic and social centre once known as the capital of Labrador. A government-sponsored relocation program in the 1960s, coupled with the rise of the frozen and fresh fish industries, led to the end of Battle Harbour as a permanent community and the beginning of its restoration as a National Historic District. Buildings, fisheries, churches and century-old houses have been restored to their former glory, creating a remote destination in which to experience the history of the region. Stay in the former homes of fishermen, doctors or policemen, and be entertained at night by seasonal performances and traditional Labradorean hospitality. Battle Harbour may rely on tourists, but not the kind who typically frequent Disneyland. To get there, you'll have to sail on the MV *Iceberg Hunter* across the St. Lewis Inlet from Mary's Harbour, running twice a day.

Three Bs, representing three glimpses into the storied past of Newfoundland and Labrador. Three places to take your time, feel the ocean breeze and turn off the modern world.

**START HERE:** canadianbucketlist.com/threebees

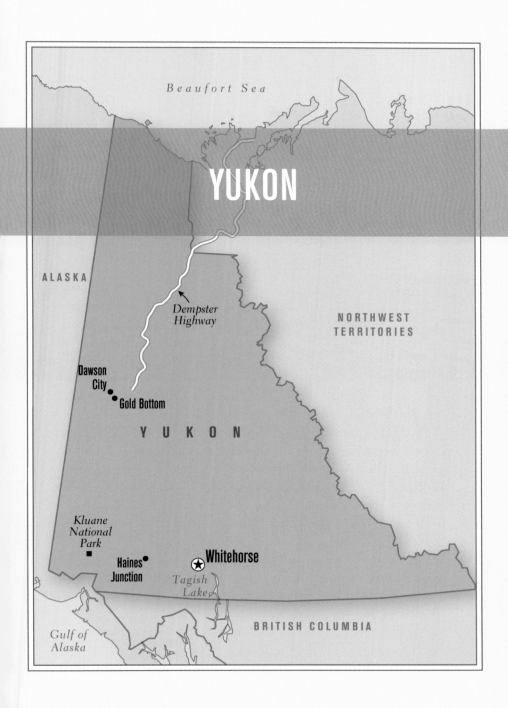

Beaufort Sea

# YUKON

ALASKA

NORTHWEST
TERRITORIES

Dempster
Highway

Dawson
City

Gold Bottom

Y U K O N

Kluane
National
Park

Haines
Junction

Whitehorse

Tagish
Lake

Gulf of
Alaska

BRITISH COLUMBIA

# DOGSLED WITH A LEGEND

Whitehorse is south of the Arctic Circle, so there is no Arctic night in late November. Still, the Yukon's capital gets light around nine a.m., dark around three p.m., and in between it's too damn cold to be outdoors anyway—unless you've arrived to go dog-sledding, in which case you'll want to drive twenty minutes outside of town to Frank Turner's Muktuk Kennels.

Although he's originally from Toronto, Frank is a venerable dog-sledding legend in the Yukon. He's the only man to have competed in twenty-three consecutive Yukon Quests, known as the "toughest race on earth," routinely placing in the top six, winning it once, and twice receiving the Vets Choice Award for his exceptional treatment of his dogs. He's the only Canadian-born person to have won the race in three decades, and he held the fastest-time record for over a decade. Joining him for an afternoon dogsled is like having a pond hockey lesson with Wayne Gretzky.

As a dogsledding virgin, I was intrigued, concerned and ignorant about the concept of harnessing dogs to pull a heavy sled across frozen tundra. When you grow up with apartment dogs, it's difficult to believe that certain breeds thrive in such extreme environments. It instantly became clear that Frank's 125 dogs are treated with as much respect as, if not more than, any suburban poodle—fed the latest naturopathic food, regularly exercised and treasured like members of a large, mostly canine family. Each Muktuk dog is lovingly named, given a kennel and cared for by the staff of international volunteers.

The dogs greet me with enthusiastic howls when I arrive, shaking off the cold, a low sun still pinking up the sky. The dogs circle their kennels amidst a cacophony of barking, making for an exciting welcome. Puppies race excitedly in a large, enclosed, wooden hamster wheel. Muktuk doesn't breed and sell its dogs, and they're made up of various crosses between husky, malamute, wolf, Labrador and tough-as-bones Yukon mutt. Turner frequently takes in local dogs that are in need of a better home, and runs an adoption program for retired sled dogs, but you have to prove yourself a worthy owner first. I inquire how an outdoor sled dog fits into an indoor family home. "Go ahead and ask one," he tells me.

Each dog has its name proudly stencilled on its individual green kennel. I hesitantly approach a husky named Falcon, and am surprised to find him as friendly and good-natured as a golden retriever. Most of them are. In fact, they are far from being savage beasts, and Turner is trained to slog through hardship. Turner is confident any one of his dogs would make a loyal, well-trained pet, and treats them as such.

It's time to suit up in layers of provided warm gear, including military-style snow boots to keep my feet warm and dry. We're heading out to a frozen river in the Takhini Valley, and I'm commandeered into the team, collecting dogs from their kennels and carrying them to a customized trailer. Turner drops nuggets of advice as we do so. "It's all about teamwork. People think it's the rider in control, but it's all about the dogs. They need to trust you. If the dogs aren't happy, you're not going anywhere." It becomes apparent that despite the spectacular surroundings and the thrill of the sport, dogsledding is more about relationships than anything else.

After a short drive, we arrive at a frozen lake. My eyes become moist, which is not ideal when the temperature is below -30°C. Once unloaded, the dogs eagerly anticipate their run. Frank gives me a brief lesson in dogsledding mechanics: yell "Gee!" for right, "Haa!" for left and "Whoa whoa!" to stop. Sleds have brakes and foot-pads to control speed. I have six dogs harnessed to my sled, and as the saying goes, unless you're the lead dog, the view is all the same.

With a whiplash jerk, the dogs set off into the snow, relishing this opportunity to release their pent-up energy. Dog power is not horsepower. Without my control, my team would run themselves senseless, exhausting their energy and possibly injuring themselves. Frank has to constantly remind me to apply the brake, to find the rhythm and flow. Once I do, the true nature of dogsledding—team-work—becomes as clear as the ice crystals clinging to the trees. Watching the effort of each dog, muscles pounding beneath thick fur, how their individual personalities influence their speed and endurance, makes me appreciate how little effort I need to expend to glide across the lake. With the dogs in their groove, I can look up and truly absorb the jaw-dropping scenery around me.

We spend a couple of hours racing along the snow and ice, and I get accustomed to my team, their personalities, their strengths. Val is a firecracker, Livingston a loyal, steadying force. Incredibly, a healthy Quest pack can travel around 160 kilometres a day, at a speed of around 15 to 20 kph, depending on conditions. I imagine

## ON THE BUCKET LIST: Frank Turner

I'd love to go to Newfoundland. My image is that it's beautiful, with small communities I can identify with, full of colourful characters. There are some similarities with the Yukon in terms of distance, and I imagine we'd both be considered different from the mainstream.

Frank Turner
Owner, Muktuk Kennels
Yukon Quest Winner

Frank's race experiences, wrapped up freezing in the sled as temperatures drop to as low as -70°C, under the bright stars and glowing northern lights. He trains hard all year to prepare his body for the sleep-deprived physical pounding of the Quest. The unprepared leader puts the team at risk, and the team comes first.

Before the sun sets, we return to the trailers, feed the dogs and crack out the hot chocolate and thermal warmers, elatedly retreating to Muktuk before the dark afternoon shadows flash-freeze our bones. With a new appreciation for life in the North, you'll be hard pressed to find happier animals—people or dogs—than on a dogsled adventure.

**START HERE:** canadianbucketlist.com/dogsled

↑

YUKON

# SWALLOW THE SOUR TOE COCKTAIL

When you're constantly dealing with different cultures, it's easy to put your foot in it. A friend had told me that a bar in Dawson City serves the most disgusting drink in the world, and I told him he was one stick short of a kebab. Live baby mice in China, boiled spiders in Cambodia, fertilized duck eggs in the Philippines—you generally have to head east to find the tattered fringes of exotic world cuisine; and besides, everyone knows that Canada's Beaver Tails are not made of real beavers. I had belittled my friend because this "Sour Toe Cocktail" could not possibly be real, with its special ingredient found nowhere on earth. Actually, it's available everywhere on earth—it's just very, very odd.

"I'm telling you," he told me, "they drop a severed human toe into a drink."

Really, I just didn't think Canada had it in her.

Dawson City boomed as a major centre of the short-lived Klondike gold rush. Between 1896 and 1898, the population swelled to 40,000,

making it the largest city north of San Francisco. By 1902, the gold had dried up, along with dreams of fame and fortune. Dawson City quickly turned into a small outpost with sinking wooden storefronts, population 1,300. In 1973, a local eccentric wanted to capitalize on the summer tourist traffic heading to the Top of the World Highway. Captain Dick, as he is known, had recently found a severed toe in an old log cabin. Now, when the temperature plummets to -55°C, hard men are known to do strange things, including, as poet Robert Service famously suggested, setting themselves on fire. Captain Dick dropped the shrivelled toe into a glass of champagne and called it the Sour Toe Cocktail. He started a club, crowning himself the Toe Captain. To join it, all you had to do was order the drink and let the toe touch your lips. Word caught on; a legend was born.

Four decades later, I walk into the Downtown Hotel, chilled to my bones. It's winter, and the icy streets of Dawson are deserted. Captain Al, tonight's Toe Captain, is awaiting new customers at the bar. Behind the counter sits the eighth reincarnation of the original toe, preserved in a jar of salt. Over the years, toes have been stolen, lost and, in some unfortunate cases, swallowed. The current toe is a sickeningly big appendage donated by an American who lost it in a lawn-mower accident. Every customer gets the same toe. I pay five dollars for the tumbler of Yukon Gold (long since replacing the more expensive champagne) and five dollars to join the club. There's no doubting the authenticity of the digit: yellowed and pickled by the

YUKON ↑

321

# The World's Grossest Foods

If the Sour Toe Cocktail makes you queasy, consider some of these treats found around the world:

1. **Fermented Shark** A delightful delicacy known in Iceland as Hákarl. It attacks the nostrils first, and leaves your taste buds for dead. Tastes like: Urine cake.

2. **Deep-fried Tarantula** Take a bite out of these popular Cambodian roadside snacks, and let the inky spider juice roll down your chin. Tastes like: Hairy bitterness.

3. **Escamoles** In Mexico, consider spiced ant larvae, collected from the agave plant, served in a taco. Tastes like: Buttery cottage cheese.

4. **Balut** Why argue which came first when you can have the egg and bird together? Filipinos wash down this fertilized duck egg with beer. Tastes like: Crunchy egg.

5. **Three Squeak Dish** This obscure Chinese dish arrives with three pink, live baby mice. The first squeak is when you pick them up with chopsticks. The second when you dip them in soy sauce, The third . . . Tastes like: Mickey Mouse's nightmare. ➤

salt, a broken nail crests the top. My stomach lurches, as Captain Al launches into a well-rehearsed ritual:

"Drink it fast or drink it slow, but either way, your lips must touch this gnarly-looking toe!"

I arch my neck, taste the sweet bourbon and indulge in this ceremony of cocktail cannibalism. Not too bad. Perhaps a little too much toe jam on the high notes.

Captain Al tells me the club has over forty thousand members. Anyone of drinking age can join, and since the Downtown Hotel is not responsible for what you put in your drink after it's purchased, the health authorities are powerless to do much about it. Tourists now visit Dawson City specifically to go toe to toe with this challenging libation, much as Captain Dick anticipated. With my name logged in a book, I receive a card confirming membership in the Sour Toe Cocktail Club. I immediately email my friend to apologize for having dismissed his story about a drink with a dismembered human appendage. In my defence, it had been one tough story to swallow, but travel writers should know better than to step on anybody's toes.

**START HERE:** canadianbucketlist.com/sourtoe

# DRIVE THE DEMPSTER HIGHWAY

There are road trips, and then there are adventures. The Dempster Highway, a ghost road built for an oil and gas boom that never came, certainly belongs in the latter category. It begins forty kilometres east of Dawson City and runs north on a narrow gravel strip for some 750 kilometres before eventually reaching Inuvik, in the Northwest Territories. By this stage, most motorists have turned back, happy to have reached the Arctic Circle, just over 400 kilometres into the journey. Considering that many will already have driven 500 kilometres from Whitehorse just to get to the starting junction, we'll forgive them.

YUKON

## The World's Smallest Desert

Crossing the Yukon by car, you might want to pop into the aptly named Carcross, located on the South Klondike Highway between Whitehorse and Alaska's Skagway. At just 642 acres, the nearby Carcross Desert claims to be the world's smallest desert, although geologists prefer to call it the sandy remains of an ancient glacial lake. Either way, the fine grain and terrific views make it ideal for the very desert-like sport of sandboarding. ➤

Decades ago, when the oil trucks abandoned the road, they left a pathway through a land of pristine mountains, valleys, plateaus and tundra. Call it the Serengeti of the North, substitute bears for lions, muskox for wildebeest, caribou for bucks, and wolves for hyenas. You'll also find Dall sheep, wild horses and some two hundred species of birds.

The landscape and wildlife are a perk, but the main priority is getting in and getting out in one piece. This is not the road for just one spare tire. Motorists tell tales of four blowouts in a matter of miles, leaving you stranded as close to the middle of nowhere as you'd ever want to get. Sharp shale shreds tires, and three or even four spares are recommended for the journey. There are no emergency pullouts, and fuel stops can be spaced hundreds of kilometres apart. The name of the highway itself serves as a warning for the unprepared: Corporal Dempster was an RCMP officer who found an RCMP patrol frozen to death after getting lost without a First Nations guide.

Parks Canada has supplied some spartan campgrounds along the way, with no electricity and pit toilets. They're a welcome refuge, but they won't save you from the relentless bugs in summer.

Pitching a tent can be more trouble than it's worth, what with the bears and wolves, so many drivers opt to sleep in their cars. The road unfolds over a landscape that does, however, yield its rewards: epic views of mountains, rivers and valleys; wildlife crossing the road; fireweed exploding at the end of the short summer. The few motels and gas stations cater to passing traffic, pearls of survival on the endless gravel string. Fresh water is trucked in, and accommodation can fill up quickly. Gravel is replaced by thick mud, with dreaded punctures just a speedometer click away. No wonder so many drivers turn back at the Arctic Circle, their adventure quotient filled to the brim.

If you keep going, the mountain roads become even more challenging, aided by weather that threatens visibility and sticky mud waiting like flycatchers for cars. In summer, there are ferry services over several rivers, while winter allows cars to drive directly over the ice, including those braving the legendary ALCAN 5000 Rally race. The final stretch to Inuvik consists of a couple of hundred kilometres of tundra before the highway connects to a paved road. After days of dicey gravel, it feels as if the car is floating on air.

So why is such a gruelling road trip on the National Bucket List? For starters, it's a lifeline through some of the most desolate and remote scenery you'll find anywhere in the world. A personal challenge of skill, perseverance and sense of adventure. Canada's North, and all its creatures, awaits you on a rocky road you'll never forget.

**START HERE:** canadianbucketlist.com/dawson

YUKON ↑

# SKATE ON A CRYSTAL LAKE

Hopefully, you've noticed that the items that make up the Great Canadian Bucket List rely on things that you can actually do, as opposed to fantasy scenarios that are fun to imagine and all but impossible to experience. This is why you will not find the following:

- Watch a dolphin somersault over a harbour seal during an eclipse.
- Star in a big-budget superhero movie filmed in Vancouver.
- Watch the Toronto Maple Leafs hoist the Stanley Cup (ouch!).

When I saw a YouTube clip of a bunch of guys shooting a puck to each other on a mirror-ice lake, surrounded by mountains and with fish swimming beneath them, I had to wonder: can you really do this? Yes, you can. Or, more cleverly, yes, Yukon. Granted, the conditions have to be goldilocks, and this does not happen every year. It has to be early winter, when the temperature drops for weeks, the lakes freeze up, but the snow is yet to fall. Alternatively, snow has fallen but heavy wind has scattered the flakes before they can scratch up the smoothness of the lake surface. Every three years or so you'll find these conditions at one of several lakes not far from Whitehorse: Kluane Lake, in the national park, Fish Lake, Kusawa Lake, and the scene of the video that went viral and dropped jaws around the world, Windy Arm on Tagish Lake. It's part of a chain of lakes that form the headwaters of the Yukon River, framed by dramatic mountains that create a tunnel for the wind to barrel through, hence its name.

Local photographer Peter Maher takes his family out every year searching for this type of magic. He'll arrive at the shore and check the ice. Just ten centimetres will do it, since trucks can drive on fifteen centimetres and thrill-seekers might go out on as little as five. Strong winds keep snow off the ice and the surface as smooth as freshly cut glass. Once you're skating, it's a window that reveals schools of grayling or trout swimming beneath you, or bottom-feeders drifting along the sandy depths. Ice bubbles create beautiful art in the ice, smooth pockets of air suspended like frozen thought balloons. You can skate for miles on this pond hockey rink of dreams, although strong winds might blow you farther than you intended.

## Gather Round, Ye Sourdoughs

You can't just show up in Whitehorse and call yourself a sourdough. The term dates back to the Klondike gold rush, when the name of the hard, fermented bread eaten by locals was bestowed on those who managed to stick around from the freeze of fall to the thaw of spring. Everyone else, well, they were just a bunch of *cheechakos*, a Chinook word for a newcomer. ➤

Peter might have someone drive the car ten kilometres down the road to avoid the family having to skate against the wind, which I'm sure his three kids appreciate. He'll whip out his camera and take some remarkable photos.

Once word gets out, locals start showing up with their skates and sticks. There used to be dozens of people, but with Facebook and YouTube spreading the good news, these days there might be hundreds, not to mention people coming in from farther away. Of course, on a lake that stretches over a hundred kilometres, there's plenty of room for everyone, with games of pond hockey featuring twenty or thirty players, all bundled up, carrying Thermos flasks with hot chocolate (or something stronger), gliding on their reflections in a real-life fantasy.

"This is one of the things that makes being a Canadian so special," says Peter. And while you may not be able to show up and do this every winter, it's special enough, distinctly Canadian enough and real enough to make it onto the bucket list.

**START HERE:** canadianbucketlist.com/windyarm

# PAN FOR GOLD

The Klondike gold rush of 1898 was a boom that could be heard around the world. Although it was short-lived, you can still hear the faint whispers of its allure—the seductive promise of instant wealth—with a visit to Dawson City and a half-hour drive to Gold Bottom. Once a town of five thousand people, Gold Bottom has just five residents these days, all still involved in active gold mining. During the summer months (-40°C weather doesn't draw too many people), you can sign up for a panning tour and sift through real pay dirt, with the bonus of being able to keep whatever you find.

As you slip on your rubber boots and load your 36-centimetre metal pan with rocks and gravel, spare a thought for the hardened prospectors who came before you. When word finally got out about streams of gold discovered up north, some 100,000 people flocked to the Yukon in search of glory. Dawson City, a ramshackle outpost, became the largest Canadian city west of Winnipeg. The boom was such that a single room in Dawson might rent for $100 a month, when a four-bedroom apartment in New York City could be had for only $120. Only 40,000 people accomplished the 400-kilometre journey through the rugged winter landscape. To stake a claim on the Klondike and surrounding rivers, they had to bring everything with them and face months of dirty, back-breaking work. Unfortunately, by the time the majority of prospectors arrived, most of the claims had been staked, the gold extracted, poems written and fortunes already made. It didn't take long for booming Dawson to sink back into the ghost towns of history, its proud salons literally sinking into the permafrost.

Parks Canada and the government came to the rescue in the 1960s, restoring the town as a National Historic Site, preserved for the thousands of tourists who visit each year. People come from around the world for the history, the quirks (see Sour Toe Cocktail, page 320), the scenery, the drives and the boom-time legends. Such as Chris Johansen, a miner on Hunker Creek, who offered one Cecile Marion her weight in gold if she would be his wife—an offer that cost him $25,000 when the 61-kilo beauty agreed.

It was the same Hunker Creek where David Millar is now bent over and facing upriver, explaining how to pan the pay dirt. His family has been operating the Gold Bottom mining camp for over three decades, expanding it with rustic log cabins and daily tours, rain or shine. Calf-deep in the muddy brown water, he fills the pan with water, shaking it gently at first while picking out the big rocks. Dipping the pan at a 45-degree angle, he adds more water, the pan is spun and shaken, the gravel slowly rinsed and discarded. Gold is

## Tips for Panning for Gold

1. Fill your pan halfway to three-quarters of the way to the top with silt. Pick out the bigger rocks, looking for nuggets as you do so.
2. Find a spot where the river flows strongly enough to carry away the silt from your pan. Sit on a log or rock unless you're particularly bendy.
3. Dip your pan in the water, using your fingers to sort the dirt and moss. Heavy gold will sink to the bottom of your submerged pan.
4. Shake the pan while it's submerged, breaking up the silt even more, allowing any gold to sink and silt to rise to the top.
5. Tilt the pan downwards, shaking the pan some more.
6. Submerge the pan again, shaking it up and down and left to right, allowing the river to wash away the lighter material. Tilt occasionally, rinse and repeat. Keep checking to see if any gold has sunk to the bottom.
7. Use tweezers or a wet finger to extract your treasure.
8. Cash it in, and blow it all at the local saloon. ➤

nineteen times heavier than water, so you'll know you've got something when you spot tiny flakes resting at the top of the pan. It's a slow process for first-timers, and you might walk away with anywhere between one and ten flakes.

In the meantime, expect to learn about the entire process, hear about the gold rush, and even see mammoth bones, teeth and tusks that have been discovered by miners digging into the permafrost. There's an eight-centimetre nugget on display in the mine's Gold Lodge, and enough value in the area to keep several mines in profitable operation. As you walk away with a vital keepsake, your hard-won treasures certainly won't be worth much in value, but panning at Gold Bottom, unlike prospecting in the nineteenth century, is all about the experience.

**START HERE:** canadianbucketlist.com/goldpan

YUKON ↑

# FLY OVER KLUANE NATIONAL PARK

About two hours' drive from Whitehorse along the famed Alaska Highway lies the sleepy little town of Haines Junction. There's not a heck of a lot going on, besides hikers and climbers hanging out at the bakery and an impressive new cultural museum celebrating the life and times of the region's Champagne and Aishihik people. The town receives a fair amount of passing traffic made up of RVs, motorbikes and cars making their way north, enjoying hour after hour of snow-capped mountains, valleys and glaciers, as well as the occasional moose or elk. From the road, you simply have no idea what lies beyond those first peaks—the striking and magnificent wilderness encompassed by the 22,000-square-kilometre Kluane National

Park and Reserve. And although you can stop for a hike around the crystal-clear Kathleen Lake, even climbing a nearby peak, there are limits to where your legs can take you.

Which is why I'm sitting in a six-seat Cessna 205 operated by Sifton Air, embarking on a one-hour flightseeing tour. Call me a Robin with a bird's-eye view of the world's largest non-polar ice caps, the continent's tallest mountains and an alien world of rock and ice.

The altimeter wobbles at six thousand metres when we first see the Kaskawulsh Glacier, a massive river of moving ice that S-curves through a chain of mountains, carving out a valley with all the patience in the universe. Eighty-two percent of Kluane's surface area consists of mountain and ice. The scale of this natural beauty even has our pilot reaching for his camera, a man who flies this route daily during the summer tourist season. In the context of endless ice, giant rockfalls and shark-fin granite peaks, our plane feels as small as a gnat, and my adjectives thin as toothpicks. We fly up the glacier, hoping for a glimpse of Mount Logan to the east. Almost six kilometres tall, the largest mountain in Canada also boasts the largest base circumference of any mountain on earth, including the giants found in the Himalayas. The tallest peak on the continent, Mount McKinley, takes up residence farther north, in Alaska, and together with other plus-5,000-metre peaks found in the area, it's clear why climbers have been coming here for decades.

Today, fortunately, is not one for ropes and harnesses, to cling to life by my fingertips. Although the Cessna bounces around in the thermals, rattling and roller-coastering, I've learned that such turbulence presents as much of a problem for planes as small bumps in the road do for cars. Even though it's a crisp summer day, Mount Logan is hidden in the clouds, so we bank left and make our way towards Kluane's most impressive wall of ice, the 70-kilometre-long, 5-kilometre-wide Lowell Glacier. When moist Pacific air collides

## Canada's Highest Mountain

Located within Kluane National Park is Canada's Mount Logan, towering at 5,959 metres. Even if it does take second place to Alaska's Mount McKinley, North America's highest mountain, Logan is still higher than any mountain in Africa, Europe or Oceania. It has the largest base circumference of any non-volcanic mountain on Earth. ➤

with these Arctic air masses, it results in huge amounts of snow, compacted over time into glaciers. Lowell's surges and ice dams have resulted in devastating floods, with local legends recalling whole villages being washed away by tsunamis of mountain water.

Down below I see deep crevices, cut like scars into the ice, and pools of ice-blue water, among the purest drinking water on Earth. We trace the glacier, watching it break apart into braided streams and muddy silt, and continue the journey over stunted forests of aspen, spruce and poplar. I'm keeping my eyes peeled for bear and moose, and spot a half-dozen white Dall sheep, the park's most abundant mammal, impossibly perched high atop a mountain.

The hour-long flight is almost complete, and I've seen just a fraction of this vast open space, the flora and fauna hidden from above like secrets. Most of Kluane is accessible only by air, hence the flightseeing options available in Haines Junction. Hop on board a plane or helicopter and witness the blue ice and black rock brush strokes on a truly spectacular Canadian canvas.

**START HERE:** canadianbucketlist.com/kluane

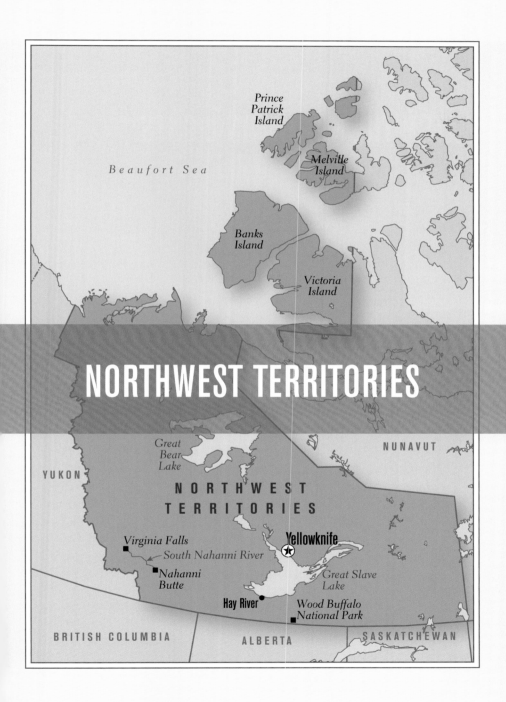

Prince
Patrick
Island

*Beaufort Sea*

Melville
Island

Banks
Island

Victoria
Island

# NORTHWEST TERRITORIES

Great
Bear
Lake

NUNAVUT

YUKON

N O R T H W E S T
T E R R I T O R I E S

Virginia Falls
South Nahanni River

Yellowknife

Nahanni
Butte

Great Slave
Lake

Hay River

Wood Buffalo
National Park

BRITISH COLUMBIA

ALBERTA

SASKATCHEWAN

# WATCH THE NORTHERN LIGHTS

It's my tenth failed attempt to see the northern lights, and here's my conclusion: When you live in cold, sparsely populated northern climes, surrounded by unimaginable amounts of space, your mind begins to untangle. Brain unwinding, it fires relaxing neurons into the backs of your eyeballs, resulting in beautiful hallucinations that can best be described as "lights dancing across the sky." When a traveller arrives from out of town with hopes of experiencing such a phenomenon, here's what he'll hear:

1. You should have been here last week, they were incredible!
2. You should be here next week, they'll be incredible!

Being here right now, on the other hand, results in clear skies with no dancing lights, or foggy skies with no dancing lights, or rainy nights with twelve Japanese tourists looking glumly towards the sky. This was my experience when I spent two weeks in Alaska. Ditto for a week in the Yukon. Likewise a week in northern Saskatchewan, and now, during a week in the best place to view the alleged natural light show, right below the aurora belt in Yellowknife.

Adding to my misery is the fact that my dad has flown up from Vancouver to join me, as viewing the aurora borealis has been the number one item on his bucket list ever since he saw an awful eight-ies movie called *St. Elmo's Fire*, which does not actually feature the aurora borealis but does contain the light going out of Ally Sheedy's acting career. Bucket lists are personal, and I'm not one to question, but we still pass on Grant Beck's offer to visit his comfortable Aurora Watching cabin on a cold, rainy night when Yellowknife is consumed by a permanent cloud. Grant, a champion dog musher who also runs mushing tours, is being wonderfully optimistic. "Sometimes the clouds break, and we get a beautiful show!" he tells us. You can almost hear those nerves crackling behind his retinas.

We would spend the night with a dozen Japanese tourists, who visit Yellowknife in the belief that procreating beneath the north-ern lights ushers in extremely good luck for any resulting babies. Of course, they're not seeing the lights if they're actually procreating, at least not in front of us.

Northerners tell us that the fabled northern lights are the result of electrical storms caused by solar flares smashing into Earth's mag-netic field. Yellowknife sits directly under the aurora oval, where these lights can be seen at their most brilliant, attracting tourists from around the world in the hope that they too will share in this mass hallucination. Every local I meet is eager to share a story of the sky

NORTHWEST TERRITORIES

337

exploding in luminous shades of green, red and blue, "like, just last week, on the day before you arrived."

The rain continues to fall, but it doesn't dampen the spirits of Carlos Gonzalez at Yellowknife Outdoor Adventures. After all, we'd just spent the day fishing on Great Slave, and Carlos has seen the skies part like the Red Sea before. Just not tonight. The weather forecast is looking fantastic, however, for the day after we leave.

Thanks to Buffalo Air, we are now in Hay River. It's cloudy, of course, which makes for poor (that is, impossible) aurora viewing. Before retiring for the night at the town's Ptarmigan Inn, we ask the friendly receptionist, half-heartedly, to call us if he notices, oh, a natural fireworks display in the sky. Imagine, then, our reactions when the hotel phone wakes us shortly after midnight with exciting news! The sky, would you believe, is absolutely clear—but there are no lights in it. Seriously, guy?

At two a.m., the phone rings again. Something about lights in the sky. My dad is at the door before I open my eyes, and I meet him in the parking lot, looking somewhat perplexed, repeatedly asking: "Where, where, where?" I direct his attention to a faint glow above us, and the fact that we're standing under a rather bright street light. We walk a couple of blocks to the river, where there's less light pollution, and sure enough, a huge green band is glowing in the sky. To our right, spectacular bolts of lightning are firing on the horizon. To our left, a bright, half-crescent yellow moon bobs in the purple sky. My dad puts his arm around me, a huge smile on his face. "Will you look at that!" he says in amazement. Yep, I can see it clearly.

We've officially spent too much time in the North, and now we're starting to hallucinate too.

**START HERE:** canadianbucketlist.com/aurora

# FLY WITH BUFFALO AIR

You don't need a hit international TV show to see that Yellowknife's Buffalo Airways is the world's coolest airline. With a fleet of over fifty planes, including a dozen DC-3s and DC-4s, no other airline can transport you back to the Golden Age of Flying the way these folks do. It's why guys like Andrew Bromage sit in Buffalo's humble departure lounge, having flown all the way from Liverpool to fly Buffalo Air on his birthday. Why Germans, Americans and Australians arrive almost daily to walk among planes that have as much character as the people who operate them. All decked in a distinctive "Northern Light" green, with the fragrance of grease and sound family values.

# Your Pilot May Look Familiar

*The Deadliest Catch, Ice Road Truckers, Flying Wild Alaska*: TV audiences love the extreme lifestyles and personalities of men and women of the North. With its retro colours, larger-than-life characters and dangerous working environment, it was just a matter of time before Buffalo Air flew high in the world of television. Originally produced for the History Channel by Vancouver-based Omni Film (the same company that produced my own series *Word Travels*, using many of the same crew), *Ice Pilots* has been seen on networks including National Geographic around the world, making stars of its very authentic owners, managers, pilots and maintenance crew. There's even an Ice Pilots roller coaster in Denmark's Legoland Park. When these old birds are flying, though, you can rest assured the folks at Buffalo Air are more concerned with service and safety than with television ratings. ➤

Operating largely as a supply lifeline to remote northern communities, Buffalo's "ice pilots" and planes are renowned for handling conditions that would freeze the cockpit off a commercial jet. Fortunately, they also fly a scheduled passenger service across Great Slave Lake to Hay River, a short flight I was eager to board. Once the stalwart of World War II–era air forces and airlines, Buffalo's tail-wheel DC-3s look like props from an Indiana Jones movie. Tilting upwards, the lime-coloured interior features large windows and an open cockpit. With Chief Pilot Justin Simle at the helm, we're in exceptionally safe hands. Buffalo operates the world's largest fleet of DC-3s, which is why it was well known to plane enthusiasts long before it became the focus of the hit reality show *Ice Pilots*.

"It's the planes that are the stars of the show," says Justin, although credit must be given to the airline's distinctly human element, starting with founder "Buffalo Joe" McBryan. He's taken only two days off in forty-two years, and one of them was for his honeymoon. The family are all involved: youngest son Mikey is the general manager, Rod is the director of maintenance, and daughter Kathy runs operations in Hay River. Visitors are invited to visit the hangar and take a look around, where they'll be surprised to learn the characters on TV are very much the characters in real life. Crusty Chuck is literally

greasing the wheels, while Sophie the mutt wanders about, a dog that has logged more flight time than many commercial pilots.

Justin shows me around the interior of a powerful Lockheed Electra, as well as Buffalo's water bombers (sorry, Mordecai Richler's ghost, but it's impossible for a bomber to suck up a swimmer in a lake). I'm itching to get in the air, and it's time for the four-thirty departure to Hay River. While Buffalo operates according to the same regulations as any commercial airline in Canada, the age of its planes and the attitudes of its crew are distinctly different. "We've got little interest in modern aviation. That's like sitting in a doctor's office," explains Mikey. "Most pilots want to be in a suit walking through a terminal. Our guys love adventure."

How refreshing to see pilots in jeans, and the formalities taken care of with the distinct understanding that, yes, I know how to operate a seat belt, and no, handstands in the aisles during turbulence is not a wise idea. The props roar to life, and in a surprisingly short take-off the DC-3 tilts forward and gently floats into the big northern sky. It's a smooth ride at 1,500 metres above the lake, and with the pilot's permission, passengers can poke their head into the cockpit, perhaps even take the jump seat and ask some questions. The 45-minute flight to the small transport hub of Hay River is fun, fascinating and, I suppose, what flying used to be like.

Fortunately, Buffalo's influence now extends to ensuring there's something to do in Hay River when you get there. Together with her husband Fraser and stepson Spencer, Kathy McBryan has launched Hay River's first tour operator, 2 Seasons Adventures. Guests can spend the night in a yurt or cabin on the sandy beaches of Great Slave, hop aboard an ATV, go fishing, or ski, snowmobile and ice-fish in the winter; take a jet boat to Louise Falls, party on a barge, spend the night watching the northern lights, or enjoy a barbecue on the boat as they float up the Mackenzie River. "There's so much to do here," says hunky Spencer as he cuts a Polaris ATV into the forest. All you need are locals with the right toys, toys that 2 Seasons has in abundance.

Back in Yellowknife, the distinctly green DC-3 lands on the runway. Nobody is quite sure what possessed Joe to adopt the colour, and four decades of aviation life in the northern extremes have blurred fact and myth, even for the founder. Maybe it's because he was born on St. Patrick's Day, or perhaps it was to remember the first green planes he ever flew. One thing's for sure: it makes for memorable merchandise in the gift shop. "People would come and demand souvenirs, and it's just grown from there," explains Peter in the merchandise store. Everyone's wearing something that says Buffalo, and by the end of my visit it's hard to distinguish who's a passenger, a visitor, a pilot or a member of the crew.

For making flying fun again—on the ground, in the air and on TV too—Buffalo Air buzzes the Great Canadian Bucket List.

**START HERE:** canadianbucketlist.com/buffaloair

# EXPLORE CANADA'S LARGEST NATIONAL PARK

Wood Buffalo National Park, split between Alberta and the Northwest Territories, has an area of 44,807 square kilometres. In Europe, they might call that a country, a country the size of Denmark, and bigger than Switzerland. Wood Buffalo, I might add, has no people living in it.

Established in 1922 as northern Canada's first national park, and the country's largest, Wood Buffalo is a massive stretch of land that protects, among other creatures, the last free-roaming wood bison herds in the world. Bison were once prolific, roaming in boreal forests from Saskatchewan to British Columbia and all the way north

# Canada's Largest National Parks

Vast amounts of space, and the bane of spelling bees everywhere.

1. Wood Buffalo, NT/AB
2. Jasper, AB
3. Wapusk, MB
4. Aulavik, NT
5. Tuktut Nogait, NT
6. Ukkusiksalik, NU
7. Auyuittuq, NU
8. Kluane, YK
9. Sirmilik, NU
10. Quttinirpaaq, NU

to the Yukon, Alaska and the Northwest Territories, but unchecked hunting and severe winters took them to the very brink of extinction. At the end of the nineteenth century there were fewer than 250 animals left. Thanks to the efforts of conservationists and Parks Canada, their numbers have rebounded to around 10,000, with half of those living in Wood Buffalo National Park.

Joining them in this vast expanse of wilderness are bears, moose, wolverines, beavers, otters and the world's largest wolves. Fortuitously, the park also provides protection for a migratory flock of whooping cranes, another species flying back from the brink. In 1941, there were just 21 left in existence. Today, Wood Buffalo is home to some 300 whooping cranes, nesting in a remote corner of the park. Birdwatchers rejoice!

I drive the long road in from Hay River, carving through dense forests of aspen, poplar, spruce and Jack pine, hoping to see some animals. Canadian wildlife can be painfully shy at the best of times, never mind in the country's biggest national park. Still, I catch a glimpse of a black bear, and a sassy red fox welcomes me to Fort Smith, Wood Buffalo's nearest town.

Here, I meet Parks Canada's Richard Zaidan, who takes me on an introductory visit into this vast, protected wilderness. Our first stop is the Salt River Day Area, the trailhead for five popular hikes, where we stroll the 750-metre Kartsland Loop. Gypsum and lime-stone have created an extensive cave system beneath our feet, of special benefit to our slithery friend, the red garter snake. Similar to the dens in Narcisse (see page 123), hundreds of snakes hibernate in these sinkholes and cracks for the winter. Next we drive to Salt Plains and Grosbeak Lake, finding mineral-rich mud with a dust-ing of white salt, the landscape looking distinctly Martian. Glaciers deposited thousands of rocks in the copper-red mud, mud that is ideal for capturing our footprints along with those of other recent visitors—bison, wolf and human. Then we visit the public campsites at Pine Lake, where algae have turned the water a rich shade of aquamarine. Easy to see why it's so popular in the summer months, but it's the drive home that introduces us to the park's star attraction.

Three large bulls stand on the side of the dirt road, each hulk-ing rump carrying an enormous head. If the bugs are bad enough to necessitate us donning bug nets at times, these beasts have no chance. Clouds of blackflies surround them, forcing one to rub itself in the dust for relief. Parked just metres away, their bulk is intimidat-ing, even from the relatively safe confines of the pickup truck. It's quite the moment, staring down some of the biggest wild bison in the world, here in Canada's biggest national park. Wood Buffalo has a space on the bucket list, and it's a very large space indeed.

START HERE: canadianbucketlist.com/woodbuffalo

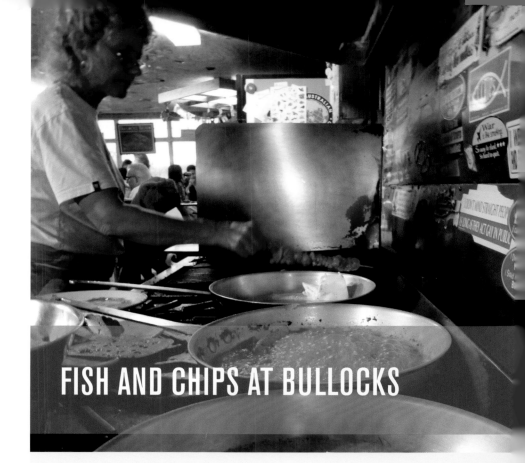

# FISH AND CHIPS AT BULLOCKS

After years in the ho-hum drum, Canada's food scene has blossomed. We've got some of the finest restaurants on the continent, operated by rock star chefs of wildly diverse backgrounds. When a restaurant becomes synonymous with a provincial capital, it demands investigation—especially when reports range from "essential" to "avoid at all costs." Such is the case with Bullocks Bistro, a ramshackle fish shack in Old Town Yellowknife. With a reputation for serving the most expensive fish 'n' chips in Canada, and an open kitchen run by a legendary local character, it demanded a culinary investigation.

Established by husband and wife Sam and Renata Bullock in 1989, the bistro has grown from a simple wooden fish shack into a larger wooden fish shack, covered in bumper stickers, notices and the satisfied scrawling left by decades of happy customers. The potato chipper is against the wall, the cold beers are in the fridge, and the place has the feel of a warm, frathouse family kitchen. The menu consists of northern seafood delights—pickerel, whitefish, lake trout, Arctic char—grilled, pan-fried or deep-fried. For the carnivore, there's also grilled caribou, muskox and bison steaks. No chicken, no beef, only food you can find in the North, all served with fresh salad and homemade fries. Sam sources and personally fillets all the fresh fish, mostly caught in Great Slave Lake, just a block away. Renata is the wisecracking chef on the other end of the long wooden counter, unhurriedly carving huge hunks of meat, prepping, grilling, frying and chatting with the customers. "The North is hot and cold, like menopause," she jokes, and apparently her mood can swing that way too. Tonight she's hot, cackling away with a motherly warmth while Jewel and Junior (and occasionally a customer at the counter) serve the dishes to the busy tables, packed with Japanese tourists and adoring locals.

"Nothing in Yellowknife comes close to this sort of quality," enthuses a mining consultant. Quality *and* quantity, for the portions are noticeably large. Slabs of meat cover the dinner plates, while fish fillets are as large as a basketball player's hands. A patron next to me receives her dish, and Renata adds another large piece of fish because her huge portion didn't look huge enough.

I order Arctic char sashimi to start, a lovely salmon-like fish best enjoyed up north. Next up is the pan-fried pickerel. Renata uses a large chunk of butter, so much that the fish isn't so much fried as poached. It is cooked to perfection, prepared with a sweet-spicy garlic herb mix that hits all the right notes. The salad is fresh and simple, with the choice of a house-made vinaigrette or a rich, creamy feta cheese dressing. Crispy fries taste like real potatoes.

The secret, according to Renata, is the cold waters of Great Slave. The colder the water, the sweeter and fresher the fish. With a dozen meals on the go, she chats away, somehow finding time to show some Japanese tourists where the bathroom light is. The meat is medium rare, the fish melts in your mouth. With a cold Pilsner from the fridge, I read the bumper stickers:

Do you know why divorce is expensive? Because it's worth it!

Mall Wart: Your Choice for Cheap Plastic Crap.

Prices Subject to Customer Attitude.

I'd been forewarned about the cost of visiting Bullocks. A meal for two typically costs around $125. Renata shrugs it off. This is Yellowknife, the nearest big city is 1,700 kilometres away. The fish is as fresh as it gets (the Arctic char is flown in daily), and hey, she reminds me, "If you want an experience, it's gonna cost you!"

An experience is right. Some people might balk at the prices, others at the attitude. But having eaten in hundreds of restaurants around the country, I can say with confidence that few meals are as synonymous with their city, or as memorable, as Bullocks Bistro.

**START HERE:** canadianbucketlist.com/bullocks

# RAFT THE NAHANNI

ell's Gate, Deadmen Valley, Funeral Range, Headless Creek: rafting the South Nahanni River sounds lawless, wild and untamed. It's certainly attracted its fair share of adventurers, from crusty prospectors and Pierre Trudeau to today's modern bucket-lister. Awaiting all is 500 kilometres of untouched Northwest Territories, comprising vast mountain chains, 1,400-metre-high canyons, evergreen forests and twisting waterways. It's not easy to get there: first you have to get to Yellowknife, then fly or drive to Fort Simpson, and from there charter a float plane over the Nahanni mountain range to the base of Virginia Falls. It's quite the starting line: a spectacular 96-metre-high waterfall, almost twice the height

↑

NORTHWEST TERRITORIES

349

of Niagara Falls. Early explorers wrote how they could hear its thunder from over thirty kilometres away. Bucket-listers—as opposed to hard-core rafters, who might start much farther up the river—typically employ the services of professional raft operators who take care of the logistics, portages, cooking and rafting. All you have to do is go along for the ride, and although you'll pass rapids (including one eight-kilometre stretch and a particular churning soup called the Figure Eight, or Hell's Gate), professional help means the excursion is manageable for virgin rafters.

Each morning, the week-long trip presents a scenic jewel, as you float with the current down a series of four spectacular canyons. Within the stunted tundra, there is also hope of spotting some northern wildlife: bears, Dall sheep, caribou, wolves. Passing through a hairpin known as Big Bend, you'll begin to encounter the more sinister aspects of the Nahanni, such as Headless Creek, where the decapitated skeletons of two prospecting brothers were found in 1908. Wrote R.M. Patterson in his seminal journals exploring the region in the late 1920s: "a country lorded over by wild mountain men . . . the river fast and bad." Lured by a gold rush but forewarned of treacherous conditions, especially travelling upriver, many prospectors perished, hence the morbid place names. All of that is in contrast to the modern experience, as you drift in a protected national park reserve recognized by UNESCO as one of its four earliest World Heritage Sites. Operators such as Nahanni River Adventures make sure their clients are well fed on gourmet snacks, dozing in the twenty-two hours of daily summer sunshine as the world passes by.

After travellers bath in the Kraus Hot Springs, the rafts gradually make their way to the islands of the Nahanni Delta, an area known as the Splits or, less kindly, Bug Hell Island. The hordes of awaiting mosquitoes are legendary, rendering bug suits essential. These are mosquitoes that take to DEET like toddlers to apple juice. But they don't seem to bother the locals in the first settlement you'll see all week, the small community of Nahanni Butte. This is where most raft journeys conclude, a welcome float plane or van waiting to return tired, sunburned, bitten and fully inspired rafters back to civilization. Budget some time to adjust after completing one of Canada's great outdoor adventures.

**START HERE:** canadianbucketlist.com/nahanni

# HOOK A NORTHERN PIKE

Life is too short not to do what you're passionate about, which in Carlos Gonzalez's case is fishing, cooking and introducing visitors from around the world to the beauty and bounty of Great Slave Lake. His log cabins rest on its shores, his boats zip about its rocky islands, and Carlos loves nothing more than catching-and-releasing the prize trophy in the world's ninth-largest lake, the great northern pike.

Great Slave (the name has nothing to do with slavery, but is attributed to the Slavey First Nation) covers an area of 27,000 square kilometres, a very big lake for very big fish. The largest of them all, sitting at the top of its underwater food chain, is the great northern

# Freedom on Great Slave Lake

It's certainly not the most digestible name for a lake, but you can relax: Great Slave Lake has nothing to do with slavery. *Slave*, in this case, should be pronounced *Slavey*, after the indigenous people who lived there when English explorer Samuel Hearne stumbled upon the lake in 1771. It is fed by Slave Lake, which should also consider adding an accurate and innocuous y to its name. ➤

pike. Dark green with yellow spots, they can grow up to 1.5 metres, weigh as much as 30 kilos, and are prized by sport fishers for their aggressive, fighting nature. With teeth as sharp as sharks, northern pike (also known as jackfish) patrol the waters preying on trout, whitefish and other unlucky creatures. Over the years, Carlos has seen some monsters, but he runs a strict catch-and-release operation. Such is his respect for the pike that if someone is after a trophy, he's happy to lose the revenue.

Kitted out in rain gear, we speedboat out of his base in Yellowknife's Old Town. Backs to the wind, Carlos manoeuvres us through the dozens of islands that dot the north arm of Great Slave. It's easy to see how treacherous these channels can be, the shallow rocks lurking beneath the waters like predators. After forty-five minutes, he finds a quiet spot, hands our small group some rods and instructs us how to cast, reel and jerk for pike. There's no time to sit back and drink beers. We stand on one side of the boat, repeatedly casting our lines, with no bait and a single hook. Within minutes, Jason from Korea snags a beauty! "That's Emily," says Carlos, holding the fish up so Jason can pose for photographs. No sooner has he released the fish back into the water than my dad snags his first of the day, introduced by Carlos as "George." Next up is Jennifer, Samuel (my first catch) and Big Bertha, a beast of a beauty, about one metre in length. By the time we break for lunch, we have caught and released

a total of eight pikes, have let a dozen get away and are well satisfied with our accomplishments.

Fishing is only half the fun. With his background in restaurants, Carlos takes shore lunches seriously. Although he has picnic tables and firepits on various islands, we head to the comfort of the warm, fully stocked cabin for a barbecue of lake trout marinated in olive oil, basil, garlic and lemon fusion.

"Some friends of mine amassed small fortunes, and always said they'd do things when they retired, but then they started dropping dead, literally," says Carlos. What's it all for if you're not doing what you want with it? From a small fishing operation set up in 1991 to keep him busy during the summers, his Yellowknife Outdoor Adventures has grown into one of the region's top outfitters, offering aurora viewing at the cabin, snowmobile adventures and trips to Nahanni National Park. Having moved north from Montreal thirty years ago to "escape the traffic," he's clearly enjoying himself—and so are we.

The biggest fish I've ever caught, on one of the most spectacular lakes I've ever seen. Now that's one for the bucket list.

**START HERE:** canadianbucketlist.com/pike

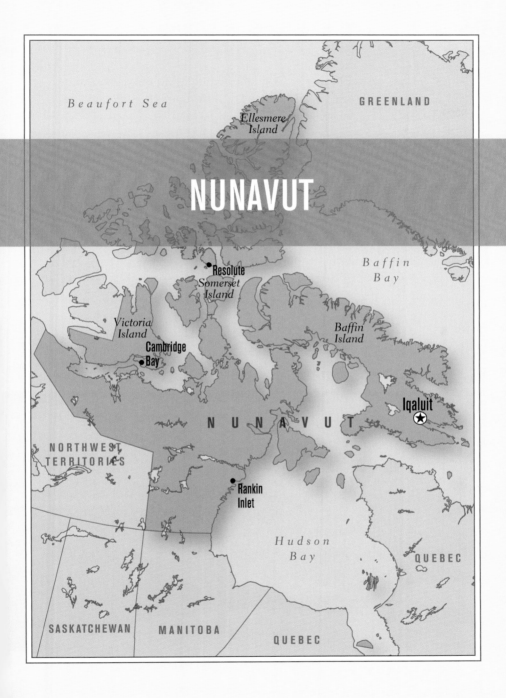

# NUNAVUT

Beaufort Sea

GREENLAND

*Ellesmere*
*Island*

● **Resolute**
*Somerset*
*Island*

*Baffin*
*Bay*

*Victoria*
*Island*

**Cambridge**
● **Bay**

*Baffin*
*Island*

N U N A V U T

**Iqaluit**
★

**NORTHWEST**
**TERRITORIES**

● **Rankin**
**Inlet**

*Hudson*
*Bay*

**QUEBEC**

**SASKATCHEWAN**      **MANITOBA**

**QUEBEC**

Before we get to the list, it might be helpful to put a few things in perspective. There is a country in Europe called Macedonia, sometimes confused with *macadamia*, which is a type of nut. Macedonia occupies an area of roughly 25,000 square kilometres and has a population of over two million people. To explore Canada's most recent federal territory, we're heading off to Somerset Island. It too is roughly 25,000 square kilometres. This week, there are 32 people on the island. In a few months, there will be nobody.

Just how big is Nunavut? It's bigger than the three largest mainland U.S. states—California, Texas and Montana—combined. It's bigger than western Europe, bigger than the secrets of the Cold War, bigger than the appetite of a wolverine, 1.8 million square kilometres shaped like a hammer pounding into Canada's Great White North. A hammer that's bigger than Mexico, which has 112 million people. Nunavut is having none of it. Just 32,000 people live in "Our Land," as it is called in the Inuktitut mother tongue. If you're looking to get away from it all, you've come to the right place.

# VISIT THE WORLD'S MOST NORTHERLY ECO-LODGE

Arctic Sunwest Charters' de Havilland Dash 8 takes off from Yellowknife on the 1,500-kilometre journey north into the neighbouring territory of Nunavut. On board are tourists from Connecticut, New Mexico, Scotland, New York and California, along with a group of Canadian geologists and some marine scientists from Mystic Aquarium. Our destination is Arctic Watch, a unique beluga whale observation post and eco-lodge located 800 kilometres north of the Arctic Circle.

As a launch pad for a once-in-a-lifetime Arctic safari, the Watch boasts several attractions: the most comfortable remote facilities in the High Arctic (private tented cabins, gourmet meals, Internet), a variety of tundra toys, an impeccable location and the fact that it

NUNAVUT

357

is owned and operated by Richard Weber and his family. Weber is the most travelled North Pole explorer on the planet, the first man to trek to the North Pole six times, including unsupported expeditions that have never been equalled. His wife, Josée, has led six expeditions herself, and both have also trekked to the South Pole (Richard kite-sledded out). Both sons are in the business as well: Tessum holds the distinction of being the youngest person to trek to the North Pole, while Nansen is an accomplished wildlife photographer. These are people who live and love the Arctic, sharing this passion with their summer camp overlooking the purple inlet of the Cunningham River. During the short summer months, when the sun burns twenty-four hours a day, a charter flight lands once a week on the tundra runway. It switches over the week's guests, bringing with it a load of fresh food and supplies. I'm as north as I've ever been, nigh an elf toss from Santa. The desolate tundra looks like the moon, and fittingly, a moon buggy is waiting to greet us.

# WATCH BELUGAS PLAY IN A RIVER MOUTH

Our group piles into the back of a bright yellow Unimog, a fifty-year-old four-by-four truck that somehow weathers one of the harshest climates on the planet. It's a short drive to the lodge, comprising a large dome-shaped communal and dining tent, bathrooms and hot showers, a fully equipped restaurant-grade kitchen and an equipment room. Adjacent individual living quarters, with double beds, sinks and marine toilets, sit outside like milk chocolate Hershey kisses. Every summer, up to two thousand beluga whales gather at the mouth of the Cunningham River for a natural body wash and to feed on rich nutrients in the flowing Arctic meltwaters. We excitedly put on rubber boots and walk over the rock and estuaries to the river mouth, drawn to the water boiling with life up ahead.

NUNAVUT

We're in luck: ice at the mouth of the inlet has finally cleared and the whales have arrived, hundreds of them, arching their backs, popping their heads out of the water, rolling and rubbing their bodies on the gravel below. Belugas, among the most social of all whales, cackle and chirp with delight, as marine scientists tell us their exfoliating gravel skin rub is actually pleasurable. I can almost hear David Attenborough's voice narrating the phenomenon of these Arctic ghosts, and you can if you watch BBC's *Frozen Planet*, which filmed a beluga segment right here at Arctic Watch. Fittingly, it turns out that two of the guys on my plane are actually BBC nature filmmakers. I love nature documentaries and often wonder: "Where in the world is that?" What a remarkable feeling when you realize *that* is right in front of you.

# SLEEP UNDER THE MIDNIGHT SUN

Considering the nearest grocery store is 1,500 kilometres away, chef Jeff Stewart and the staff serve up magnificent fare: roast lamb, braised ribs, pickled Arctic char, adobo chicken, butter-smooth tenderloin, fresh salads and vegetables. There is homemade bread, mayonnaise and yogurt. Much like my experience at Skokie Lodge (see page 73), I'm eating like royalty in the wilderness.

We're introduced to the Webers and the young, attractive staff. It's easy to make yourself at home when it feels like a home, complete with Josée, the nurturing mom. Our groups span a wide range of ages (eight to seventy) and interests (birders, scientists, hikers, photographers), and the Watch does its best to make sure everyone is accommodated. We're chatting in the main lodge, getting to know each other, when I make two rather dumb comments:

What not to say in the High Arctic summer, Part 1: **Damn, I just realized I forgot my headlamp!**
What not to say in the High Arctic summer, Part 2: **Wow, we're so remote, the stars are going to be epic tonight!**

## ON THE BUCKET LIST: David Suzuki

You should visit Pond Inlet, Nunavut, have an Inuit guide take you on the ice floe. I couldn't believe it, there were narwhal everywhere! When we got back, there were polar bear prints right through our camp.

David Suzuki
Science Broadcaster, Environmentalist

There are no stars, of course, for the same reason I won't need to worry about a flashlight. This far north, the sun wheels across the sky, roughly fifteen degrees every fifteen minutes. It never sets, and so the sky never so much as gets mildly dusky. The midnight sun is disorienting but energizing. Still, with the white fabric of our sleeping tents, I quickly realize:

What not to say in the High Arctic summer, Part 3: **I forgot my eye mask!**

The comfortable beds have heavy duvets and warm fleece sheets. Yet high winds shake the tents, and polar bears stalk my dreams. I awake constantly on my first night, panicking that I've overslept for the morning's activities. It's okay, it's only two a.m., bright as day. Sleeping without night is an early afternoon nap that never ends.

# SWIM IN AN ARCTIC WATERFALL

Tessum Weber greets me with a freshly made cappuccino in the morning. Each day, the youngest man to trek to the North Pole is my personal barista. After a hearty breakfast, we go for a walk to some local waterfalls. The tundra is sweeping, a desert of shale skipping stones and crushed limestone—desert, that is, were it not for the bright blue streams, mineralized with rock flour into shades of green and turquoise. The local waterfall is a fifteen-metre beauty, surrounded by sharp-cut canyon walls. Farther up, a series of smaller but just as striking cascades invite a swim. If God put us on earth to endure supermarket lineups and mortgages, He wanted us to take Arctic waterfall showers too.

I strip down and take a refreshing dip in water pure enough to bottle and sell to Fiji. Thanks to warming temperatures and shrinking Arctic ice, mosquitoes have invaded the island for the first time. They're as big as oil rigs, ready to drill, but fortunately, their small numbers are nothing compared with bug net hell down south.

We continue our walk, familiarizing ourselves with the landscape. Although the island is covered in a sheet of ice for much of the year, life stubbornly resists in the form of small plants, flowers and white candy balls of Arctic cotton. We walk through a valley, giving a wide berth to a sandpiper protecting her nest. A hot lunch awaits, the ATVs are fuelled, and there just might be a larger form of life lurking sixteen kilometres away, at Polar Bear Point.

## Five Arctic Creatures that Turn White for Winter

For greater warmth and protection against predators, animals in the Arctic go through a remarkable transformation in the winter.

**Arctic hare:** brown and black during summer months
**ermine:** world's smallest weasel flips brown to white
**Arctic fox:** nature's most northerly fox is brown-grey in summer
**barren ground caribou:** predominantly brown in summer, predominantly white in winter
**rock ptarmigan:** moults brown to white in winter, keeping its brown or black tail

# ATV TO ANCIENT ARCTIC RUINS

The Watch is as small as a poppy seed on a basketball court. To get around, we'd need the Unimog, rafts and tough ATVs built for such a terrain. I salute our opposable thumbs, which gave humanity the dexterity to evolve beyond the apes, build tools, text messages and accelerate on ATVs.

We drive up along the coast, crossing streams and crunching rocks, past an old scientific observation cabin and slowly towards the famed Northwest Passage. The path is lined by inukshuks, piled stones used by Inuit for millennia as a form of communication and guidance. The stone guardians ensure we are travelling in the right direction. In the distance are icebergs, along with floating crusts of slowly melting sea ice.

Tessum stops off at a small circular mound of rocks, explaining that these are the archaeological remains of thousand-year-old Thule hunting stations. Dozens of similar stations line the coast, where Inuit

ancestors hunted whales and seals. We can still see the heavy bones of bowhead and beluga whales. I tell Tessum I've seen UNESCO World Heritage Site status awarded for less, but he says such remains are fairly common up the coast, where many of the stations have not been excavated.

We continue to the point, racing along the beach, slaloming between beached chunks of ice. Two large icebergs are drifting just offshore. We stop to observe the ice, hopping between the giant floating slabs. Steve from Santa Fe spots something through his binoculars, and sure enough, it's a polar bear. One of the staff always carries a rifle just in case, and we're given bear spray in case we decide to wander off, but since the lodge opened in 2000, there has never been any problem with the bears. In fact, in all of Richard Weber's expeditions to the North Pole, he has never even seen a bear, although he has come across their tracks. They're out there, but with this much space, no two species have to cramp each other's style.

# HIKE IN THE TUNDRA

Eight thousand years ago, the vast plains of the tundra that buttress Cunningham Inlet were under the sea. We can see this hiking among the fossils and shells on its distinctly seabed landscape. Once past the rocks that have been gathered downstream by the river, the ground becomes soft and spongy with moss, sprouting tufts of grass like hair on the face of a teenage boy. A finger-thick branch of Arctic willow, growing low on the soil, might be a century old. Only the hardiest of life can survive here. Arctic sorel (with leaves that taste like strawberry), Arctic poppies and glossy yellow buttercups whisper a fragile beauty in this unforgiving starkness.

We hike along the blue river that cuts through Gull Canyon, spotting boisterous Arctic hares on the mossy green slopes. There's no need to carry a water bottle; we simply drink from the streams. Mucks, the insulated rubber boot of choice at Arctic Watch, prove

**An Ode to My Mucks**

You keep my feet warm and dry
Your weight in gold one cannot deny
Crossing streams and mud, moss and gravel
Without you, my piggies unravel!
My Arctic boot, my rubber soul
Let's take this tundra, es-rock and roll!

# The Mysteriously Doomed Voyage

You can't visit the High Arctic without getting swept up by the mystery of Captain John Franklin's doomed quest to find the Northwest Passage. It has besotted the public since 1845, when Franklin's ships, the *Erebus* and HMS *Terror*, set off from England and were never seen again. Both ships were fully kitted out with supplies and the best technology available at the time, and one would think the 134 men on board would have fancied their chances to make history. Five men were sent back along the way (call them the lucky ones), while the remaining 129 sallied forth into a desolate adventure that would ultimately see the elements pick them off, one by one, like victims in an Agatha Christie novel.

Spurred on by Franklin's devoted wife, British and American rescue ships were sent in vain, some on their own doomed voyages, and over the next 150 years the fate of Franklin's crew was slowly pieced together. Although the ships have never been found, it's widely believed they were crushed by the ice, causing the crew to scatter on foot, starve (traces of cannibalism have been found), suffer and die. Joyous stuff it's not, but fascinating reading for any visitor to the Arctic. ➤

invaluable across this terrain. At one point they magically keep water out after a river crossing that went up to my knees. I haven't had such appreciation for a product since I discovered the iPod.

We walk to Sunday Lake ("because we used to visit here on Sundays," explains Josée) across a badlands landscape, discovering the scattered remains of bowhead whales miles inshore. Arctic fox cubs were spotted in a nearby den a few weeks ago, but today it is abandoned. The white skull of a baby fox on the tundra is a reminder that life is tough in the wild, and only the strongest survive. We walk past more bones. "Members of the Franklin expedition?" I joke, recalling the ill-fated British mission to discover the Northwest Passage, a mission that scattered the frozen, scurvied and emaciated remains of 129 men throughout the region.

A strong, biting breeze is picking up, so we return to the Watch, appreciating the hot roasted veggies and sweet desserts more than ever. Some primeval instinct has given me a huge appetite, as if it expects no further supply planes to arrive.

# PADDLE A CRYSTAL ARCTIC STREAM

Canada is baking in a mid-July heat wave, but the Arctic turns on us. Gale force winds rock our tents, stinging rain attacks the windows of the lodge, as the temperature plummets and snow begins to fall. We huddle up with coffee and hot chocolate in the lodge as the Mystic marine scientists give a presentation about beluga behaviour and Richard Weber takes us on a journey to the North Pole.

Having received numerous awards and honours, no less than Sir Ranulph Fiennes has called Richard, and his partner Misha Malakhov, the "greatest of all Arctic travellers." Listening to tales of his military-like preparation and experience is fascinating, a battle against the harshest elements on the planet. The keys to his success

NUNAVUT

369

are efficiency, the right caloric intake, walking distances, body-fat ratio, gear, equipment and attitude. His words are efficient too, an Arctic general with no time or energy to waste.

Next up, Jeff Turner and Justin Maguire show us an Attenborough-narrated BBC documentary they filmed in British Columbia. They captured wolves attacking a grizzly, and spent months waiting for those jaw-dropping shots you see on TV. One guest is a bestselling photographer, another a bond trader obsessed with great migrations. Everyone is having a bucket list sort of week.

Although it's still chilly and grey, by the following day the weather has softened enough to allow us to head upstream on the Unimog to meet river rafts and a kayak. The river is as smooth as glass, so after a lunch in the field (heartwarming borscht) I hop in the kayak with a Belarusian named Rus and expertly snap the steering pedal. We head over some gentle rapids backwards, but the current is generous and smooth, and so, straightening up, it shepherds us along the canyon under the watchful gaze of a rough-legged hawk. The others follow us in the rafts, berthing on the gravel after someone spots a muskox. Although they've been hunted for their fur and meat, today we stalk these shaggy beasts of the tundra with our cameras.

With another storm blowing in, we retreat to base, where the brave decide to bear the icy winds to spend more time with the belugas. I opt for beluga-shaped ice cubes in a glass of Iceberg vodka with a teaspoon of honey. It keeps the Arctic chill at bay.

## ON THE BUCKET LIST: Cory Trépanier

Cory Trépanier is a well-known artist and filmmaker with a passion for capturing the Canadian wilderness on canvas. He has explored and painted many of our spectacular, and remote, national parks. Here are his favourites:

1. Quttinirpaaq (NU) for unequalled vastness
2. Pukaskwa (ON) for pristine water and ancient coastlines
3. Ivvavik (YK) for hiking back in time
4. Auyuittuq (NU) for feeling very, very small
5. Gros Morne (NL) for rugged beauty

NUNAVUT ↑

# FISH FOR ARCTIC CHAR

Freezing rain or shine, there is one day left to head deeper into the tundra, on rugged Bombardier all-terrain vehicles. I've ridden ATVs before, but never on a landscape so complementary to their capabilities: muddy, rocky, wet, no trees for thousands of kilometres. Warned never to underestimate the Arctic, I layered up to the point of absurdity (three pairs of socks, two layers of merino wool long underwear). Our destination, Inukshuk Lake, is a three-hour ride away, where we will pull out rods and attempt to catch some tasty Arctic char. Similar to salmon, Arctic char is lighter, whiter and rarer to find on your plate.

Just minutes outside the Watch, I'm once again feeling the isolation, desolation and striking beauty of the tundra. We cross rivers and estuaries, and ride on the spines of ridges, even as a light snow begins to fall. Tessum stops up ahead and points out two muskox in the valley below. They appear to be running towards us, disappearing on the slope before popping up thirty metres away. They're not snorting or stamping their feet, but it's unusual for these huge Arctic creatures to get so close. They trot along onto the path in front of us, and for the next ten minutes they clear our way, like squad cars leading a motorcade. Finally they vanish into a valley below, leaving us elated from the encounter.

After roller-coasting up and down muddy banks and rocky hills, we arrive at the lake. Low cloud hovers on the hills, draining all colour. Then the sun breaks through for a moment, pouring turquoise dye into the water. Sven and Tessum prepare the rods, and after soup, sandwiches and coffee we're casting our lines from the shore. Landlocked char grow slowly, and a strict quota is in place. Our goal is to catch four medium-sized fish for the kitchen and catch-and-release the rest. It's Sven, Arctic Watch's shaggy-haired handyman, who reels in the first couple of char. As for me, let's just say if you teach this man to fish, he's still not going to catch anything.

On the long ride back (when did you last spend six hours on an ATV?), with my right thumb on the throttle, I find myself zoning out. Life seems very simple: get back to the warmth of the Watch, eat, survive. This is the way of the Arctic north.

Considering its size, I explored but a fraction's fraction of Nunavut. I did not get the opportunity to spend time with its Inuit people, nor to visit their towns and settlements. Yet as small as my Arctic dosage was, it was in the company of people who love it, explore it and are devoted to introducing us Southerners to its wonders. Nunavut before you die? You'd be a macadamia not to.

**START HERE:** canadianbucketlist.com/nunavut

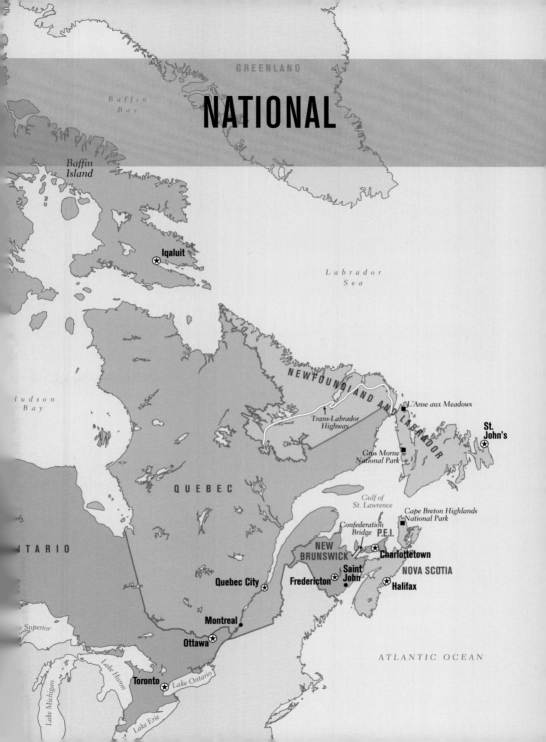

NATIONAL

GREENLAND

Baffin
Bay

Baffin
Island

⊛ Iqaluit

Labrador
Sea

Hudson
Bay

NEWFOUNDLAND AND LABRADOR

■ L'Anse aux Meadows

St.
John's ⊛

Trans-Labrador
Highway

Gros Morne
National Park

QUEBEC

Gulf of
St. Lawrence

Cape Breton Highlands
National Park

ONTARIO

Confederation
Bridge      P.E.I.

NEW
BRUNSWICK

Charlottetown

NOVA SCOTIA

Quebec City ⊛

Fredericton ⊛

Saint
John ■

Halifax ⊛

Montreal

Lake Superior

Ottawa ⊛

Lake Huron

Lake Michigan

Toronto ⊛

Lake Ontario

Lake Erie

ATLANTIC OCEAN

# SEE CANADA WITH THE CANADIAN

I've been fortunate to experience some of the world's great, and not so great, train journeys. The Trans-Siberian, the Trans-Mongolian, the Tazara from Zambia to Dar es Salaam, Tanzania. Trains across Croatia, Poland and Hungary. Trains through western Europe and India. I find long train journeys a pleasant mode of transport—far less stressful than driving, far more comfortable than buses, much slower than airplanes but with the benefit of actually seeing something other than the seat in front of you. VIA Rail's Canadian is a 4,466-kilometre journey that slices the country from east to west, and vice versa. The four-night, three-day passage is rightly regarded as one of the world's great train voyages, and if people from around the world are boarding, it certainly demands investigation for the bucket list.

It's eight p.m. on a Friday night in June at Pacific Central Station in Vancouver. My wife and I arrive in a typical west coast downpour, the summer determined to hide no matter how much everyone seeks

it. Like other passengers in the waiting room, we each have a carry-on piece of luggage, with larger items checked in, along with pets, bikes and equipment. We're shown to our Touring Class cabin, which features two bunks, a basin, storage and a toilet. The two classes of sleeping cars are named after English settlers or French explorers. Car 213 is called Bliss Manor, not for the state of mind it will later induce but for a commissary in the Revolutionary War and New Brunswick settler named Daniel Bliss.

This week's configuration of the Canadian consists of twenty-one cars, 644 metres long, weighing a total of 1,540 tons. We have two engine machines, one to pull the train and one to power the cars. Configurations might vary depending on demand, but expect panoramic-view cars and double-storey domed viewing cars, dining cars, activity cars and a wonderfully retro Park Car at the back, complete with a bar and view of the tracks left behind. The showers and toilets are clean, the food outstanding, and activity co-ordinators hold beer and wine tastings, movies, games and interpretation sessions. During the eleven days I spent on a train in Russia, I could only dream of such facilities and services, confined as I was to a sleeper car with stale noodles, dirty washrooms and rough attendants showing all the hospitality of aggravated vampire bats.

Despite many renovations over the years, VIA Rail's cars still carry the pastel colours, industrial carpets, stainless steel and boxiness of the 1950s glory days, before airfares were affordable and the Trans-Canada Highway was complete. The cross-country journey was initially offered by two competing railway companies: Canadian Pacific Railway's Canadian and Canadian National Railway's Super Continental. As passenger numbers declined, CPR hoped to discontinue the service, forcing the federal government to take over with its VIA Rail Crown corporation. In 1990, the train moved from the CPR route through Calgary and Regina to the CN route via Edmonton and Saskatoon. While trainspotters will no doubt love all this information, my wife and I were simply looking forward to some quality time together, enjoying the soporific effect of the world passing us by, and the opportunity to see Canada's landscape transform before our eyes.

It takes a night or two to get used to sleeping on a train—the rocking, the sounds, the feeling of hurtling forward at 130 kph with your eyes closed. I wake up shortly before dawn to find the tracks running alongside semi-arid cliffs and a swollen Thompson River. Heavy rains have resulted in the river breaching its banks in some areas, and the water level seems alarmingly high. As dawn breaks, an American tourist, enthusiastically taking photos out the front of the dome car, joins me. We high-five like kids after skirting a particularly steep cliff and when exiting especially long and dark tunnels.

I return to the cabin for a few hours of sleep, and wake for an excellent breakfast (crab hollandaise eggs Benedict) and a day touring through the most dramatic part of the journey: the Coastal Range, Selkirks and Canadian Rockies. It's my third visit to the Rockies this

## The Right Side of the Tracks

- Canada has the third-largest rail network in the world, handling the fourth-largest volume of goods.
- On average, one train moves the same tonnage of freight as 280 big trucks.
- According to the Transportation Safety Board of Canada, rail is the safest means of ground transportation in the country.
- New technology on the railways includes LED lights at crossings, trains depositing lubrication on the rails for enhanced quietness and efficiency, X-ray scans at the border and real-time Internet tracking.
- Between 2010 and 2012, more than $22 million was invested in modernizing the Canadian, which receives around 100,000 passengers a year. ➤

year, but the expressions on the faces of my fellow passengers remind me of the impact these mountains have on those from afar. The viewing cars come into their own.

In the course of its journey, the Canadian will make ten major stops for servicing and changing of crew and engineers. Additional stops take place in small towns such as Clearwater, B.C., Unity, Saskatchewan, and Winnitoba, Manitoba, if there are passengers or cargo to service. Stops range from fifteen minutes to stretch your legs on a dusty platform to an hour or more to explore the town of Jasper or the Forks in Winnipeg. With a good book, a bottle of wine, a comfortable bed, tons of writing to do and a lovely wife to spend time with, I never feel bored. The only responsibility we have is to show up for the three daily meals in the dining car. Time on a train is time in movement, literally barrelling through boreal forests, mountains and prairies. Just to prove its time is so malleable, the Canadian goes through four time zones. And yet everything runs like clockwork. The attendants are helpful and friendly, the meals consistently excellent and varied (rosemary lamb chops, pan-seared scallops, quinoa salad with goat cheese). Crossing Siberia, all I had to feast on was cheap instant noodles, cheaper vodka and a never-changing landscape of farmland.

Out our window, we see the world in perpetual green motion blur, forest and fields punctuated by urban development, marshes or copper brown lakes reflecting Simpsonesque clouds against a sunny blue sky. When we step outside in Hornepayne, Ontario, we're attacked by blackflies, grateful they cannot penetrate the heavy steel doors of our comfortable air-conditioned bubble. Occasionally the attendants will announce a moose or bear sighting, the animals visible only for the briefest of moments. From time to time I spot trucks and cars on the Trans-Canada Highway, and I feel fortunate I can pass them without having to keep my eyes on the road. Wherever they're going, we're Canadians on the move inside the Canadian, perpetually on the move too.

As I write these words in the activity car, a lady opposite me begins to chat. She's come up from Florida with her husband, and together they've been overwhelmed by the size, beauty and nature of the Canada we have experienced outside the window. I ask her why, of all the options available to them, they decided to hop on board the Canadian.

"Travel by train lets you actually see a country," she says. "Really, this should be on everyone's bucket list."

She has no idea just how much I agree with her.

**START HERE:** canadianbucketlist.com/canadian

# EPILOGUE

"What are you so afraid of?"

—Morgan Freeman in *The Bucket List*

In 2005, when I first set out to tick off my Global Bucket List, I decided to ask everyone I'd meet three questions, and take their picture. It was a way of remembering each person, and learning from them. I capped out at 1,732 people from 46 countries, including many characters as illuminating and inspiring as the places in which I met them. I asked each one to finish three sentences:

1. **I am inspired by** ... This was my attempt to see what gets people out of bed in the morning.
2. **I regret** ... This was to learn what mistakes people make, and how we can learn from them.
3. **Today I am grateful for** ... This was to elicit a positive recognition of something that's important.

Across a staggeringly diverse range of cultures, ages, languages, religions and nationalities, the answers were beautifully universal. Parents and heroes, the beauty of nature and the simple act of waking up all seemed to be common sources of inspiration. Folks were grateful for friends, family, health and opportunities. When it came to regret, hardly anyone rued not working harder, making more money or being more successful. No, the most common answers were regretting the things they hadn't done, the opportunities missed and, most of all, that they hadn't travelled more.

As I hope this book illustrates, it needn't be travel to far-flung countries or on exotic adventures; there's plenty to do and see where you live too. And rest assured, there's no danger of actually finishing the list. After I fulfilled my bucket list, I happily discovered that one experience only inspires another. Tick off one item and three more sprout on top.

Over the years I was researching this book, I asked many people about their Canadian Bucket List—where they want to go, and what they want to do before they proverbially kick the bucket. It's a deeply personal question, and everyone is different. This book comprises activities and destinations I personally found interesting, given my experience and profession. Skipper Jim in Newfoundland told me his bucket list included finishing his shed, which I thought was as admirable an answer as any I'd heard.

My Great Canadian Bucket List is expansive, but it is also a living document. You met many people in this book, and learned about destinations you may not have known existed. In the years to come, many details will no doubt change, and new items will be added, which is why I pushed all the practical information, along with bonus photos and video, online, where it will be easier to update.

While researching this list, I began to create a new one, evolving once more. Six weeks after my wife joined me on my research trip aboard VIA's Canadian train route, my personal bucket list altered course significantly. Instead of chasing adventures around the world, my list of desired achievements now begins with: *Be a great dad.*

Regardless of whether you tick off adventures on the Great Canadian Bucket List, finally build the shed, spend time with the kids or simply finish reading this book, it's never too late, or early, to fill your bucket with the experiences that make living worthwhile.

Robin Esrock
robin@robinesrock.com

# ACKNOWLEDGEMENTS

Researching, experiencing and surviving to write this book would not have been possible without the support, help, participation, humour and vision of many people and organizations across Canada. With links provided after each item, I encourage you to find out more about these destinations, characters and activities, including practical advice on how to follow in my footsteps. Behind the scenes, I'd like to thank, in no particular order:

BRITISH COLUMBIA: Destination British Columbia, Greg McCracken, Amber Sessions, Jorden Hutchison, Janice Greenwood-Fraser, Andrea Visscher, Lana Kingston, Susan Hubbard, Liz Sperandeo, Teresa Davis, Josie Heisig, Luba Plotnikoff, Geoff Moore, Heidi Korven, Cindy Burr, BC Ferries, Morgan Sommerville, Holly Wood, Dee Raffo, Sarah Pearson, CMH guides Rob, Mikey and Bob, and powder ski buddies Natman, David, Dave, Mike, Jim and Larita. The WCT crew: Kyle, Jarrod, Robbie, Andrew, Chris and James.

ALBERTA: Travel Alberta, Jessica Harcombe-Fleming, Anastasia Martin-Stilwell, Amy Wolski, Hala Dehais, Vanessa Gagnon, Charlie Locke, Tricia Woikin, Mary Morrison, Tessa Mackay, Doug Lentz, ski instructors John Jo and Kaz, Go RVing, Neil English and Isabel, Nancy Dery, Bin Lau, Ralph Sliger.

SASKATCHEWAN: Tourism Saskatchewan, Jonathan Potts, Carla Bechard, Kari Dean, Jennifer Nelson, Corporal Dan Toppings, the RCMP, Tyrone Tootoosis, Alexandra Stang.

MANITOBA: Travel Manitoba, Julia Adams, Gillian Leschasin, Jillian Reckseidler, Linda Whitfield, the Castle Boys, Tricia Schers, Lynda Gunter, Derek, Neil, Brie and Julia on the Tundra Buggy at Frontier North.

ONTARIO: Ontario Tourism Marketing Partnership, Jantine Van Kregten, Kattrin Sieber, Vanessa Somarriba, Ann Swerdfager, Melanie Wade, Melanie Coates, Michael Braham, Henriette Riegel, Irene Knight, Sue Mallabon, Niagara Parks, the Toronto Maple Leafs, Paul Pepe, Cathy Presenger, Larry Lage, Steve Kristjanson.

QUEBEC: Tourisme Québec, Patrick Lemaire, Paule Bergeron, Magalie Boutin, Gillian Hall, Catherine Binette, Pierre Bessette, Gilbert Rozon, everyone who joined me for Carnaval and on the Via Ferrata.

NEW BRUNSWICK: Tourism New Brunswick, Alison Aiton, Margaret MacKenzie, Joan Meade, Kurt Gumushel, Jocelyn Chen, the traffic officer who pulled us over and didn't ruin our day.

NOVA SCOTIA: Nova Scotia Tourism Agency, Pam Wambeck, Andrea Young, Monica MacNeil.

PRINCE EDWARD ISLAND: Tourism Prince Edward Island, Pamela Beck, Robert Ferguson, Andrea Kolber, Eza Paventi.

NEWFOUNDLAND & LABRADOR: Newfoundland & Labrador Tourism, Gillian Marx, Monica MacNeil (thanks again!), the Anchor Inn (Hunter's Gold!), Munju Ravindra, that moose for not killing me.

YUKON: Travel Yukon, Jim Kemshead, Denny Kobayashi, Peter Mather, Marten Berkman.

NORTHWEST TERRITORIES: Northwest Territories Tourism, Julie Warnock, Spencer Pike, Frazer Pike, Kathy McBryan, Mikey McBryan, Justin Simle (he flies planes and picks up hitchhikers).

NUNAVUT: Nunavut Tourism, Sara Acher, Richard Weber, Tessum Weber, Nansen Weber, Josée Auclair and everyone at Arctic Watch.

NATIONAL: VIA Rail, Josephine Wasch.

Special thanks to the photographers for the generous use of their images: Rock, TJ Watt, Ian Mackenzie, Gary Kalmek, Joe Kalmek, Ana Esrock, Lee Newman, Bhaskar Krishnamurthy, Ruslan Margolin, Paul Vance, Neil MacLean, Mandy Poole, Nansen Weber, Gretchen Freund, Gillian Salazar, Eva Holland, Peter Mather, Ed English, Peter Maher, Chrystal Kruszelnicki, Éliane Excoffier, Sean Cable, Neil MacLean, Zach Williams, and the photographs provided by various operators and tourism boards.

Several chapters have appeared in a different form in the following publications. Special thanks for their support: Zebunnisa Mirza and Melissa Morra at Bell, Jim Byers at the *Toronto Star*, Sarah McWhirter at the *Globe and Mail*, Matt Robinson at *Outpost*, Ross Borden at the *Matador Travel Network* and Anne Rose at *Westworld* magazine. Thanks to Fairmont Hotels and Resorts for their ongoing support.

Several stories were researched while filming the TV series *Word Travels*, which taught me how to travel hard, write hard and chase a good story. A big shout-out to Heather Hawthorne-Doyle, Julia Dimon, Leah Kimura, Caroline Manuel, Sean Cable, Deb Wainwright, Mike Bodnarchuk, Mary Frymire, Peter Steel, Zach Williams, Ian Mackenzie, Paul Vance all at Omni Film, and Patrice Baillargeon.

Thanks to Ann Campbell, Randall Shirley, Linda Bates, Ron Barker, Ian Mackenzie, Gloria Loree, Kate Duffy, the Canadian

Tourism Commission, Ken Hegan, the Travel Media Association of Canada, the Vancouver and Burnaby Public Libraries, Chris Lee, Minty Thompson, Kimberley Morton, Elyse Mailhot, Karen Margolese, Jon Rothbart, Jarrod Levitan, Marc Telio, and everyone else who helped me shape an unlikely career over the past decade. My thanks to Rock for all his video and photo help.

Thanks interns Kaicea Pitts and Lyda Mclallen. This travel writing is hard work!

After years of pitching a book without success, it was an editor who approached me to write *The Great Canadian Bucket List*, after reading my column in the *Globe and Mail*. He retired shortly afterwards, but my eternal thanks to Patrick Crean for recognizing the potential. For a high-flying first-time author, Thomas Allen Publishers was a very fortunate place to land. My gratitude to Jim Allen, Janice Zawerbny, Krista Lynch, David Glover, Catherine Whiteside, Heather Goldberg, Bonita Mok, and everyone at TAP who made this a fun project to work on. Thanks to John Sweet, Linda Pruessen, Beth Crane and Wendy Thomas for their time, skills and patience. Tania Craan did a magnificent job designing the book. Thanks to Mary Rostad for the maps, and Prasad and team at rtCamp for the rocking website.

Being friends with a travel writer is not easy. Somehow, while travelling around the planet five times, I've managed to maintain relationships that mean the world to me: Jarrod, Robbie, Brad, Rock, Chris, Rob, Geoff, Greg, Bruce, Ian, Karen, Sean, Andrea, Lili, Brian, Grant, Erin, Tamar, Mary, Kristen, April, Steve, Chandra and the crazy Brazilians (you know who you are). My family has supported me since the beginning, holding me up when I was sworn in as a Canadian citizen, battered and bruised from my accident the previous day, giving me the encouragement and space to prove I could make a living travelling the world. With love and *nachas*: Mom, Dad, Bradley, Staci, Gary, Abby, Erin, Bobba, Cecile, Alex and Ian. My late grandfather once told me that he'd always wanted to see the world, but by the time he could afford to, he was too old. I got the message, Abie Esrock. Finally, to my wife, Ana Carolina, who put up with a husband flying off to the Calgary Stampede a couple of days after our wedding, calling from a car in the Rockies so he wouldn't fall asleep at the wheel and constantly living out of a duffel bag. She had to make the biggest sacrifice of all, and I'll always love her for doing so. This book is part of our lives in more ways than one: in true Canadian fashion, our daughter, Raquel, was conceived ticking off the Great Canadian Bucket List.

# PHOTO CREDITS

Cover images: Robin Esrock; Nansen Weber; Chrystal
    Kruszelnicki/RCMP; T.J. Watt; Éliane Excoffier, Ed English
Maps:    Mary Rostad
    iii    Robin Esrock, Rocky Mountaineer
    iv    Robin Esrock, Neil MacLean/EWM,
        Ottawa Tourism
    v    Robin Esrock, Gretchen Freund, Tourism NWT,
        Newfoundland & Labrador Tourism
    vii    Robin Esrock, Ana Esrock
**Sail in Haida Gwaii**
    2    Robin Esrock
    5    Robin Esrock
**Hike the West Coast Trail**
    7    Robin Esrock
    9    Robin Esrock
    10    Robin Esrock
**Dive a Sunken Battleship**
    11    Lee Newman
**Surf in Tofino**
    15    Robin Esrock
    17    Word Travels
**Track the Spirit Bear**
    18    Robin Esrock
    20    Robin Esrock, Bhaskar Krishnamurthy
**Snorkel with Salmon**
    23    Destiny River Adventures
    24    Robin Esrock
**Listen to Bob Marley in a Cold Sauna**
    26    Shawn Talbot Photography/Sparkling Hills
    28    Shawn Talbot Photography/Sparkling Hills
**Explore an Old-Growth Forest**
    29    TJ Watt
    31    TJ Watt
**Go Heli-skiing**
    32    Brad White/Canadian Mountain Holidays
**Powder Down in Whistler**
    35    Mike Crane/Tourism Whistler
    37    Steve Rogers/Tourism Whistler
**Stroll the Seawall**
    38    Thinkstock
    39    Gary Kalmek
**Taste the Okanagan**
    40    Ana Esrock
    41    Robin Esrock
**Let it Hang Out on Wreck Beach**
    42    Robin Esrock
**Float the Penticton River Channel**
    44    Melissa Barnes/Tourism Penticton
    45    Melissa Barnes/Tourism Penticton
**Climb the Grind, Hike the Chief**
    46    Grouse Mountain Resorts
    47    Grouse Mountain Resorts
    48    Zebunnisa Mirza
**Experience the Calgary Stampede**
    50    Ian Mackenzie
    52    Ian Mackenzie

**Ski in a UNESCO World Heritage Site**
    53    Scott Rowed/Ski Big3
    55    Richard Hallman/Ski Big3
**Hunt for Dinosaurs**
    56    Robin Esrock
**Heli-yoga in the Rockies**
    59    Word Travels
    60    Word Travels
**Be the Cowboy on a Ranch Vacation**
    62    Word Travels
    63    Robin Esrock
**RV the Icefields Parkway**
    66    Robin Esrock
    68    Robin Esrock
    69    Joe Kalmek
**Hit Your Target at the West Edmonton Mall**
    70    West Edmonton Mall and Edmonton
        Economic Development Corporation
**Hike or Ski into Skoki Lodge**
    73    Robin Esrock
    75    Robin Esrock
    76    Robin Esrock
**Board the Rocky Mountaineer**
    77    Rocky Mountaineer
    78    Rocky Mountaineer
**Swallow a Prairie Oyster**
    79    Ian Mackenzie
    81    Ana Esrock
**Salute the RCMP**
    84    Robin Esrock
    87    Chrystal Kruszelnicki/RCMP
    88    Chrystal Kruszelnicki/RCMP
**Support Rider Nation**
    89    Ana Esrock
**Float in Canada's Dead Sea**
    92    Robin Esrock
**Visit a Haunted Grove**
    95    Robin Esrock
    97    Ana Esrock
**Star Gaze in a Dark Sky Preserve**
    99    Robert Postma/Tourism Saskatchewan
**Explore North America's Largest Sand Dunes**
    102    Davin Andrie/Tourism Saskatchewan
**Horseride with Bison**
    105    Thinkstock
    106    Thinkstock
**Meet the First Nations**
    109    Robin Esrock
    111    Robin Esrock
    112    Robin Esrock
**See Polar Bears from a Tundra Buggy**
    114    Robin Esrock
    116    Robin Esrock
    117    Robin Esrock
**Crack the Hermetic Code**
    118    Robin Esrock

PHOTO CREDITS